HANDBOOK OF

GENEALOGICAL SOURCES

by

George K. Schweitzer, Ph.D., Sc.D.
407 Ascot Court
Knoxville, TN 37923-5807

WITHDRAWN

Wordprocessing by
Anne M. Smalley

ISBN 0-913857-13-0

TABLE OF CONTENTS

1. Introduction 3
2. About beginning 6
3. Adoptions 14
4. Ads in genealogical
   magazines 15
5. American Genealogical
   Lending Library 16
6. Archives 17
7. Associations, organizations,
   and societies 19
8. Atlases 20
9. Bible records 24
10. Biographies 25
11. Birth records 27
12. Black genealogy 32
13. Bounty land records 34
14. Burned county records . . 35
15. Canadian genealogy 37
16. Card/computer catalogs . 39
17. Cemetery records 40
18. Census 1790-1840 43
19. Census 1850 46
20. Census 1860 48
21. Census 1870 49
22. Census 1880 51
23. Census 1890 53
24. Census 1900 54
25. Census 1910 55
26. Census 1920 57
27. Census integrated indexes 59
28. Church archives 60
29. Church records 63
30. City directories 67
31. City histories 70
32. City panoramic views . . . 71
33. City research 71
34. Civil War records 73
35. Claims 77
36. Colonial families 79
37. Colonial war records . . . 80
38. Computer indexes 84
39. Computer programs 87
40. Computer/modem
    facilities 89
41. County atlases 91
42. County courthouses 91
43. County histories 92
44. County landowner maps . 93
45. County records 94
46. Court records 95
47. DAR records 99
48. Death records 100
49. Deed records 105
50. Directories 106
51. Divorce records 107
52. Encyclopedias 111
53. Emigration records 112
54. English/Welsh genealogy 113
55. Ethnic genealogy 116
56. Family History Centers . 118
57. Family History Library . . 123
58. Family investigations . . . 125
59. Family organizations . . . 127
60. Family publications 128
61. Farm and ranch censuses 128
62. Finding aids 129
63. Foreign genealogy 130
64. Fraternal and occupa-
    tional organizations 135
65. Gazetteers 140
66. Genealogical book
    sources 142
67. Genealogical columns . . . 145
68. Genealogical compi-
    lations 145
69. Genealogical periodicals . 146
70. Genealogical periodical
    indexes 148
71. Genealogical publica-
    tions 149
72. Genealogical societies . . 150
73. German genealogy 151
74. Group theory 154
75. Guardianships 155

76. Hired researchers 156
77. Historical societies 157
78. Homestead records 157
79. Immigrant ancestor
origins 158
80. Immigration records 159
81. Indian genealogy 160
82. International genea-
logical index 162
83. Irish genealogy 163
84. Jewish genealogy 166
85. Land grants 167
86. Land records 169
87. Large genealogical
libraries 170
88. Legal appeals 173
89. Libraries 174
90. Locating an ancestor ... 176
91. Manufactures censuses .. 177
92. Manuscripts 178
93. Maps 179
94. Marriage records 181
95. Migration patterns 186
96. Military records 190
97. Mortality censuses 195
98. Mortuary records 196
99. National Archives 196
100. National Archives
Field Branches 197
101. Naturalization records .. 198
102. Newspapers 199
103. Orphans 201
104. Other local
repositories 201
105. Passport applications ... 202
106. Passenger lists 202
107. Patriotic and hereditary
societies 205
108. Pension records 206
109. Published genealogies .. 208
110. Revolutionary War
records 209
111. Scots-Irish genealogy ... 212
112. Scottish genealogy 214

113. Slave-holder censuses .. 216
114. Soundex system 217
115. Special censuses lists ... 219
116. Spelling variations 219
117. State and special
censuses 224
118. State archives 225
119. State indexes and
finding aids 227
120. State libraries 227
121. State society libraries .. 229
122. State source guides 230
123. State university
libraries 236
124. Surname indexes 237
125. Tax lists 237
126. Territorial records 239
127. Town records 241
128. War of 1812 records ... 241
129. Ward maps 243
130. Will and probate
records 244
131. WPA records 246
132. Writing source
citations 247

███████████

1. Introduction

███████████

The joy of genealogy rests in the deepest need of the human personality, the need to belong. It is belonging that gives us our sense of security and psychological well-being. In doing genealogy, in researching your family's history, you are developing a knowledge of the long lines of ancestry to which you belong. And you will find, and continue to find, that with this knowledge comes an immense gratification. Your appreciation for this personal history will grow as your investigations ferret out more and more detail on your forebears and establish connections further and further back. You will discover yourself bound into a network of persons who jointly gave you your being and made you what you are today. You will come to share your ancestors' joys and sorrows, their successes and failures, their struggles and accomplishments, and their outlooks and dispositions. And in the process, you will realize again and again things you have inherited from them: physical characteristics, mental outlooks, psychological attitudes, emotional predispositions, likes and dislikes, as well as activities you are good at and those you are not. All of this will emerge from what you will discover about their births, marriages, deaths, living places, church activities, land transactions, military service, tax payments, court cases, migrations to new locations, occupations, organization memberships, and inheritances.

The purpose of this small handbook is to facilitate your family investigations. It is intended to help you to locate the largest amount of ancestor information in the shortest time with the smallest expenditure of money. It lists the major types of genealogical records, describes what you may expect to find in them, and tells you where they are located. Further, the major repositories (archives and libraries) where records are kept are described and information on what materials they have is given. In addition, there are numerous sections which describe for you research techniques, especially ones to assist you in solving difficult problems.

The major places in which materials for genealogical research are to be found are libraries (Library of Congress, state libraries, county libraries, city libraries, town libraries, university libraries, historical society libraries, genealogical society libraries, private libraries), archives (National Archives, state archives, university archives, church archives, private archives), governmental office buildings (US courts, US Immigration Service, state courts, state attorneys general, county courthouses, city halls, town halls), and certain private offices (abstract companies, associations, attorneys, businesses, cemeteries, churches, ethnic organizations, fraternal organizations, hereditary societies, hospitals, mortuaries, newspapers, patriotic societies). This source book refers to numerous original records, microform-copied records (microfilms, microfiche), and published records (books, journal articles, computer disks), along with many indexes, all of which are available in the places mentioned above. Several possible ways are open to you for obtaining materials: (1) visiting the places yourself, (2) borrowing microform-copies and/or published materials, (3) writing to the places, and (4) hiring genealogical researchers in the appropriate places to do the work for you. In general, the best approaches are the first and the second. The reasons follow.

Obviously, visiting the various record locations yourself is the most satisfactory. You will be more interested in finding what you are seeking then anyone else and will probably be more thorough. The second alternative, borrowing materials, is a good option, because there are several sources which have immense holdings. The most important is The Family History Library (FHL) in Salt Lake City, UT. They will lend you microfilm copies of records from the largest genealogical record collection in the world. They will send these microfilms to any of their several hundred branch Family History Centers located all over the US. In addition, the National Genealogical Society (NGS, Arlington, VA) and the New England Historic Genealogical Society (NEHGS, Boston, MA) lend to their members volumes from their large holdings of published genealogical records. Further, the American Genealogical Lending Library (AGLL, Bountiful, UT) will lend directly to you or to your local library microfilm copies of many major records. And your local library may also borrow microfilm copies of a number of important federal records from the National Archives Census Microfilm Rental Program (Annapolis, MD).

The third alternative, writing for records, sometimes works, but usually not. The majority of personnel at the various archives, libraries, and other repositories simply do not have the time to do any detailed work for you. Sometimes they can answer short, to-the-point questions which require only a bit of time. And sometimes they can supply you with a copy of a record if you can tell them exactly where in their materials it is located. The fourth approach, hiring a researcher, deprives you of the pleasure of the hunt and is often costly. But there are occasions when it may be needed, especially when the only source of a record is a long way from you. Details on all these will appear in later sections.

Every aspiring genealogist should read a good book on beginning genealogy. Among the better ones are:

_J. Cerny and A. Eakle, ANCESTRY'S GUIDE TO RESEARCH, Ancestry Publishing, Salt Lake City, UT, 1985.
_R. Crandall, SHAKING YOUR FAMILY TREE, Yankee Publishing, Dublin, NH, 1986.
_N. E. Wright, PRESERVING YOUR AMERICAN HERITAGE, Brigham Young University Press, Provo, UT, 1981.

Every starting genealogist should also subscribe to three special country-wide information, query, ad, and technique journals:

_E. S. Mills, editor, NATIONAL GENEALOGICAL SOCIETY QUARTERLY, National Genealogical Society, 4527 Seventeenth St., North, Arlington, VA 22207-2399.
_V. N. Chambers, editor, THE GENEALOGICAL HELPER, PO Box 368, Logan, UT 84323-0368, bimonthly.
_L. K. Meitzler, editor, HERITAGE QUEST, PO Box 329, Bountiful, UT 84011-0329, bimonthly.

As your interests continue to develop, you need to add the first book below to your library. It is an indispensable guide to state, county, city, and town genealogical sources for the US. Then, the other two books should be read in order to enhance your abilities to compare and evaluate genealogical data. When you realize their value, you may wish to purchase them also.

_A. Eichholz, editor, ANCESTRY'S RED BOOK, Ancestry Publishing, Salt Lake City, UT, latest edition.
_N. C. Stevenson, GENEALOGICAL EVIDENCE, Aegean Press, Laguna Hills, CA, latest edition.
_M. Rubincam, PITFALLS IN GENEALOGICAL RESEARCH, Ancestry Publishing, Salt Lake City, UT, 1987.

If your interests develop and you continue to gain satisfaction in your genealogical quest, there are some further reference works which will guide you in doing more efficient work. They can be added to your guidebook shelf as funds become available. They are listed in the order in which they should be purchased.

_A. Eakle and J. Cerny, THE SOURCE, A GUIDEBOOK TO AMERICAN GENEALOGY, Ancestry Publishing, Salt Lake City, UT, latest edition.
_J. Cerny and W. Elliott, THE LIBRARY, A GUIDE TO THE LDS FAMILY HISTORY LIBRARY, Ancestry Publishing, Salt Lake City, UT, latest edition.

_Staff of the National Archives, GUIDE TO GENEALOGICAL RESEARCH IN THE NATIONAL ARCHIVES, National Archives and Records Service, Washington, DC, latest edition.

The abbreviation SASE means a long, self-addressed, stamped envelope. The genealogical research community generally accepts the very thoughtful and courteous custom that anytime and every time you ask anyone for any free information you send them an SASE.

The next section, Section 2, is devoted to instructing you on how to begin your genealogical research. If you are not a beginner and are well acquainted with how you move your ancestral lines back 3 or 4 generations, you may skip Section 2. If you are just beginning or are still working on your 4-generation chart, you ought to carefully read the section.

2. About beginning   At the outset of your genealogical adventure, you need to recognize how very important it is to adhere to the fundamental genealogical research principle. This principle is that you start with one of your grandchildren or children or yourself and that you work backward in time generation by generation. You must not succumb to the temptation to skip one or more generations back to someone who bears the surname you are working on. This usually leads to diverting you from a procedure which allows you to prove each and every connection in your ancestor's lines. And a genealogy without good proofs is essentially worthless since no one can know that it is in any way accurate.

The first step that a beginner should take is to obtain or draw out on a sheet of 8.5" x 11" paper a 5-generation ancestor chart similar to the one labelled Figure 1. You put the name of your grandchild or child or yourself in pencil on the line following the number 1. The name should appear as the last name (surname) in all capital letters, then a comma, then the first and middle names. In pencil, write the birth date of this person on the line which starts with the letter b. It should be entered in the order day-month-year, with the day indicated by two numerals (such as 04 or 07 or 14 or 31), the month abbreviated with three letters (such as Jan or Apr or Jul or Nov), and the year with four numerals (such as 1924 or 1950 or 1981). Then, in pencil, write the birth place on the line below the birth date. Indicate it by writing the city or town, then a comma, then the county, then another comma, and finally the two capital-letter abbreviation for the state (such as MO or IL or TN). If the birth place

ANCESTOR CHART NO. _1_

```
                                                      16: GREAT-GREAT GRANDFATHER
                                                          b_____ p_____
                                   8: GREAT GRANDFATHER    m_____
           4: GRANDFATHER          b_____              d_____
           b_____               p_____          17: GREAT-GREAT GRANDMOTHER
           p_____               m_____              b_____ p_____
           p_____               p_____              d_____
           d_____               d_____          18: GREAT-GREAT GRANDFATHER
           p_____            9: GREAT GRANDMOTHER      b_____ p_____
    2: FATHER                      p_____              p_____
    b_____                      d_____          19: GREAT-GREAT GRANDMOTHER
    p_____                      p_____              b_____ p_____
    m_____                                             d_____
    p_____                                         20: GREAT-GREAT GRANDFATHER
    d_____                      10: GREAT GRANDFATHER  b_____
    p_____                      b_____              m_____ p_____
           5: GRANDMOTHER          p_____              d_____
           b_____               m_____          21: GREAT-GREAT GRANDMOTHER
           p_____               p_____              b_____ p_____
           d_____               d_____              d_____
           p_____            11: GREAT GRANDMOTHER  22: GREAT-GREAT GRANDFATHER
                                   b_____              b_____ p_____
1: SCHWEITZER, Hallie Keene        p_____          23: GREAT-GREAT GRANDMOTHER
b 11 Jun 1986                      d_____              b_____ p_____
p Dallas, Dallas Co., TX           p_____              d_____
m_____                                             24: GREAT-GREAT GRANDFATHER
p_____                                                 b_____
d_____                          12: GREAT GRANDFATHER  m_____ p_____
p_____                          b_____              d_____
           6: GRANDFATHER          p_____          25: GREAT-GREAT GRANDMOTHER
           b_____               m_____              b_____ p_____
           p_____               p_____              d_____
           m_____               d_____          26: GREAT-GREAT GRANDFATHER
           p_____            13: GREAT GRANDMOTHER      b_____ p_____
           d_____               b_____              m_____
           p_____               p_____              d_____
    3: MOTHER                      d_____          27: GREAT-GREAT GRANDMOTHER
    b_____                      p_____              b_____ p_____
    p_____                                             d_____
    d_____                                         28: GREAT-GREAT GRANDFATHER
    p_____                      14: GREAT GRANDFATHER  b_____
           7: GRANDMOTHER          b_____              m_____ p_____
           b_____               p_____              d_____
           p_____               m_____          29: GREAT-GREAT GRANDMOTHER
           d_____               p_____              b_____ p_____
           p_____               d_____              d_____
                                15: GREAT GRANDMOTHER  30: GREAT-GREAT GRANDFATHER
                                   b_____              b_____ p_____
                                   p_____              m_____
                                   d_____              d_____
                                   p_____          31: GREAT-GREAT GRANDMOTHER
                                                          b_____ p_____
                                                          d_____ p_____
```

b = born
m = married
d = died
p = place

Figure 1a.

ANCESTOR CHART NO. _1_

16: SCHWEITZER, George Robert
  b 25 Dec 1864 p Lawrence, Douglas Co., KS
8: SCHWEITZER, Francis John   m 30 Jun 1888 p Newaygo, Newaygo Co., MI
b 16 May 1893   d 01 Feb 1962 p Poplar Bluff, Butler Co., MO
4: SCHWEITZER, George Keene   p Fremont, Newaygo Co., MI   17: HEINOLD, Alelia Elsia
b 05 Dec 1924   m 24 Dec 1921   b 26 Jul 1868 p Fremont, Newaygo Co., MI
p Poplar Bluff, Butler Co., MO   p Poplar Bluff, Butler Co., MO   d 08 Sep 1945 p Farmington, St. Francis Co., MO
m 06 Jun 1948   d 14 Jan 1985   18: KEEN, William Thomas
p Poplar Bluff, Butler Co., MO   p Knoxville, Knox Co., TN   b 25 Feb 1862 p Rockingham Co., NC
d _____   9: KEEN, Ruth Elizabeth   m 14 Jan 1891 p Dexter, Stoddard Co., MO
p _____   b 05 Sep 1899   d 31 Mar 1943 p St. Louis Co., MO
2: SCHWEITZER, Evie George   p Dexter, Stoddard Co., MO   19: SISLER, Mary Josephine
b 09 Feb 1957   d 23 Feb 1987   b 30 Jun 1867 p Catlin, Vermilion Co., IL
p Knoxville, Knox Co., TN   p Knoxville, Knox Co., TN   d 09 Mar 1952 p Poplar Bluff, Butler Co., MO
m 24 Nov 1979   20: PRATT, William Lapp
p Plano, Collin Co., TX   b 25 Aug 1847 p Bermondsey, London, England
d _____   10: PRATT, Franklin Talmadge   m 04 Apr 1868 p St. Louis, St. Louis Co., MO
p _____   b 04 Feb 1882   d 13 Nov 1892 p St. Louis, St. Louis Co., MO
5: PRATT, Verna Lee   p St. Louis, St. Louis Co., MO   21: Fitz RANDOLPH, Marietta
b 27 Aug 1927   m 04 Jul 1905   b 07 Nov 1849 p Newark, Essex Co., NJ
p Sedalia, Pettis Co., MO   p Oswego, Labette Co., KS   d 01 Jul 1923 p Parsons, Labette Co., KS
d _____   d 18 Feb 1946   22: MASHBURN, Levi
p _____   p St. Louis, St. Louis Co., MO   b 18 Nov 1844 p McMinn Co., TN
  11: MASHBURN, Rosa Belle   m 02 Oct 1866 p Cleveland, Bradley Co., TN
1: SCHWEITZER, Hallie Keene   b 18 Dec 1884   d 07 Jun 1907 p Parsons, Labette Co., KS
b 11 Jun 1986   p Crawford Co., KS   23: BREWER, Julia Ann
p Dallas, Dallas Co., TX   d 01 Dec 1957   b 28 Apr 1842 p Davidson Co., NC
m _____   p Overland, St. Louis Co., MO   d 10 May 1922 p Sedalia, Pettis Co., MO
p _____   24: MATHER, Edward Strong
d _____   b 09 Apr 1868 p Amherst, Hampshire Co., MA
p _____   12: MATHER, Edward Whiting, Sr   m 31 Dec 1890 p Malden, Middlesex Co., MA
  b 17 Jun 1895   d Dec 1928 p Knoxville, Knox Co., TN
6: MATHER, Edward Whiting, Jr   p Weston, Middlesex Co., MA   25: BLACKMAN, Clara
b 23 Nov 1925   m _____   b 1866 p Jackson, Jackson Co., MI
p Winston-Salem, Forsyth Co., NC   d 22 Apr 1968   d 25 Feb 1958 p Franklin, Macon Co., NC
m 29 Nov 1952   p Bradenton, Manatee Co., FL   26: MELVIN, William H.
p San Antonio, Bexar Co., TX   13: MELVIN, Suda Mae   b May 1864 p Bladen Co., NC
d _____   b 17 May 1897   m _____   p _____
p _____   p Fork, Dillon Co., SC   27: MOORE, Susan P.
3: MATHER, Sharon Ann   d 25 Jun 1939   b Sep 1863 p Robeson Co., NC
b 08 Sep 1955   p Knoxville, Knox Co., TN   d _____   p _____
p San Antonio, Bexar Co., TX   28: STRIEBER, William F.
d _____   b Dec 1871 p Indianola, Calhoun Co., TX
p _____   14: STRIEBER, Leslie John   m 27 May 1895 p Yorktown, DeWitt Co., TX
  b 25 Jan 1898   d 07 Jun 1940 p Karnes Co., TX
7: STRIEBER, Johanna Lou   p Yorktown, DeWitt Co., TX   29: ECKHARDT, Johanna
b 27 Aug 1931   m Aug 1921   b _____   d 1901 p Yorktown, DeWitt Co., TX
p San Antonio, Bexar Co., TX   p Yorktown, DeWitt Co., TX   30: CROSS, George W.
d _____   d 28 Apr 1987   b 13 Mar 1868 p Nolanville, Bell Co., TX
p _____   p San Antonio, Bexar Co., TX   m 28 Apr 1889 p Thrifty, Brown Co., TX
  15: CROSS, Emma Alta   d 03 Sep 1864 p Austin, Travis Co., TX
  b 27 Apr 1899   31: ALLEN, Martha Louise
b = born   p Thrifty, Brown Co., TX   b 25 Oct 1871 p Flatonia, Fayette Co., TX
m = married   d 07 Dec 1936   d 14 Jul 1955 p Yorktown, DeWitt Co., TX
d = died   p Bexar Co., TX
p = place

Figure 1b.

ANCESTOR CHART NO. _19_

76: SISLER, Lewis
b
p
m
p
d 22 Jun 1851
p East Aurora, Erie Co, NY

152:
b
m
p
d
p
b

304:
b _____ p _____
m _____ p _____
d _____ p _____

305:
b _____ p _____
d _____ p _____

306:
b _____ p _____
m _____ p _____
d _____ p _____

38: SISLER, James Alonzo
b 08 Dec 1834
p Erie Co, NY
m 12 Feb 1860
p Brookston, White Co, IN
d 16 May 1894
p Dexter, Stoddard Co, MO

77: MARSH, Margaret
b
p   PA
d 28 May 1872
p Summit Co, OH

153:
b
p
d
p

154:
b
p
m
d
p

155:
b
m
d
p

307:
b _____ p _____
d _____ p _____

308:
b _____ p _____
m _____ p _____
d _____ p _____

309:
b _____ p _____
d _____ p _____

310:
b _____ p _____
m _____ p _____
d _____ p _____

311:
b _____ p _____
d _____ p _____

19: SISLER, Mary Josephine
b 30 Jun 1867
p Catlin, Vermilion Co, IL
m 14 Jan 1891
p Dexter, Stoddard Co, MO
d 09 Mar 1952
p Poplar Bluff, Butler Co, MO

78: STEWART, Russell
b 21 Feb 1813
p Henry Co, KY
m 02 Feb 1835
p Henry Co, KY
d 01 Jun 1884
p Iconium, St Clair Co, MO

39: STEWART, Elizabeth
b 31 Aug 1838
p Henry Co, KY
d 04 Jan 1892
p Dexter, Stoddard Co, MO

79: NEVILL, Nancy
b
p Henry Co, KY
d 18 Sep 1854
p White Co, IN

156: STEWART, Asa
b 18 Mar 1787
p Fauquier Co, VA
m 06 Jul 1808
p Henry Co, KY
d 06 Apr 1859
p Henry Co, KY

157: DAVISS, Lindy Judah
b
p
d 23 Oct 1856
p Henry Co, KY

158: NEVILL, Stewart
b
p
m 12 Mar 1811
p Henry Co, KY
d
p

159: DAVIS, Lucy
b 05 Aug 1794
p
d 06 Sep 1860
p Henry Co, KY

312: STEWART, John, Sr
b _____ p _____ VA
m _____
d Oct 1826 p Henry Co, KY

313:
b _____ p _____
d _____ p _____

314:
b _____ p _____
m _____ p _____
d _____ p _____

315:
b _____ p _____
d _____ p _____

316: NEVILL, Thomas
m 31 Jul 1772 p Fauquier Co, VA
d Jul 1806 p Henry Co, KY

317: STEWART, Mary
b _____ p _____ VA
p _____

318: DAVIS, John
b _____ p _____
m _____ p _____
d _____ p _____

319:
b _____ p _____
d _____ p _____

b = born
m = married
d = died
p = place

Figure 1c.

was out in the county (not in a city or town), simply write the county and the state. Now, in pencil, enter the marriage date on the line beginning with m (using the same form as for the birth date), the marriage place on the line below it (using the same form as for the birth place), and recognize that the next two lines are for the death date and the death place. The reason that entries are made in pencil is that your personal knowledge is the source of the information. Only after you have obtained records which substantiate the entries should they be changed to ink.

The space labelled 2 is for the father of 1, and the space labelled 3 is for the mother. Spaces 4 and 6 are for the grandfathers and 5 and 7 for the grandmothers. Notice also that 4 and 5 are the parents of 2, and that 6 and 7 are the parents of 3. The great-grandfathers are put in spaces 8, 10, 12, and 14, and the great-grandmothers are put in spaces 9, 11, 13, and 15. And spaces 16, 18, 20, 22, 24, 26, 28, and 30 are for the great-great-grandfathers, with spaces 17, 19, 21, 23, 25, 27, 29, and 31 for the great-great-grandmothers. Pay attention to the fact that in all cases except number 1 the men are even-numbered (2, 4, 6, 8, etc.) and the women are odd-numbered (3, 5, 7, 9, etc.).

Continue filling in the blanks, as many as you can, from your personal knowledge and from any records you may have. All information is to be entered in pencil until you get records which confirm the data. The second step can now be taken. Contact as many family members as you can (siblings, cousins, parents, aunts, uncles, grandparents, grand aunts, grand uncles), especially the oldest. Ask them for further information which will assist you in making additions in pencil to the chart. Inquire about birth, marriage, and death dates and places, burials, parents of various persons, places lived, moves, education, churches, jobs, war service, organization memberships, divorces, court suits. Take careful notes. Especially ask if they know of anyone who is working on the family genealogy. Ask for photocopies of any documents they might have. Such items might include diaries, letters, photographs, legal papers, birth and marriage and death certificates, military papers, naturalization documents, passports, diplomas, employment records, Bible, newspaper clippings, announcements, membership cards, funeral cards, estate papers, hospital records, business licenses, tax receipts and returns. Also inquire about old household and personal items which could carry ancestral information: pictures, uniform, ribbons, medals, furniture, tableware, rings, watches, books, engraved jewelry, awards. Add all the data to the chart.

Now, with numerous names, dates, and places on your ancestor chart, you are ready for the third step, the setting up of a record keeping system. Careful, detailed attention must be paid to this, else you end up with a box full of scrambled miscellaneous data. Your requirements are few: a 8.5" x 11" loose leaf ring notebook, a supply of punched narrow-lined 8.5" x 11" paper for it, an inexpensive cardboard file box to hold 9" x 12" file folders, and a supply of 9" x 12" file folders (for 8.5" x 11" sheets). In the notebook, put the ancestor chart first, then label one sheet at the top for each person on your ancestor chart. Give the ancestor's number and name exactly as listed on the chart. These sheets are to record brief statements (usually a line or two) on all sources you consult and all information you obtain on the ancestor. Each statement must be accompanied by a brief reference to exactly where you got the data. In the file box, you should place a file folder for each progenitor (ancestor, forebear) on your ancestor chart. The folders should be labelled also, each bearing a number and name exactly as listed on the chart. Into these folders, you should place research notes, photocopies of documents, copies of correspondence, and other material relating to the pertinent forebear.

The fourth step begins your documentation. For every person on your ancestor chart obtain birth, marriage, and death certificates or records. These are available from state vital records offices, county offices, and/or town offices. Birth and death records are available from most state offices back to about 1900/10, farther back for some states, much farther back for a few states. Before that time, you must contact the counties, towns, or cities. Marriage records are obtainable from most counties or towns back to the time of their origin (except for some few states such as PA, NY, and SC). Details on the exact offices to write and the time spans for which records are available are given in later sections of this Handbook. These sections are entitled Birth records, Death records, and Marriage records. When you receive copies of certificates back, change the entries in your ancestor chart from pencil to ink, record the information briefly on the proper page of your notebook, and file the documents in the proper file folder. You will discover when you receive these certificates that they often list the parents which will supply data on the next generation back. Don't forget to put these data in three places: (1) on your ancestor chart, (2) on the proper page in your notebook, and (3) in the proper file folder in your file box. In most states, the birth and death records will eventually play out on you, but not in all. You will find that in some states, particularly those in New England, they will go back to the very beginning. The situation is similar for marriage records, although you will discover that they usually play out farther back. When these vital records (as birth, marriage, and death records are called) fail you, then other records will have to be sought. This leads us to the fifth and sixth steps.

The fifth step is based on the possibility that someone has already done all or a part of your genealogy and has published it. The best ways to ascertain this is to look into numerous indexes and reference works which list large numbers of published family histories or published genealogical data. The major places to look include books by Kaminkow, Munsell, Rider, the staff of the Newberry Library, and the Catalog of the NY City Public Library; the IGI and surname indexes at your local Family History Center; the Family Group Records Archives in the Family History Library; and card and computer catalogs in the states, counties, cities, and towns where each of your progenitors lived. You need to look up every name on your ancestor chart in all these finding aids. Details regarding where to find these reference sources and how to use them will be found in the sections of this Handbook which are labelled Card and computer catalogs, Computer indexes, Family History Centers, Family History Library, International genealogical index (IGI), Published genealogies, and Surname indexes.

When you reach this point, you may have had the good fortune of discovering the parents of one or more of the persons listed on the right edge of your ancestor chart (numbers 16 through 31). Let us suppose you have discovered the parents of number 19. Where do you put their names? Very simply; what you do is copy the number 19 and the name following it into the first space on the left on a new ancestor chart. And you label it Ancestor Chart No. 19 at the top. The next two places are labelled 38 (19 x 2) and 39 (19 x 2 plus 1). The four places in the next column are labelled 76 (38 x 2), 77 (38 x 2 plus 1), 78 (39 x 2), and 79 (39 x 2 plus 1). The parents of 19, you see, are 38 and 39, and the grandparents of number 19 are 76, 77, 78, and 79. The next column contains the eight great-grandparents of 19 (152, 153, 154, 155, 156, 157, 158, 159), and the last column contains the sixteen great-great-grandparents of 19 (304, 305, 306, 307, 308, 309, 310, 311, 312, 313, 314, 315, 316, 317, 318, 319). Please carefully note that the father of any number is double the number, and the mother of any number is double the number plus one. Similar additional charts can be set up for ancestors 16, 17, 18, 20, 21, 22, 23, 24, 25, 26, 27, 28, 29, 30, and 31. Remember the even numbers are men (fathers), and odd numbers are women (mothers). Also note that wives have numbers one higher than husbands. The process can be continued as needed to accommodate any number of ancestors.

The sixth step to push your forebear's lines back further will now be described. Birth, marriage, and death records will often cease to be available, and so you will need to turn to other pertinent records that will locate the parents of the people farthest back on your ancestor chart. In order to do this, you must use the census records (or schedules as they are called) to locate the counties and/or towns where your progenitors lived. The reason you need to know these places is that the best records for moving your lineage back are usually to be found in the counties and/or towns. In addition, you will usually find that the censuses themselves give direct or indirect evidence of parents. The US took censuses (lists of people) in the years 1790, 1800, 1810, 1820, 1830, 1840, 1850, 1860, 1870, 1880, 1890, 1900, 1910, 1920, and so on. All those listed by number are available except the 1890 ones, which were destroyed. The 1790-through-1870, the 1900 and 1920 censuses are indexed by state, the 1880 is partially indexed by state, and the 1910 is indexed for 21 states. There are overall indexes for the combined 1790-1800-1810 censuses, the 1820, the 1830, and the 1840; and the 1850 censuses are indexed in three separate lists. Soon all the 1880 censuses will be completely indexed. All these indexes make the census records fairly easy to search.

The 1790-through-1840 censuses list only the head of the household by name along with the numbers of persons living in the household in various age brackets. The 1850-through-1920 censuses list all persons with age, sex, and birth state or foreign country. The 1880-through-1920 censuses also give the states or counties of parents' births. And the 1900 censuses show the birth month and year, years married, years in the US, and whether naturalized. The 1910 census omits the birth month and year. Look in the pertinent census indexes for all ancestors on your ancestor chart, then examine in detail the actual census entries. For those census years for which there are only partial indexes, your census record search will be somewhat time-consuming, but persevere, because your reward will probably be more good data. You will undoubtedly find parents of many ancestors, and then parents of those and so on, since the censuses have the potential to carry you back to 1790. All finds should be added to your ancestor chart and your notebook, and copies of the census records should go in your file folders. Details on the censuses are given in later sections of this Handbook.

The <u>seventh</u> step is now before you. This involves the use of many other types of records in order to find parents which the vital records and censuses have failed to locate for you. In addition, you will want to flesh out your ancestors' lives by finding records of their many activities in the communities in which they lived. And eventually, you will want to track them overseas. All this is done by using many other sorts of records which are available to you. There are <u>federal</u> governmental records: land grants, military service, military bounty land, military pension, and passenger lists. There are <u>state</u> governmental records: censuses taken by the state, court, divorce, estate, land grant, military, tax, will. There are <u>county</u> governmental records: court, deed, divorce, estate, mortgage, naturalization, probate, tax, will. There are <u>town</u> governmental records: early land, militia, proprietors, poor, selectmen, tax, town meeting, and sometimes deed and probate. And there are <u>private</u> records: Bible, biography, cemetery, church, city directory, city history, county history, genealogical compilations, genealogical periodicals, genealogical society publications, manuscript, mortuary, newspaper, organization and association records, published genealogies, record transcripts, surname indexes. As you push your ancestral lines farther and farther back, you will find it important to use all of these as well as a number of other sources. To learn more about these records, read the many sections which follow this one. There you will discover what these records will tell you, where they may be found, and how to use them.

3. Adoptions

Adoption records are usually found in courts at the county level. These courts are usually the probate court, but in some states other county-level courts have jurisdiction. In general, adoption did not become a process requiring a court action and generating court records until 1848 or after, the date varying from state to state. The records include such things as name, birth date, birth place, residence, custody, sex, race, siblings, guardian, and parents of the child, plus information on the new adopting parents such as names, ages, marriage date, and data indicating their qualifications to adopt. In most cases, these records are enclosed in an envelope, packet, or file folder called the case file. The case files may be found by looking through the court docket, the court minutes, or the index, if available. There you will find a case number under which the case file is filed. Most adoption records before the 1920s/1930s are open to the public, but some are restricted or partly restricted. After this date, you can expect to find access prohibited or restricted in most places. It will be necessary for you to ask the individual court just what its regulations are. Fewer court records of the type

containing adoption data have been microfilmed, transcribed, or abstract-
ed than of some other types, so the county courthouse is often the only
source of them. Four useful guidebooks which will give you detailed
search instructions are:
_J. Askin, SEARCH: A HANDBOOK FOR ADOPTEES AND BIRTH
PARENTS, Harper and Row, New York, NY, latest edition.
_M. J. Rillera, THE ADOPTION SEARCHBOOK, Tri-adoption
Publications, Westminster, CA, 1985.
_C. Alexander-Roberts, THE ESSENTIAL ADOPTION HANDBOOK,
Taylor Publ. Co., Dallas, TX, 1993.
_ J. U. Brink, THE ADOPTION SEARCH: BASICS FOR ADOPTEES
SEARCHING FOR THEIR ROOTS, Family Historian Books,
Tacoma, WA, 1994.

4. Ads in genealogical magazines
Many genealogical societies, agencies, and some individuals publish journals (magazines, periodicals) devoted to family research. A number of them accept ads or queries from persons who are working on their family lines. The purpose of an ad or query is to discover other people who have information on an ancestor of yours. The advertising or inquiry fees are usually very reasonable or free. Consider sending your ad or query to five types of periodicals: (a) a genealogical journal with national coverage, (b) a genealogical journal with state coverage, (c) a genealogical periodical with regional or local coverage, (d) a local newspaper, and (e) a genealogical periodical dealing with the surname you are interested in.

Your ad or query must be carefully worded. Make it brief, but give sufficient information so that readers will not confuse your ancestor with unrelated people of the same name. Be sure to give full names, dates (births, marriages, migrations, deaths), location, parents, and children to the extent that you know them.

The leading national genealogical periodicals have circulations in the tens of thousands. These are THE GENEALOGICAL HELPER and HERITAGE QUEST. No other national magazines even begin to approach them in the number of readers they reach. Therefore, send them an SASE and request an ad form to fill out and return. Write:
_Bureau of Missing Ancestors, THE GENEALOGICAL HELPER,
Everton Publishers, PO Box 368, Logan, UT 84323-0368.
_Queries, HERITAGE QUEST, PO Box 329, Bountiful, UT 84011-0329.

To locate genealogical periodicals and publications in specific states, regions, counties, and cities where you ancestor lived, and to find journals dealing with specific surnames, consult the following reference works. When you find what appears to be a pertinent periodical, send them an SASE and a request for information on placing an ad or inquiry.
_E. P. Bentley, THE GENEALOGIST'S ADDRESS BOOK, Genealogical Publishing Co., Baltimore, MD, latest edition.
_V. N. Chambers, editor, THE GENEALOGICAL HELPER, Everton Publishers, Logan, UT, listings of family-surname periodicals in the latest Mar-Apr issue, listings of locality genealogical periodicals in the latest May-Jun issue.
_M. K. Meyer, DIRECTORY OF GENEALOGICAL SOCIETIES IN THE USA, with their periodicals, Libra Publications, Linthicum Heights, MD, latest edition.
_J. Konrad, A DIRECTORY OF GENEALOGICAL PERIODICALS, Ye Olde Genealogie Shoppe, Indianapolis IN, latest edition.
_J. Konrad, DIRECTORY OF FAMILY ONE-NAME PERIODICALS, Ye Olde Genealogie Shoppe, Indianapolis IN, latest edition.
_A. C. Milner, NEWSPAPER GENEALOGICAL COLUMN DIRECTORY, Heritage Books, Bowie, MD, latest edition.
_J. Konrad, LIST OF NEWSPAPERS AND PERIODICALS WITH GENEALOGICAL QUERY COLUMNS, Ye Olde Genealogie Shoppe, Indianapolis IN, latest edition.
For newspapers now being published in towns and cities, consult:
_GALE DIRECTORY OF PUBLICATIONS, Gale Research, Detroit, MI, latest annual edition.

5. American Genealogical Lending Library

The American Genealogical Lending Library (AGLL) is a commercial organization specializing in the rental and sale of microfilm/microfiche copies of many major genealogical records and indexes and computer disks of many major genealogical indexes. Both you and your local library may borrow these records from them at very reasonable fees. The over 250,000 microfilms, microfiche, and computer disks which are available from them include vital records (birth, marriage, death), federal census records (1790-1920 including indexes), federal military records (from the Revolution, War of 1812, and Civil War), federal ship passenger lists, state censuses, church records, tax lists, county records (birth, marriage, death, deed, probate, will), county histories, American Indian records, Black records, and family histories. To order records yourself, you need

to join their club, which has a small fee, and includes their large catalog. To order through your local library, you do not need to.join. For details, send an SASE and an inquiry to:
_American Genealogical Lending Library, PO Box 329, Bountiful, UT 84011-0329. Phone 1-(801)-298-5446.
In addition to the above services, they maintain a very useful computer bulletin board, publish the GENEALOGY BULLETIN, and publish HERITAGE QUEST.

6. Archives An archives is a place where original records are collected, preserved, organized, and indexed. Archives may also collect books, microfilms, microfiche, computer data, and periodicals which duplicate, abstract, annotate, index, or supplement their original documents. There are many archives in the US, both governmental and private, which have records of value for genealogical research. These include, along with their record holdings:
_The National Archives in Washington, DC, and its eleven Field Branches in major centers throughout the US: federal government censuses, military, immigration, passenger list, and naturalization records.
_The State Archives, one in each state at the state capital: state governmental birth, census, court, death, estate, immigration, land, map, marriage, military, naturalization, tax, and will records; also often private records such as Bible, cemetery, church, ethnic, manuscript map, mortuary, and newspaper records; also often county, city, and town records of the types mentioned next.
_County, City, and Town Archives (in courthouses, city halls, town halls, and sometimes separate record repository buildings): birth, court, death, divorce, estate, land, marriage, military, tax, and will.
_Private Archives: records of organizations and associations (businesses, churches, companies, ethnic groups, fraternal societies, genealogical societies, hereditary societies, historical societies, insurance companies, mortuaries, patriotic societies, professional societies); records of special types (such as city directories, diaries, letters, maps, newspapers, steam boat records, wagon train records); these archives include ones at colleges, universities, museums, military parks, churches, cemeteries, newspapers, mortuaries, and organizations (local, regional, state, and national).

The major archives mentioned above will be treated in greater detail in later sections of this Handbook. Among these are the ones entitled Church archives, County courthouses, Manuscripts, National Archives, and State archives, as well as several others. Practically all archives in the US along with their holdings are described in:

_P. M. Hamer, A GUIDE TO ARCHIVES AND MANUSCRIPTS IN THE US, Yale University Press, New Haven, CT, 1961.

_DIRECTORY OF ARCHIVES AND MANUSCRIPT REPOSITO-RIES IN THE US, National Historical Publications and Records Commission, Oryx Press, Phoenix, AZ, latest edition.

_NATIONAL UNION CATALOG OF MANUSCRIPT COLLEC-TIONS, Library of Congress, Washington, DC, annual volumes since 1959-.

When you go into an archives, register, then ask for and read the regulations. Next, request the main catalog, which may be a card catalog, a computer catalog, a microfiche catalog, or an indexed guidebook. These are generally alphabetically arranged according to one or more of the categories suggested by the five letters in the word SLANT: by Subject, by Locality (state, county, city, town), by Author (or compiler or editor or collector of the material), by Name, and by Title. Now, search this main catalog for the names of your ancestors, the localities where they lived, and the subjects which relate to their activities, and, if pertinent, you should also look under appropriate titles and authors (or compilers or editors or collectors). When you find pertinent references, copy the name of the source and its code numbers (and/or letters), and use them to request the records from an attendant or an archivist. Following this, ask for other finding aids, such as smaller catalogs, typescript lists, inventories, registers, calendars, guides, files, and indexes. Examine them also under all of the above categories (SLANT) that apply, copy the code numbers, and request the records. When you receive the materials, treat them with extreme care so that no damage is done to them, and return them in the condition in which you received them. Some archives have published guides to their collections. Before visiting any archives, be sure to send an SASE and ask if there is a published guide, and if so, obtain it and use it before going.

In smaller archives, such as many county, city, and town record repositories, the access to records may be much simpler. There may be only one or a few sets of indexes, and they may be in book form. Further, the records could simply be located on specific shelves in certain offices, record rooms, or vaults. Or the indexes may be out for public use, with you having to request that the records be brought to you.

7. Associations, organizations, and societies

Beginning in the earliest times, many associations, organizations, and societies were established in the American Colonies and the US. These associations, organizations, and societies were composed of people with a common interest of one sort or another. Such associations, organizations and societies are of many types: agricultural, alumni, ancestral, art, athletic, benevolent, burial, business, college, colonial, commercial, cultural, early family, early settler, educational, ethnic, family, fraternal, genealogical, health, hereditary, historical, hobby, honorary, labor, lineage, medical, military, musical, nationality, occupational, patriotic, pioneer, political, professional, public affairs, recreational, religious, retiree, royal descent, scholarly, scientific, social, sports, technical, university, veterans, wars. Some of them no longer exist, but a large number are still active. There are four kinds of these groups which can be of assistance to genealogical researchers. They are:

_Genealogical and historical societies (national, state, regional, and local). These are societies interested in fostering genealogical and historical research in their areas. They often collect and publish records, publish a newsletter and/or a journal, and offer help to researchers. These will be discussed in detail in later sections.

_Family organizations usually deal with one particular surname or the descendants of one particular ancestor. They often collect and publish records, act as a clearing house for data on the line, provide lineages, and usually publish a newsletter. A more detailed discussion appears later.

_Fraternal and occupational organizations are composed of groups with interests in some particular benevolence or service or other unifying concern, or of groups with the same occupation or profession or vocation. Their membership records sometimes contain genealogical information. A later section goes into detail on these organizations.

_Lineage and hereditary societies are made up of people with ancestors from some historical event, organization, place, or time. They usually require their members to trace their lines back to the event, organization, place, or time. Hence, their records can be excellent sources of ancestral lines. They usually publish lists of their members, lineages, and/or lists of their ancestors. Some of them also publish records which can assist genealogists trace progenitors back to the pertinent event, organization, place, or time. More detail on these societies appears in a later section.

In the various later sections which deal with these many groups, you will be told exactly what sorts of records they hold and how to obtain those records. In addition, you will be informed of reference books which will give your their addresses. There is a good general reference work to many of the associations, organizations, and societies mentioned above. There you will find details on them along with their addresses.

_K. E. Koek and S. B. Martin, ENCYCLOPEDIA OF ASSOCIATIONS, Gale Research Co., Detroit, MI, latest edition.

Other more specialized reference works on genealogical, historical, family, hereditary, lineage, and fraternal organizations will be indicated in later sections.

8. Atlases   An atlas is a book of maps. Fives types of atlases contain maps which are of value to genealogical researchers: (a) historical atlases, (b) national atlases, (c) state atlases, (d) county atlases, (e) city atlases. Historical atlases of the US are made up of maps and text which illustrate and describe the settlement of the country, the development of the colonies, the ownership (Spanish, French, British, US) of the lands, the westward expansion, the addition of new areas, the development of territories and states, the battle lines in wars, the transportation (rivers, trails, canals, roads), migration routes, population movements, types of land (plains, mountains, deserts, river bottoms, timbered, prairie), and the rise and growth of towns and cities. All of these are exceptionally pertinent to your ancestral research since they provide you with an understanding of your progenitor's world. Among the best of the historical atlases are the following:

_H. H. Kagan, THE AMERICAN HERITAGE PICTORIAL ATLAS OF US HISTORY, American Heritage Publishing Co., New York, NY, 1966.

_C. O. Paullin, and J. K. Wright, ATLAS OF THE HISTORICAL GEOGRAPHY OF THE US, Carnegie Institution, Washington, DC, 1932.

_National Geographic Society, HISTORICAL ATLAS OF THE US, The Society, Washington, DC, 1988.

_J. T. Adams and K. T. Jackson, ATLAS OF AMERICAN HISTORY, Charles Scribner's Sons, New York, NY, 1984.

_R. H. Ferrell and R. Natkiel, ATLAS OF AMERICAN HISTORY, Facts on File, New York, NY, 1993.

_W. H. Goetzmann and G. Williams, THE ATLAS OF NORTH AMERICAN EXPLORATION, Prentice-Hall, New York, NY, 1992.

_Readers Digest Association, THESE UNITED STATES: OUR NATION'S GEOGRAPHY, HISTORY, AND PEOPLE, Readers Digest Association, Pleasantville, NY, 1968.
_HAMMOND'S AMERICAN HISTORICAL ATLAS, Hammond and Co., Maplewood, NJ, 1963.
_F. W. Hewes and H. Gannett, SCRIBNER'S STATISTICAL ATLAS OF THE US, Scribner's Sons, New York, NY, 1885.
These will be found in most large libraries, Most can also be borrowed as microfilms from the Family History Library.

National atlases can be of assistance to you in locating counties, cities, towns, and villages. They can also inform you about the relationship between an area your ancestor left and the area to which he migrated. The current atlases with the greatest detail are:
_RAND McNALLY COMMERCIAL ATLAS AND MARKETING GUIDE, Rand McNally, New York, NY, latest annual edition.
_US Geological Survey, THE NATIONAL ATLAS OF THE USA, US Geological Survey, Washington, DC, 1970.
Sometimes you will be unable to locate a place in these atlases because it no longer exists or its name has been changed. In such an instance, you will need to consult an older atlas, such as:
_M. Carey, CAREY'S MINOR ATLAS, M. Carey, Philadelphia, PA, 1810.
_J. C. Carey and I. Lea, A COMPLETE HISTORICAL, CHRONO-LOGICAL, AND GEOGRAPHICAL AMERICAN ATLAS, Carey and Lea, Philadelphia, PA, 1823.
_T. G. Bradford, AN ILLUSTRATED ATLAS OF THE US, Grant and Co., Philadelphia, PA, 1838.
_H. D. Rogers, ATLAS OF THE US OF NORTH AMERICA, Stanford, London, England, 1857.
_JOHNSON'S NEW ILLUSTRATED FAMILY ATLAS, Johnson and Ward, New York, NY, 1862.
_ASHER AND ADAMS NEW COMMERCIAL ATLAS AND GAZETTEER OF THE US, Asher and Adams, Philadelphia, PA, 1872 and later editions.
_O. W. Gray, THE NATIONAL ATLAS, Gray and Son, Philadelphia, PA, 1875, and later editions.
_S. A. Mitchell, MITCHELL'S NEW GENERAL ATLAS, Mitchell, Philadelphia, PA, 1878.
_THE PEOPLE'S ILLUSTRATED AND DESCRIPTIVE FAMILY ATLAS OF THE WORLD, People's Publishing Co., Chicago, IL, 1884.

These atlases will be found in most large libraries. They can also be borrowed as microfilms from the Family History Library.

State atlases are generally of greater value to you because they give you maps with even finer detail than national atlases, revealing places and topographic features that do not appear on larger scale maps. They contain maps which show county lines as of the date on which they were published. The following reference volume lists most of those that exist for dates before 1900, which is the period for which most genealogists need the information.

_C. E. LeGear, US ATLASES, Library of Congress, Washington, DC, 1950/3, 2 volumes.

An exceedingly useful atlas is one which shows the existing counties in each state and territory along with their boundaries during each of the census years (1790, 1800/10/20/30/40/50/60/70/80, 1900/10). The information it displays on county formations and changes during this period of time can be very helpful in locating your forebears.

_W. Thorndale and W. Dollarhide, MAP GUIDE TO THE US FEDERAL CENSUSES, Genealogical Publishing Co., Baltimore, MD, 1987.

Several other atlases, specialized books, and a computer program contain details on county origins and changes.

_J. H. Long, HISTORICAL ATLAS AND CHRONOLOGY OF COUNTY BOUNDARIES, 1788-1980, G. K. Hall, Boston, MA, 1984, 5 volumes. [14 states only]

_J. H. Long and P. T. Sinko, ATLAS OF HISTORICAL COUNTY BOUNDARIES, Simon and Schuster, New York, NY, 1992-. One volume per state.

_J. N. Kane, THE AMERICAN COUNTIES: ORIGINS, CREATION, ORGANIZATION, AREA, POPULATION, HISTORICAL DATA, AND PUBLISHED SOURCES, Scarecrow Press, Metuchen, NY, 1972.

_A. Eichholz, ANCESTRY'S REDBOOK: AMERICAN STATE, COUNTY, AND TOWN SOURCES, Ancestry Publishing, Salt Lake City, UT, latest edition.

_ANIMAP COUNTY BOUNDARY HISTORICAL ATLAS FOR WINDOWS, Computer program, Gold Bug, Alamo, CA, 1994.

State atlases can be located in large libraries, especially ones in the state being considered. The state library and state university library are usually the best. They can also be borrowed from the Family History Library.

For even greater geographical detail on areas on which your progenitor lived, you can consult county, city, and town atlases. Such volumes of maps have been published for many, but not all, counties, cities, and towns. Sizable numbers of county atlases began to be published shortly before the Civil War. These books contain maps, township plats, sometimes city plans, sometimes names of property owners, land boundaries, roads, railroads, lakes, streams, and rivers. Some have historical sketches of the counties, biographies of inhabitants, patrons directories, pictures of businesses, farms, and homes, portraits of leading citizens, and business directories. As a genealogist, you will find in them many clues to family relationships. To discover if atlases were available for the county in which your progenitor lived, consult:

_C. E. LeGear, US ATLASES, Library of Congress, Washington, DC, 1950/3, 2 volumes.

Microfilm copies of numerous early county atlases are also available. These are listed in:

_J. J. Walsh, MICROFORMS IN PRINT, Microforms Review, Westport, CT, latest issue, classifications 240 and 280.

The best sources for county atlases are the pertinent county and state libraries, with the state university library also being very good. They may also be borrowed as microfilms from the Family History Library. Another helpful atlas, which can be found in large libraries, shows township detail for counties. It is:

_J. L. Andriot, TOWNSHIP ATLAS OF THE US, Andriot Associates, McLean, VA, 1987. [Not all states included.]

City, and town atlases can also give you valuable aid if your ancestor lived in either of these jurisdictions. Atlases as near the dates of your ancestor as possible should be sought. The city atlases contain detailed maps showing streets, buildings, ward boundaries, and sometimes names of individual land owners and/or business tenants. City atlases are indispensable for locating ancestors in census records, since the census schedules are arranged by wards, and city atlases give these wards, saving you hours of searching. To discover what atlases were published for your progenitor's city or town, consult:

_C. E. LeGear, US ATLASES, Library of Congress, Washington, DC, 1950/3, 2 volumes.

Very good repositories for these atlases are the relevant state, state university, county, city, and town libraries. And the Family History Library will lend microfilms of them to you.

9. Bible records

During the past 200 years it was customary for many families with religious affiliations to keep vital statistics on their members in the family Bible. These records vary widely, but among them the items that may be found are names, dates, and places of birth, christening, confirmation, baptism, marriage, death, burial, and sometimes military service and divorce. Although most Bibles containing recorded information probably still remain in private hands, some of the information has been submitted for publication and some has been filed in libraries and archives. Your <u>first</u> move is to make extensive inquiries within your family to see if anyone has an old Bible which has been passed down.

The <u>second</u> searches should be in the local region of your forebear, because local organizations are the most likely ones to know of the existence of Bible records pertaining to their areas. Therefore, send an SASE and an inquiry to as many of these organizations as you can find: nearby local genealogical societies, libraries, and historical societies. Ask them about available Bible records and the possibility of having them searched for you. Their names and addresses will be found in:

_V. N. Chambers, editor, THE GENEALOGICAL HELPER, Everton Publishers, Logan, UT, latest Jul-Aug issue, for genealogical societies and libraries.

_M. K. Meyer, DIRECTORY OF GENEALOGICAL SOCIETIES IN THE USA AND CANADA, The Author, Pasadena, MD, latest edition.

_J. Konrad, GENEALOGICAL SOCIETIES AND HISTORICAL SOCIETIES, Ye Olde Genealogie Shoppe, Indianapolis IN, latest edition.

_E. P. Bentley, THE GENEALOGIST'S ADDRESS BOOK, Genealogical Publishing Co., Baltimore, MD, latest edition.

_American Library Association, AMERICAN LIBRARY DIRECTORY, R. R. Bowker, New York, NY, latest issue.

_American Association for State and Local History, DIRECTORY, HISTORICAL SOCIETIES AND AGENCIES IN THE US AND CANADA, The Association, Nashville, TN, latest issue.

The <u>third</u> set of searches should be carried out at the state level. Inquiries and SASEs should be sent to the State Archives, the State Library, and the State Genealogical Society. In some of these repositories, there may be a special index or alphabetical Bible record file, or as is more often the case, data from Bibles may be listed in indexes or alphabetical files labelled something other than Bible records. The most likely labels are family records, genealogies, manuscripts, names, sur-names. Also a look needs to be taken in the major card and computer indexes in these repositories for the names you are seeking. The names and addresses of these repositories are given in later sections of this Handbook. The sections are entitled Genealogical societies, State archives, and State libraries.

The fourth investigations involve a search of genealogical periodical indexes. These are described in this Handbook in a section by that title. Careful attention must be paid to periodicals in your forebear's state, county, and city. You can also contact genealogical publications which deal with the specific surname you are investigating. For details, read the later section entitled Family publications.

The final investigations are essentially at the national level. Two large libraries have unusually good collections of Bible records or copies of them. These are the Family History Library in Salt Lake City, UT, and the DAR Library in Washington, DC. You can examine some indexes to many of the Bible and other family records in the DAR Library and at the Family History Library:
_National Society, DAR, DAR LIBRARY CATALOG, The Society, Washington, DC, 1982/6, 2 volumes.
_Family History Library, FAMILY HISTORY LIBRARY CATALOG, LOCALITY SECTION, The Library, Salt Lake City, UT, latest edition. On microfiche and computer. Also at every Family History Center. Search under state, county, city, and town.
You should write the DAR Library (SASE) and ask if they have Bible record compilations for your progenitor's area. Then check the surname and locality indexes at your nearest Family History Center (branch of Family History Library) for your ancestor's name, state, county, and city. The address of the DAR Library is:
_National Society of Daughters of the American Revolution, 1776 D Street, NW, Washington, DC, 20006. Also see later sections on the DAR.
The locations of Family History Centers, all of which have the indexes referred to above (indexes to the items in the Family History Library) are given in a later section entitled Family History Centers.

---

10. Biographies

Many biographical compilations have been pub-lished. These volumes present biographical sketches on persons who have attained national, state, county, or city prominence in the fields of law, agriculture, business, politics, medicine, engineering, industry, science, military, manufacturing, teaching, government, public service, or philanthropy. Over 600 national biographical works have been indexed in a large microfiche and computer set which contains more than 7 million entries. This set is available in numerous large libraries, and is added to annually:

_BIOBASE, Gale Research, Detroit, MI, latest edition. On both microfiche and computer. And/or see M. C. Herbert and B. McNeil, BIOGRAPHY AND GENEALOGY MASTER INDEX, Gale Research Co., Detroit, MI, 1980-, and supplements.

There are also biographical compilations for citizens of states. The best sources of these are state libraries and state university libraries. Consult a later section entitled State libraries for the addresses of these institutions. In addition, biographical compilations have been published for local regions, counties, towns, and cities. As you might imagine, these are best located by contacting the libraries in these places. Addresses will be found in:

_AMERICAN LIBRARY DIRECTORY, R. R. Bowker, New York, NY, latest edition.

Biographical sketches are also often found in state, regional, county, town, and city histories. These can be easily located in:

_M. J. Kaminkow, US LOCAL HISTORIES IN THE LIBRARY OF CONGRESS, Magna Carta Book Co., Baltimore, MD, 1975, 5 volumes.

_P. W. Filby, BIBLIOGRAPHY OF COUNTY HISTORIES IN AMERICA, Genealogical Publishing Co., Baltimore, MD, 1985.

_The Newberry Library, THE GENEALOGICAL INDEX OF THE NEWBERRY LIBRARY, G. K. Hall, Boston, MA, 1960, 4 volumes. 500,000 names.

About 170,000 names taken from 340 state, regional, county, and city histories and biographical directories are indexed in:

_THE LIBRARY OF CONGRESS INDEX TO BIOGRAPHIES IN STATE AND LOCAL HISTORIES, 40 reels of microfilm, Magna Carta Book Co., Baltimore, MD, 1979.

This index is only partial; it does not by any means index all state and local histories, there being far more than 340.

11. Birth records

Official birth records have been kept by colony, state, territory, district, county, city and town agencies. These records at their best include name, date, place, sex, hospital, father's name, mother's name, mother's maiden name, parents' ages, parents' occupations, legitimacy of the birth, and data on other children born to the mother. As the records get earlier, the amount of information usually gets less. Every state initiated birth registration at some date between 1841 and 1920. For records after this date, you should write to either the state registration agency or the state archives. Below are listed these dates for the various states and the names and addresses of the agencies that should be contacted for the records. The date appears [in brackets] and the agency follows. Then information regarding the source of official birth records before this date is given.

_In AL [1908] AL Department of Public Health, PO Box 5625, Montgomery, AL 36130. From 1881-1908, very incomplete registration in counties. Before 1881, a few records in county probate courts.

_In AK [1913] AK Bureau of Vital Statistics, PO Box 10675, Juneau, AK 99811. Before 1913, church records are the best source.

_In AZ [1909] AZ Vital Records Section, PO Box 3887, Phoenix, AZ 85030. They also have abstracts of some county records before 1909. Some births in county superior courts before 1909.

_In AR [1914] AR Division of Vital Records, 4815 West Markham Street, Little Rock, AR 72205. They also have some Little Rock and Fort Smith births from 1881.

_In CA [1905] CA Vital Statistics Branch, 304 Street, Sacramento, CA 94244. For 1850-1905, records are in counties, in most for only part of this period.

_In CO [1910] CO Vital Records Section, HSVRD-VR-A1, 4300 Cherry Creek Dr., South, Denver, CO 80222. For 1872-1910, some counties have some records, mostly for only part of this time.

_In CT [1897] CT Vital Records Section, 150 Washington St., (First Floor), Hartford, CT 06106. For 1640-1897, contact town or city clerk, or CT State Library.

_In DE [1861-3, 1881] For records after 1920 DE Bureau of Vital Statistics, State Health Building, PO Box 1401, Dover, DE 19901. For records 1861-3 and 1881-1920 DE State Archives, Dover, DE 19901.

_In DC [1871] DC Vital Records Section, 613 G St., N.W., Ninth Floor, Washington, DC 20001. Earlier records very poor.

_In FL [1917] FL Office of Vital Statistics, PO Box 210, Jacksonville, FL 32231. Also some records 1865-1917. A few counties have records 1875-1917, mostly for only part of this time.

_In GA [1919] GA Vital Records Unit, Room 217-H, 47 Trinity Avenue, SW, Atlanta, GA 30334. Atlanta 1887-1919, Savannah 1890-1919, Macon 1891-1919 from county health departments. A few counties have earlier records.

_In HI [1853] HI State Health Department, 1250 Punchbowl Street, Honolulu, HI 96813. Early records incomplete. Records 1853-1896 also at HI State Archives.

_In ID [1911] ID Vital Statistics Unit, 450 West State, Boise, ID 83720. For 1907-1911 county recorder.

_In IL [1916] IL Division of Vital Records, 605 West Jefferson Street, Springfield, IL 62702. For 1877-1916, contact counties. For Chicago 1871-1916, contact county. A few counties have earlier records.

_In IN [1907] IN Division of Vital Records, PO Box 1964, Indianapolis, IN 46206. For 1882-1907, contact counties. A few counties have earlier records.

_In IA [1880] IA Vital Records Section, Lucas State Office Building, Des Moines, IA 50319.

_In KS [1911] KS Department of Health, 900 South West Jackson, Topeka, KS 66612. For 1880-1911, some counties have some records, mostly for a part of this time.

_In KY [1911] KY Office of Vital Statistics, 275 East Main Street, Frankfort, KY 40621. For 1852-1911 KY Department for Libraries and Archives, 300 Coffee Tree Road, Frankfort, KY 40601, or contact counties. Louisville 1898-1911, Covington 1898-1911, Newport 1890-1911, Lexington 1906-1911 at city health departments.

_In LA [1914] LA Division of Vital Records, PO Box 60630, New Orleans, LA 70160. New Orleans 1790-1914 very incomplete, available from city.

_In ME [1892] ME Office of Vital Records, State House, Station 11, Augusta, ME 04333. For 1892-1955 also at ME State Archives, State House, Augusta, ME 04333. For 1635-1892, records incomplete, contact towns.

_In MD [1898] MD Division of Vital Records, PO Box 68760, Baltimore, MD 21215. For 1898-1978 and Baltimore 1875-1978 also at MD State Archives, 350 Rowe Boulevard, Annapolis, MD 21401. For earlier records, contact MD State Archives.

_In MA [1841] For 1896 and later, MA Registry of Vital Records and Statistics, 150 Tremont Street, Room B-3, Boston, MA 02111. For

1841-1896 MA State Archives, 220 Morrissey Boulevard, Boston, MA 02125. For 1620-1896, consult town or city. Most records published.

_In MI [1867] MI Office of the State Registrar, PO Box 30195, Lansing, MI 48909.

_In MN [1908] MN Section of Vital Statistics, 717 Delaware Street, SE, Minneapolis, MN 55440. For 1870-1908, contact county, or contact health departments in St. Paul and Minneapolis.

_In MS [1912] MS Bureau of Vital Statistics, PO Box 1700, Jackson, MS 39215.

_In MO [1909] MO Bureau of Vital Records, PO Box 570, Jefferson City, MO 65102. For 1863-1909, contact counties. For St. Louis 1870-1910 or Kansas City before 1909, write city vital records departments.

_In MT [1907] MT Bureau of Records and Statistics, PO Box 200901, Helena, MT 59620. For 1878-1907, some counties have some records, usually only for a part of this time.

_In NE [1904] NE Bureau of Vital Statistics, PO Box 95007, Lincoln, NE 68509.

_In NV [1911] NV Section of Vital Statistics, 505 East King Street, Carson City, NV 89710. For 1887-1911, contact counties.

_In NH [1901] NH Bureau of Vital Records, 6 Hazen Drive, Concord, NH 03301. Also has some records since 1640. For 1640-1901, contact towns. Also NH State Library, 20 Park Street, Concord, NH 03301.

_In NJ [1848] For 1848-1923 NJ State Archives, 185 West State Street, Trenton, NJ 08625-0307. For after 1923, NJ State Registrar, CN 370, Trenton, NJ 08625.

_In NM [1920] NM Vital Statistics Office, PO Box 26110, Santa Fe, NM 87502.

_In NY [1880] NY Vital Records Section, Room 244, Corning Tower Building, Albany, NY 12237. For records before 1914 in Albany, Buffalo, and Yonkers, and for records before 1880 for Rochester, Syracuse, and Utica, contact city registrar. For New York City records since 1898, contact Bureau of Vital Records, 125 Worth Street, New York, NY 10013. For Manhattan records 1865-1897, contact Municipal Archives, 31 Chambers Street, New York, NY 10007.

_In NC [1913] NC Vital Records Branch, PO Box 29537, Raleigh, NC 27626. A few counties have some incomplete records during 1870-1913.

_In ND [1907] ND Division of Vital Records, 600 East Boulevard Avenue, Bismarck, ND 58505. Also have some incomplete records 1893-1907. For before 1907, also consult counties.

_In OH [1908] OH Department of Health, PO Box 15098, Columbus, OH 43215. For 1867-1908, consult probate court offices in counties.

_In OK [1908] OK Vital Records Section, PO Box 53551, Oklahoma City, OK 73152. A few counties have incomplete records before 1908.

_In OR [1903] OR Vital Records Unit, PO Box 14050, Portland, OR 97214. For Portland records 1864-1903 contact OR State Archives, 1005 Broadway, NE, Salem, OR 97130.

_In PA [1906] PA Division of Vital Records, PO Box 1528, New Castle, PA 16103. For 1860-1915 Philadelphia records contact Vital Statistics, City Hall Annex, Philadelphia, PA 19107. For 1870-1906 incomplete records of Allegheny City, Easton, Harrisburg, Pottsville, Pittsburgh, and Williamsport, contact cities. Some early records also with county registers of wills.

_In RI [1853] RI Division of Vital Records, Cannon Building, 3 Capitol Hill, Room 101, Providence, RI 02908. For 1636-1853, consult town clerks. Also 1636-1850 mostly in book by J. N. Arnold.

_In SC [1915] SC Office of Vital Records, 2600 Bull Street, Columbia, SC 29201. For 1877-1915 Charleston, 1895-1915 Florence, and 1895-1915 Newberry records, contact county health departments.

_In SD [1905] SD Health Statistics Program, 445 East Capitol, Pierre, SD 57501. Some incomplete earlier records available in counties.

_In TN [1914] TN Division of Vital Records, Cordell Hull Building, Nashville, TN 37247. Also have 1908-1912 records and 1881-1914 records for Chattanooga, Knoxville, and Nashville. For incomplete 1874-1914 Memphis records, contact city health department. For 1881-1914 some counties and larger cities have incomplete records.

_In TX [1903] TX Bureau of Vital Statistics, 1100 West 49th Street, Austin, TX 78756. A few counties have incomplete earlier records.

_In UT (1905) UT Bureau of Health Statistics, PO Box 16700, Salt Lake City, UT 84116. Some counties have incomplete records 1887-1905. For Salt Lake City and Ogden 1890-1904, contact city health departments.

_In VT [effectively 1857] VT Public Records Division, PO Box 70, Burlington, VT 05402 for index, abstracts, and microfilm copies for 1760-1954. But original record must be obtained from town clerk.

_In VA [effectively 1853] VA Division of Vital Records, PO Box 1000, Richmond, VA 23208. There is a gap of no records 1896-1912. For the few records before 1853, contact VA State Archives, 11th and Capitol Streets, Richmond, VA 23219. For 1896-1912, inquire at VA State Archives, county, and city.

_In WA [1907] WA Center for Health Statistics, PO Box 9709, Olympia, WA 98507. For 1891-1907, contact WA State Archives, 12th and Washington, Olympia, WA 98504, or county auditor.
_In WV [1917] WV Division Vital Registration Office, Capitol Complex, Building 3, Room 516, Charleston, WV 25305. For 1853-1900, contact WV Archives and History Library, Charleston, WV 25305, or clerk of county court.
_In WI [1907] WI Bureau of Health Statistics, PO Box 309, Madison, WI 53701. For 1852-1907, contact county register of deeds and State Historical Society of WI. Earlier records incomplete.
_In WY [1909] WY Vital Records Services, Hathaway Building, Cheyenne, WY 82002.

Many microfilm copies of the records before the state registration dates are available at the Family History Library, and many births are indexed in their over 200-million-entry International Genealogical Index (IGI). There are also microfilm copies of county birth records (as well as the state records) in the relevant state archives and state libraries, and sometimes in the state historical or genealogical society libraries. State libraries also often hold published copies of the records, and local libraries (county, city, town) may have their own birth records in published or typescript form.

The addresses of county courthouses, county officials, town halls, and town clerks will be found in:
_A. Eichholz, ANCESTRY'S REDBOOK, Ancestry Publishing, Salt Lake City, UT, latest edition.
_NAMES AND NUMBERS, Wiley and Sons, New York, NY, latest edition.
_L. K. Meitzler, THE US COUNTY COURTHOUSE ADDRESS BOOK, Heritage Quest, Orting, WA, 1988.
More detail on birth records in the various states will also be found here. Now, let us note a couple of important items. First, you may find that some states have restrictions on access to their birth records, especially the more recent ones. You may be required to document your use of the records or demonstrate your relationship to the person. Second, it is very important to recognize that delayed records of births were often recorded. That is, birth records were sometimes generated long after the event. For example, even though the records may start in 1852, a person born in 1812 may have registered his birth in 1853. Such records are available in some states, counties, cities, and towns. They may very well have your ancestor in them. So be sure and ask about delayed records of births.

As can be seen from the above listings, official (governmental) birth records cease to be available in most states at some time during their histories. Before these dates, you will need to seek birth information in other sorts of records. The most likely sources include records of the following types: <u>Bible</u>, biography, <u>cemetery</u>, <u>census</u>, <u>church</u>, county and city history, <u>death</u>, family records, fraternal organizations, <u>gravestone</u>, hereditary societies, <u>International Genealogical Index</u>, <u>marriage</u>, military, mortuary, <u>newspaper</u>, published genealogy. All of these are discussed in detail in other sections of this Handbook. Those that are usually the most helpful have been underlined.

12. Black genealogy

Basically, two classifications of black people must be recognized as you approach research on them: free blacks and slave blacks. There were numerous free blacks in this country from its very early years. As of the beginning of the Civil War, about 11-12% of US blacks were free. Then, of course, following the Civil War (after 1865), all blacks were free. For these people, the research procedure is very much the same as that for whites. Help in identification is sometimes given in some records which record people's color. And there are some special records which pertain to the newly-freed blacks just after the Civil War. Both free black and slave black research and data sources are discussed in several important reference works. Several should be thoroughly read and understood before you attempt any work:

_AFRICAN-AMERICAN GENEALOGY HANDBOOK, Gale Research, New York, NY, 1995.

_N. Law, AFRICAN-AMERICAN GENEALOGY WORKBOOK FOR BEGINNERS, Legacy Publ. Co., Birmingham, AL, 1993.

_H. B. Matthews, AFRICAN-AMERICAN GENEALOGICAL RESEARCH, Matthews Heritage Society, Baldwin, NY, 1992.

_D. H. Streets, SLAVE GENEALOGY, A RESEARCH GUIDE WITH CASE STUDIES, Heritage Books, Bowie, MD, 1986.

_J. Rose and A. Eichholz, BLACK GENESIS, Gale Research Co., Detroit, MI, 1978.

_C. L. Blockson and R. Fry, BLACK GENEALOGY, Prentice-Hall, Englewood Cliffs, NJ, 1977.

_J. Cerny, BLACK GENEALOGY, in A. Eakle and J. Cerny, THE SOURCE, A GUIDEBOOK OF AMERICAN GENEALOGY, Ancestry Publishing Co., Salt Lake City, UT, latest edition.

In addition, there are several key source volumes with which you need to be familiar.

_T. M. Young, AFRO-AMERICAN GENEALOGY SOURCEBOOK, Garland Publishing, New York, NY, 1987.
_GUIDE TO GENEALOGICAL RESEARCH IN THE NATIONAL ARCHIVES, The National Archives, Washington, DC, latest edition, Chapter on Records of Black Americans.
_D. L. Newman, BLACK HISTORY: A GUIDE TO CIVILIAN RECORDS IN THE NATIONAL ARCHIVES, National Archives, Washington, DC, 1986.
_BLACK STUDIES, A SELECT CATALOG OF NATIONAL ARCHIVES MICROFILM PUBLICATIONS, National Archives, Washington, DC, 1984.
_A. Eichholz, ANCESTRY'S REDBOOK, Ancestry Publishing, Salt Lake City, UT, 1989, see state sections for brief summaries of black records for their areas.
_B. K. Henritze, BIBLIOGRAPHIC CHECKLIST OF AFRICAN AMERICAN NEWSPAPERS, Genealogical Publishing Co., Baltimore, MD, 1995.

Black slave genealogical research can be quite difficult because slaves were considered as property and not as people. They usually were given only first names, although they often adopted last names within their own society. After the Civil War, the freed slaves took surnames, but sometimes this was a fitful process, resulting in their use of several surnames before they finally settled on one. The major technique that must be used to attempt to trace slaves is to identify the white owner and the plantation or farm or industry in which they worked. Every conceivable scrap of information on the owner must be ferreted out, with special effort being devoted to locating plantation records. Those that survive are widely scattered, so all possible manuscript repositories must be contacted. Sometimes slave births were registered as a means of establishing ownership of the new-born, sometimes sales records of slaves appear in property or court records, sometimes slaves are given to heirs in wills or other estate action, sometimes there are records of the freeing of slaves (manumission) in county land or court offices, sometimes there are newspaper ads offering rewards for runaways, sometimes there are ads of slaves for sale. There were anti-slavery groups in northern states and manumission societies in both the north and south which kept numerous records. And there were collections of slave stories, oral black history, and Underground Railroad materials in several places.

The 1790-1840 censuses give the numbers of slaves in the households of their owners, but no names. The 1850 and 1860 censuses have special schedules which list slave-holders and the numbers of slaves they have, but again no slave names are given. The 1870 census is notable since it is the first to list all black people by name. Blacks served in the military, beginning in early times, there being good records for the Revolutionary War forward. Many received pensions, which are on record. After the Civil War, the US set up a Freedman's Bureau to assist blacks to readjust to their new situation. Help along several lines was offered: food, clothing, shelter, employment, hospital care, land, schools, locating relatives, marriages, savings, and loans. A vast number of records were generated, and they now reside in the National Archives. All the above records and many more, plus details on research techniques are given in the works identified at the beginning of this section. You will also find there information on several large black record repositories, black ancestry collections, black lineage registries, and black genealogical societies.

13. Bounty land records

Bounty land most usually refers to land given by the colonies, the states, and the federal government as a reward for or as an inducement to military service. In colonial times, the colonies often granted land for military service or for manning frontier forts. Numerous such grants were made to participants in the French and Indian War (1754-1763). A number of the original colonies, after they became states following the Revolution (1775-1783), awarded bounty land to their veterans (GA, MA, MD, NC, NY, PA, SC, VA), but others did not (CT, DE, NH, NJ, RI). Of those states who gave grants, all but three gave land in the state, MA giving it in what is now ME, NC in what is now TN, and VA in what is now KY and OH. The veteran filed an application, and if it was approved, he received a warrant. This warrant could be exchanged for the land. The applications vary in the amount of detail, but they often carry some genealogical information. Sometimes the recipients of warrants sold them rather than personally taking possession of the land. All the above records should be sought in the appropriate state archives. Their addresses are given in a later section entitled State archives. Some of these records are also available on microfilm at the Family History Library.

For military service in the federal forces 1775-1855, the federal government awarded bounty land beginning in 1788. Major wars during this period included the American Revolution (1775-1783), the War of 1812 (1812-1815), the Indian Wars (various times in the 1800s), and the Mexican War (1846-1848). Bounty lands for Revolutionary service were in OH, and those for War of 1812 service were in IL, AR, and MO. In 1830 and 1842 federal laws were broadened finally permitting veterans to take up federal land anywhere. An application had to be sent in, and if approved, a warrant was issued. This warrant could be redeemed for land or sold, most veterans doing the latter. The most valuable document for genealogical purposes is the application, which often contains many of these records: name, age, rank, wife's name, wife's maiden name, military unit, service records, residence, dates of birth and marriage, affidavits of witnesses, discharge and other papers. To obtain bounty land records, write the National Archives where they are stored, and request a NATF Form 80. Fill it out with as much information as you have, then return it. The proper address is

_Reference Service Branch (NNIR), National Archives, 8th and Pennsyl-
    vania Avenue, NW, Washington, DC 20408.

Response from the National Archives can sometimes be slow because of the large backlog of work they often have. Instead of contacting them by mail, you may wish to hire a researcher in Washington, DC, to do the work for you. Searchers are listed in:

_V. N. Chambers, editor, THE GENEALOGICAL HELPER, Everton
    Publishers, Logan, UT, latest Sep-Oct issue.

Or you may first want to look into the bounty land records which the Family History Library has on microfilm. Microfilms of some of the records are also available at the Regional Branches of the National Archives and at some state and large genealogical libraries. See the section describing these repositories. Many further details on bounty land records will be found in:

_National Archives Staff, GUIDE TO GENEALOGICAL RECORDS
    IN THE NATIONAL ARCHIVES, National Archives, Washington,
    DC, latest edition, Chapter on Bounty Land Warrant Records.

14. Burned county records

Sooner or later practically every genealogist runs into the problems posed by the loss of records in a courthouse fire or other disaster (flood, tornado, earthquake, vandalism). This is especially devastating because the county is usually the most important governmental unit for the generation of genealogically-useful records. The problem is particularly bad in the south, but no region is without some losses. In practically all such cases, the situation is by no means hopeless simply because there are likely to be numerous other sources of genealogical information. The following steps should be taken.

First, a thorough investigation of the exact situation in the county should be made. A careful exploration for precisely what records were left is required. Sources of such information include the state library and archives, state and regional and local genealogical societies, the local library, local genealogists, county historians, and county officials. Be sure to ask what was done with the remains of damaged records. And remember that after a record-destroying disaster, the county often reconstituted records (especially land, marriage, and tax). For example, the county would ask all land owners to re-file their deeds. You will also sometimes find that someone has transcribed, indexed, or abstracted records before their loss, and that genealogists who worked in the records before the disaster included data in their materials and published family histories. It is also well to ask about family, city, county, regional, and state histories, and about dissertations and theses which may refer to the lost records or quote from them. One further item to which you need to be alert is that now and again records of one sort will be in books labelled something else. This sometimes occurred in the earliest years of a county.

Second, use of every possible state and national record is to be made. Among the important state records, most of which can be found in the state archives, are: birth, death, and marriage (usually late, but not always), state censuses (not all states), colonial (before counties), divorce (in legislature early), appeal courts, state land grants (for the 13 colonies, ME, VT, WV, KY, TN, TX, HI), legislative (claim, divorce, petition, road), military service, military pension, prison, tax (counties often sent duplicates in). Important national records are located in the National Archives, with copies in the National Archives Field Branches, state archives, state libraries, and large genealogical libraries. Included are records of these types: census, farm census, homestead, land grant (states other than those above), manufactures census, military bounty land, military pension, military service, mortality census, tax (1798 for ME, NH, MA, RI, CT, PA, DE, MD, TN, and 1862-6 all existing states).

Third, proceed to look into the records of all related counties, both in time and space. This includes the parent county or counties from which the burned county came. Parent counties sometimes kept records for new counties during several early years while the government was being set up. Also included are daughter counties because sometimes a new county would take possession of a copy or a partial copy of the records of its parent. All neighboring counties should also be searched, especially those nearest the land of the ancestor. It is also possible that your forebear had business in a nearby county, owned property there, went to church there, banked there, got his mail at a postoffice there, or that it was a shorter or easier trip to town there. Not to be overlooked are the records of the counties from which you progenitors came and to which they went. Around the times when they moved, there are often records in both the county being left and the new county, especially land sale and purchase records.

Fourth, look into non-governmental records that can give you data. Some of them can be good substitutes for lost materials. The following are among those that can be of value: abstract company records (land), atlases (land owners), attorneys' records (court cases, divorce, estate, land, probate, tax, will), biographies (birth, marriage, death, parents, children), cemetery (death, birth, marriage), church (birth, baptism, confirmation, communion, marriage, death, burial), city directories (death, age), employment (birth, marriage, death), insurance (birth, marriage, death, children, heirs), manuscripts (birth, marriage, death, other), mortuary (death, burial, marriage, birth, survivors), newspapers (birth, marriage, anniversary, court), school (birth, parents), title insurance (land). Contacts with genealogical societies, historical societies, libraries, and various businesses in the county are the best ways of locating these records (remember the SASE). Practically all of the records mentioned above are treated in detail under their respective headings in this volume.

15. Canadian genealogy

The second largest country in the world, Canada, borders the 48 contiguous states of the US on the north. It consists of ten provinces and two territories: New Brunswick (1604 F), Nova Scotia (1605 F), Quebec (1608 F), Newfoundland (1610 B), Ontario (1668 B), Alberta (1670 B), Manitoba (1670 B), Northwest Territories (1670 B), Prince Edward Island (1719 F), British Columbia (1800/10 B), Saskatchewan (1774 B), Yukon Territory (1840 B). The dates in parentheses represent the date or approximate date when the area was settled or began to be exploited by traders. The letters indicate who established the first settlement or began the first trading activity, B indicating the British and F the French. From the beginnings until 1763, the area was constantly fought over by the British and the French. The French early established and operated an extensive fur-trading enterprise out of Quebec. From this center, French fur traders, explorers, and missionaries moved down waterways into the interior regions of North America. The British strongly entered Canada in 1670 through the trading activities of the Hudson Bay Company, even though there were British settlements on the eastern coast before that date. The Hudson Bay Company operated west and northwest of the French.

In 1713 Acadia (Nova Scotia, New Brunswick, Prince Edward Island) was taken by the British, and the Hudson Bay area and Newfoundland were recognized as their lands. At the conclusion of the French and Indian War in 1763, all French Canadian lands became British. During the American Revolution (1775-1783), many Loyalists fled to Canada and settled in the eastern coastal area and Quebec. In 1791, Quebec was split into English Protestant Upper Canada (now Ontario) and French Catholic Lower Canada (Quebec). In the period 1800-1810 British Columbia was secured as British. During the 1820s and 1830s immigration from Scotland and Ireland was very heavy. Upper and Lower Canada were united in 1841 to form the Province of Canada, the two parts being renamed Canada West and Canada East. Then in 1867, the four provinces of Ontario (Canada West), Quebec (Canada East), Nova Scotia, and New Brunswick formed a federation, which received all the Hudson Bay lands in 1870. In this same year, Manitoba joined, with British Columbia joining in 1871, with Prince Edward Island in 1873, and Alberta and Saskatchewan in 1905. The Northwest Territories were obtained from the Hudson Bay Company. Newfoundland was added in 1949.

Genealogical research in Canada follows the general pattern of that in the US. The major repositories are the Canadian Public Archives, the archives of the provinces, and the Family History Library in Salt Lake City, UT. The records which are of value include these types: biography, birth, cemetery, census, church, court, death, genealogical collections, land, Loyalist, marriage, military, naturalization, newspaper, passenger lists, periodicals, probate, tax, and will. Several very good short treatments which are recommended are:
_M. Rubincam and K. Stryker-Rodda, GENEALOGICAL RESEARCH: METHODS AND SOURCES, American Society of Genealogists, Washington, DC, 1980/3, Volume 1, pages 338-389, Volume 2, pages 285-307.
_J. Cerny and W. Elliott, THE LIBRARY, Ancestry Publishing, Salt Lake City, UT, 1988, pages 359-384.
Recommended volumes for more detailed treatment include:
_A. Baxter, IN SEARCH OF YOUR CANADIAN ROOTS, Genealogical Publishing Co., Baltimore, MD, 1994.
_E. Jonasson, THE CANADIAN GENEALOGICAL HANDBOOK, Wheatfield Press, Winnipeg, Manitoba, 1983.

Several of the above should be studied carefully before you begin your quest for a Canadian progenitor.

16. Card and computer catalogs

In practically all archives, libraries, and other record repositories, the major finding aid will be one or more card or computer catalogs. A card catalog usually consists of 3 x 5 cards arranged alphabetically in the drawers of one or more large cabinets. These cards show special code numbers of the holdings of the repository which permit them to be located. A computer catalog is similar in that a computer alphabetically displays information on the holdings of the repository along with the special code numbers.

In order to make certain that you have used a card or computer catalog properly and thoroughly, that is, that you have not missed material relating to your forebears, remember the word SLANT. The letter S stands for subject, the letter L for locality, the letter A for author, the letter N for name, and the letter T for title. These indicate categories under which you should search for items which might carry genealogical data of interest to you. However, for best and quickest results, they should not be searched in the order S-L-A-N-T, but in the order N-L-S-A-T. Thus when you first begin to use the catalog search the N or name category. Look up every surname in which you are interested. If you see materials which refer to your ancestor or which you think might, copy the code numbers. These will permit you to locate the items on open shelves or will be used by an attendant to retrieve them from closed shelves or storage.

Your second search should be under the L or locality category. Search the catalog for your ancestor's county. It is usually listed alphabetically. For example, Knox County, TN will be listed under K. Sometimes, however, in certain catalogs it will be listed under Tennessee, then under Tennessee alphabetically. Again, look at every card or listing under the county, copy the codes of all promising items, then obtain and use them. Continue your locality search by looking under your progenitor's city or town. These will sometimes be found under the county, sometimes strictly alphabetically, and sometimes under the state. If you have trouble, ask the attendant. Finally, look at every card or listing under the pertinent state. You will often find a tremendous number of cards or listings, and you will feel that you have quite a long task before you. However, many, probably even most of the cards or listings will not be of genealogical interest, so you will be able to move through them fairly rapidly.

The third search is one based on the category S or subject. There are a number of subjects that it is often of value to search out in the card or computer catalog. The titles to many of the sections in this book will give you a good idea of subjects to look for (such as Adoptions, Atlases, Bible records, Biographies, etc.). Two subject headings that you must not overlook are <u>Registers of births, etc</u>. and <u>Vital records,</u> since you are likely to find birth, marriage, divorce, and death records under them. There are also certain special headings that should be looked for under the United States, and then under History. Here you will find items relating to important historical events, including the wars.

The fourth search is based on the category A or author. If you happen to know the author of a book which you want to find, it can be located alphabetically under the author's name. And the fifth search, which is based on the category T for title, reminds you that if all you know about an item is its title, that title will be alphabetically listed in the card or computer catalog. This lets you look up titles of books, periodicals, microfilms, and agencies and organizations which sponsor publications (such as DAR, UDC, WPA, US National Archives). If you conscientiously make these five searches, you can be assured that you have seen everything a given card or computer catalog has to offer you.

There are repositories in which their catalogs are split, that is, there is an author-title catalog and a separate name-locality-subject catalog. You need to be alert to this possibility, as well as other ways catalogs might be split. Sometimes you will find that a repository has more than one catalog, so never leave without asking.

17. Cemetery records

Records of burials, grave sites, and tombstone inscriptions are often obtainable from cemetery custodians. These custodians may be sextons, county officials, township officers, city employees, town officials, church officers, mortuary personnel, or private cemetery staff members. Various types of records may be kept: burial registers, plot maps, plot deeds, burial permits, biographical cards. In some cases the cemetery files will contain details on the persons buried there. In other cases, only the name, date, and site of the burial will be recorded. If the name and location of the cemetery is known, you should send them an SASE and an inquiry addressed to the custodian asking about your ancestor. Addresses of many, but not all, cemeteries in the US will be found in:

_CEMETERIES OF THE US, Gale Research Co., Detroit, MI, latest edition. Over 22,600 cemeteries.

_INTERNATIONAL CEMETERY DIRECTORY, American Cemetery Association, Columbus, OH, latest edition.

If the cemetery is unknown, or if you are unable to locate a custodian, or if you do not receive a response, send an SASE and an inquiry to the nearest local genealogical society. Give them details about your ancestor, and ask them about cemeteries in the region, cemetery records (typescript, published, manuscript, genealogical periodicals), custodians, and search costs. The locations and addresses of genealogical societies will be found in:

_M. K. Meyer, DIRECTORY OF GENEALOGICAL SOCIETIES IN THE USA, Libra PUblications, Linthicum Heights, MD, latest edition.

_E. P. Bentley, GENEALOGICAL ADDRESS BOOK, Genealogical Publishing Co., Baltimore, MD, latest edition.

_V. N. Chambers, editor, THE GENEALOGICAL HELPER, Everton Publishers, Logan, UT, latest Jul-Aug issue.

Should this not prove successful, try the same approach with the nearest local library (county, town, city) to your forebear's place of residence. Practically all libraries in the US are listed in:

_American Library Association, AMERICAN LIBRARY DIRECTORY, R. R. Bowker, New York, NY, latest issue.

If this too fails, use the same approach with the nearest local history society whose name and address will appear in:

_DIRECTORY: HISTORICAL SOCIETIES AND AGENCIES IN THE US AND CANADA, American Association of State and Local History, Nashville, TN, latest edition.

Often a funeral establishment will have old records of burials within the local region. Thus a useful approach would be to write one or more mortuaries in the immediate vicinity of your progenitor's place of residence. Names and addresses will be found in:

_THE AMERICAN BLUE BOOK OF FUNERAL DIRECTORS, Boylston Publications, New York, NY, latest edition.

Your second set of searches should be made at your nearest Family History Center, which is a branch of the Family History Library in Salt Lake City, UT. The Family History Library has microfilm copies of ₂ large number of typescript and published cemetery records. At the

Family History Center, ask for the Locality Section of the Family History Library Catalog, which is on microfiche and computer. You want the section which pertains to your ancestor's state. Move in them to your ancestor's county, then look for cemetery records. Should you find that records are available and if they look promising, have the attendant borrow them from the Family History Library for you.

The third set of searches is to be carried out at the state level. Start by sending an SASE and an inquiry to the applicable state genealogical society. Ask about available cemetery records, borrowing the records, and having the records searched. Names and addresses of the societies are given in the section of this Handbook entitled State genealogical societies. The next step is to try the state archives. Their addresses appear in this volume under a section called State archives. Similarly, try the state libraries, whose addresses appear in this Handbook under a section entitled State libraries. If still no success has been attained, contact the state historical society. Their names and addresses are in this volume in a section labelled State Historical societies. In all these contacts be sure you send an SASE and keep your letter brief. You probably will not hear from all of these organizations since some of them have little or no interest in genealogy and some are seriously short-handed.

The fourth set of searches is to be undertaken in genealogical periodicals. Local, regional, and state periodicals are likely sources of cemetery data. Initially, it is important that you look through the indexes of all local genealogical periodicals, looking under the category of cemetery records. When you write the local genealogical society and the local library (as in the second paragraph of this section), be sure to ask about cemetery records in their local genealogical periodicals. Then, make a search in the nation-wide genealogical periodical indexes which are discussed in detail in a later section. There you will be told where to find and how to use these indexes.

Finally, a few important points will be called to your attention. (a) Do not forget that many burials, especially early ones, were in church yards or church cemeteries. A knowledge of or a good guess about your progenitor's religion can often indicate appropriate cemeteries to be considered. (b) Many smaller cemeteries, including the old-time family cemeteries, have never been recorded. You may have to locate them and search them yourself, or hire someone to do it for you. (c) Useful aids in finding cemeteries are atlases and detailed maps of the pertinent area.

These are sometimes available at the county library, county highway department, the county tax office, and/or the state highway department. Town and city offices ought also to be asked. A very good series of exceedingly detailed maps, each map showing only a part of a county, is available from the US Geological Survey. Many cemeteries are shown. Details on obtaining all these maps are given in this book in a later section entitled Maps. (d) Cemeteries of burial may be found in certain other records: death certificates, obituaries, funeral notices, cemetery plot purchase records (deeds), burial permits, family Bibles, church records, mortuary records.

---

18. Censuses of 1790-1840

In the years 1790, 1800, 1810, 1820, 1830, and 1840, the US Government attempted to count the population in every county in every state and territory. In the process, they listed the names of the heads of households. No other names were listed, but the people in each household were counted according to certain categories. The data in each of the censuses, and the states for which the records survive, are:

_1790 Census [National Archives Microfilms M637 and T498, also in published volumes]: state, county, date, name of census taker, city or town or subdivision, name of head of household, number of free white males over 15, number of free white males under 16, number of free white females, number of other free persons, number of slaves [CT, ME, MD, MA, NH, NY, NC, PA, RI, SC, VT, missing for DE, GA, KY, NJ, TN, VA, substitutes for most of them reconstructed from state data, usually tax records].

_1800 Census [National Archives Microfilm M32, 52 rolls]: state, county, date, name of census taker, city or town or subdivision, name of head of household; number of free white males 0-10, 10-16, 16-26, 26-45, 45 and over; number of free white females 0-10, 10-16, 16-26, 26-45, 45 and over; number of other free persons except Indians not taxed; number of slaves [CT, DE, DC, ME, MD, MA, NH, NY, NC, PA, RI, SC, VT].

_1810 Census [National Archives Microfilm M252, 71 rolls]: content same as for 1800 [CT, DE, KY, LA, ME, MD, MA, NH, NY, NC, PA, RI, SC, TN (part), VT, VA].

_1820 Census [National Archives Microfilm M33, 142 rolls]: state, county, subdivision(s), name of census taker; name of head of household; number of free white males 0-10, 10-16, 16-18, 16-26, 26-45, 45 and over; number of free white females 0-10, 10-16, 16-26, 26-45, 45 and over; number of other free persons except Indians not taxed; number of free colored males 0-14, 14-26, 26-45, 45 and over; number of free colored females 0-14, 14-26, 26-45, 45 and over; number of male slaves 0-14, 14-26, 26-45, 45 and over; number of female slaves 0-14, 14-26, 26-45, 45 and over; number of foreigners not naturalized; number of persons in agriculture; number of persons in commerce, number of persons in manufacturer (sic) [CT, DE, DC, GA, IL, IN, KY, LA, ME, MD, MA, MI, MS, NH, NY, NC, OH, PA, RI, SC, TN, VT, VA].

_1830 census [National Archives Microfilm M19, 201 rolls]: state, county, subdivision(s), name of census taker; name of head of household; number of free white males 0-5, 5-10, 10-15, 15-20, 20-30, 30-40, 40-50, 50-60, 60-70, 70-80, 80-90, 90-100, 100 and over; number of free white females 0-5, 5-10, 10-15, 15-20, 20-30, 30-40, 40-50, 50-60, 60-70, 70-80, 80-90, 90-100, 100 and over; number of male slaves 0-10, 10-24, 24-36, 36-55, 55-100, 100 and over; number of female slaves 0-10, 10-24, 24-36, 36-55, 55-100, 100 and over; total number of persons; number of whites deaf and dumb 0-14, 14-25, 25 and over; number of blind whites; number of whites not naturalized [AL, AR, CT, DE, DC, FL, GA, IL, IN, KY, LA, ME, MD, MA, MI, MS, MO, NH, NJ, NY, NC, OH, PA, RI, SC, TN, VT, VA].

_1840 Census [National Archives Microfilm M704, 580 rolls]: state, county, subdivision(s), name of census taker; name of head of household; number of free white males 0-5, 5-10, 10-15, 15-20, 20-30, 30-40, 40-50, 50-60, 60-70, 70-80, 80-90, 90-100, 100 and over; number of free white females 0-5, 5-10, 10-15, 15-20, 20-30, 30-40, 40-50, 50-60, 60-70, 70-80, 80-90, 90-100, 100 and over; number of slave males 0-10, 10-24, 24-36, 36-55, 55-100, 100 and over; number of slave females 0-10, 10-24, 24-36, 36-55, 55-100, 100 and over; total number of persons; number of persons in agriculture; number of persons in commerce; number of persons in manufacturer (sic) and trades; number of persons in mining; number of persons in navigation; number of persons in learned professions and engineers; names and ages of Revolutionary or military pensioners; number of white males over 21 who cannot read and write; total number of persons [AL, AR, CT, DE, DC, FL, GA, IL, IN, IA, KY, LA, ME, MD, MA, MI, MS, MO, NH, NJ, NY, NC, OH, PA, RI, SC, TN, VT, VA, WI].

In the above listings a designation such as 10-15 means persons 10, 11, 12, 13, and 14 years old, but not 15; that is, it includes those 10 years old up to (but not including) 15, or, it means persons 10 and older, but under 15. The 1790-1820 censuses counted the people as of the first Monday in August, while the 1830-40 censuses did so as of 01 June.

Some notes on the censuses are on order. (1) The censuses are sometimes incomplete, sometimes inaccurate, sometimes illegible, and published copies sometimes have errors. (2) The listings under each county are often subdivided into districts, towns, townships, parishes, precincts, or hundreds. Careful attention needs to be paid to these. Cities are sometimes included in counties, sometimes appended to them, sometimes precede them. Cities are often divided into wards. (3) In some years, part or all of the records for a few states have been lost or destroyed. These include DE, GA, KY, NJ, TN, and VA for 1790; GA, IN, KY, MS, NJ, OH, TN, and VA for 1800; DC, GA, IN, MI, MS, MO, NJ, OH, and part of TN for 1810; and AL, AR, MO, and NJ for 1820. (4) Substitutes for some of these missing census records have been constructed using various state data, most usually tax records. (5) A very useful aid to census searches is an atlas which shows the county boundaries as they were in each census year and compares them to the boundaries of today.

_W. Thorndale and W. Dollarhide, MAP GUIDE TO THE FEDERAL CENSUSES, 1790-1920, Genealogical Publishing Co., Baltimore, MD, 1987.

Your search of these 1790-1840 census records has been made easy because indexes for each available state have been published for 1790, 1800, 1810, 1820, 1830, and 1840. These published indexes list under each surname the given names with a reference to the county and the page number where the entry will be found in the census records. The indexes are widely available in large libraries, especially those with good genealogical collections (large city libraries, state libraries, the larger genealogical libraries, some state archives, the Family History Library). For listings of these published census indexes, see:

_P. W. Filby, AMERICAN AND BRITISH GENEALOGY AND HERALDRY, The New England Historic Genealogical Society, Boston, MA, 1983, and periodic SUPPLEMENTS. Be sure to examine all supplements. Look in the indexes under the heading Census.

In addition, Accelerated Indexing Systems has gathered together all its 1790-1800-1810 census indexes (along with some other material) to produce an overall US index. Likewise all the 1820 censuses have been gathered to produce an overall US 1820 index. Similar overall US indexes for 1830 and for 1840 have been produced. These microfiche indexes are available in every Family History Center, one of which is close to you. Some of these published and microfiche indexes have some errors in them (omissions, misspellings, transpositions, transcription mistakes), so if two or more indexes are available, all of them should be searched. And if you do not find your ancestor in them, it does not necessarily mean he/she is not in the census.

Once you have found from the indexes where in the census records your ancestor is listed (or at least your suspected ancestor), you can obtain the actual census information in several ways. First, you may borrow the census records for a small fee through your local Family History Library (locations in a later section). Second, you may personally borrow them for a small fee from the American Genealogical Lending Library, PO Box 329, Bountiful, UT 84011. Third, any library, including your local library, can borrow them for a small fee from the American Genealogical Lending Library or from the Census Microfilm Rental Program, PO Box 30, Annapolis Junction, MD 20701. Fourth, you may find them in a large genealogical library or state library (see later sections under Large genealogical libraries and State libraries), or in a Regional Branch of the National Archives, (locations and addresses in a later section), or in the National Archives in Washington, DC. Fifth, you may hire a searcher to look at them for you at the National Archives, or its Regional Branches or at the Family History Library. Instructions for hiring a searcher are given in a later section entitled Hired searchers.

19. Census of 1850

In 1850, the US Government continued its census-taking activity by recording census data as of 01 June 1850. With this 7th federal census, there came a very significant change. The names of all free persons were recorded, not just those of heads of households. The names were listed under households, then under an enumeration district or other subdivision, then under the county, and finally under the state. Accompanying each name are the age, sex, color (white, black, or mulatto), profession or trade of each male over 15, value of real estate owned, place of birth (state, territory, or county), if married within the past year, if attended school within the year, if over 20 and unable to read and write, and if deaf, dumb, blind, insane, idiotic, pauper, or convict. The microfilm copies of the records are as follows, along with a list of the state and territories for which the census is available.

_1850 Census [National Archives Microfilm M432, 1009 rolls]: AL*, AR*, CA, CT, DE*, DC*, FL*, GA*, IL, KY*, LA*, ME, MD*, MA, MI, MN Territory, MS*, MO*, NH, NJ, NM, NY, NC*, OH, OR Territory, PA, RI, SC*, TN*, TX*, UT Territory, VT, VA*, WI. States marked with an asterisk * have separate census records of

slave-holders which are included with the above records. For details
see the later section entitled Slave-holder censuses.

Your search of the 1850 census records has been made easy
because an index for each of the above states or territories has been
published (books, microfiche, CDs). These published indexes list under
each surname the given names with a reference to the county and the
page number where the entry will be found in the census records. The
indexes are widely available in large libraries, especially those with good
genealogical collections (large city libraries, state libraries, the larger
genealogical libraries, some state archives, the Family History Library,
larger Family History Centers). For listings of these published indexes,
see:
_P. W. Filby, AMERICAN AND BRITISH GENEALOGY AND
    HERALDRY, The New England Historic Genealogical Society,
    Boston, MA, 1983, and periodic SUPPLEMENTS. Be sure to
    examine all supplements. Look in the indexes under the heading
    Census.
In addition, Accelerated Indexing Systems has gathered together all its
1850 census indexes (plus some others) to produce three consolidated
microfiche indexes. These are
_AIS Consolidated 1850 Census Index for New England and Northeast-
    ern States: CT, DE, ME, MA, NH, NJ, NY, OH, PA, RI, VT.
_AIS Consolidated 1850-60 Census Index for Midwestern and Western
    States: AZ, CA, IL, IN, IA, KS, MN, MI, MN Territory, MO, NE
    Territory, NM, ND, OK, OR Territory, OR, SD, TX, UT Territory,
    WA, WI.
_AIS Consolidated 1850 Census Index for Southern States: AL, AR, DC,
    FL, GA, KY, LA, MD, MS, NC, SC, TN, VA.
These microfiche indexes are available in every Family History Center,
one of which is close to you. Some of these published and microfiche indexes have some errors in them (omissions, misspellings, transpositions,
transcription mistakes), so if two or more indexes are available, use all of
them. And if you do not find your ancestor in them, it does not necessarily mean he/she is not in the census.

Once you have found from the indexes where in the census
records your ancestor is listed (or at least your suspected ancestor), you
can obtain the actual census information in several ways:
_Borrow the census microfilms for a small fee through your local Family
    History Center (locations in later section entitled Family History Cen-
    ters).

_Personally borrow the census microfilms for a small fee from the American Genealogical Lending Library, PO Box 329, Bountiful, UT 84011.

_Any library, including your local library, can borrow them for a small fee from the American Genealogical Lending Library or from the Census Microfilm Rental Program, PO Box 30, Annapolis Junction, MD 20701.

_You may find them in a large genealogical library (see later sections entitled Large genealogical libraries and State libraries), or in a Regional Branch of the National Archives (locations and addresses in a later section under that name), or in the National Archives, Washington, DC.

_You may hire a searcher to look at the microfilm records at the National Archives, at a National Archives Regional Branch, or at the Family History Library. Instructions for hiring a researcher are given in a later section entitled Hired searchers.

20. Census of 1860

As of 01 June 1860, the 8th US Census was taken. The names of all free persons were listed under households, then under a Post Office address, then under the county, and finally under the state. With each name were listed age, sex, color (white, black, mulatto), occupation or trade for all over 15, value of real estate owned, value of personal estate, place of birth (state, territory, or country), if married in a previous year, if attended school in previous year, if over 20 and could not read and write, if deaf, dumb, blind, insane, idiotic, pauper, or convict. The microfilm copies of the records are as follows, along with a list of the state and territories for which the census is available:

_1860 Census [National Archives Microfilm M653, 1438 rolls]: AL*, AR*, CA, CT, Dakota Territory, DE*, DC*, FL*, GA*, IL, IN, IA, KS, KY*, LA*, ME, MD*, MA, MI, MN, MS*, MO*, NE Territory, NH, NJ, NM, NY, NC*, OH, OR, PA, RI, SC*, TN*, VT, VA*, WA, WI. States marked with an asterisk * have separate census records of slave-holders. These records are included with the above records. For details see the later section entitled Slave-holder censuses.

Your search of the 1860 census records has been made easy because an index for each of the above states or territories has been published (books, microfiche, CDs). These published indexes list under each surname the given names with a reference to the county and the page number where the entry will be found in the census records. The indexes are widely available in large libraries, especially those with good genealogical collections (large city libraries, state libraries, the larger genealogical libraries, some state archives, the Family History Library, larger Family History Centers). For listings of these published indexes, see:

_P. W. Filby, AMERICAN AND BRITISH GENEALOGY AND HERALDRY, The New England Historic Genealogical Society, Boston, MA, 1983, and periodic SUPPLEMENTS. Be sure to examine all supplements. Look in the indexes under the heading Census.

In addition, Accelerated Indexing Systems has produced some consolidated microfiche indexes. Each of these consists of the census indexes of states in a certain geographical region which have been coalesced. These microfiche indexes are available in every Family History Center, one of which is close to you. Some of these published and microfiche indexes have some errors in them (omissions, misspellings, transpositions, transcription errors), so if two or more indexes are available, use all of them. And if you do not find your ancestor in them, it does not necessarily mean he/she is not in the census.

Once you have found from the indexes where in the census records your ancestor is listed (or at least your suspected ancestor), you can obtain the actual census information in several ways. First, you may borrow the census records for a small fee through your local Family History Library (locations in a later section). Second, you may personally borrow them for a small fee from the American Genealogical Lending Library, PO Box 329, Bountiful, UT 84011. Third, any library, including your local library, can borrow them for a small fee from the American Genealogical Lending Library or from the Census Microfilm Rental Program, PO Box 30, Annapolis Junction, MD 20701. Fourth, you may find them in a large genealogical library or state library (see later sections under Large genealogical libraries and State libraries), or in a Regional Branch of the National Archives, (locations and addresses in a later section), or in the National Archives in Washington, DC. Fifth, you may hire a searcher to look at them for you at the National Archives, or its Regional Branches or at the Family History Library. Instructions for hiring a searcher are given in a later section entitled Hired searchers.

21. Census of 1870
The 9th US census was taken as of 01 June 1870. The names of all persons were listed under county subdivision, then under county, then under state, with the Post Office also being shown. With each name were listed the age, sex, color (white,

black, mulatto, Chinese, Indian), profession or occupation or trade, value of real estate, value of personal estate, place of birth (state, territory, or country), if father was foreign born, if mother was foreign born, the month of birth if born within the year, the month of marriage if married within the year, if attended school within the year, if cannot read, if cannot write, if deaf or dumb or blind or insane or idiotic, if male citizen 21 or over, if male citizen of US 31 or over and right to vote denied. The microfilm copies of the records are as follows, along with a list of the states and territories for which the census is available:

_1870 Census [National Archives Microfilm M593, 1748 rolls]: AL, AZ Territory, AR, CA, CO, CT, Dakota Territory, DE, DC, GA, ID Territory, IL, IN, IA, KS, KY, LA, ME, MD, MA, MI, MN, MS, MO, MT Territory, NE, NV, NH, NJ, NM, NY, NC, OH, OR, PA, RI, SC, TN, TX, UT, VT, WA, WV, WI, WY Territory.

Your search of the 1870 census records has been made easy because an index (books, microfiche, CDs) for each of the above states or territories has been published. These published indexes list under each surname the given names with a reference to the county and the page number where the entry will be found in the census records. The indexes are widely available in large libraries, especially those with good genealogical collections (large city libraries, state libraries, the larger genealogical libraries, some state archives, the Family History Library, larger Family History Centers). For listings of these published indexes, see:

_P. W. Filby, AMERICAN AND BRITISH GENEALOGY AND HERALDRY, The New England Historic Genealogical Society, Boston, MA, 1983, and periodic SUPPLEMENTS. Be sure to examine all supplements. Look in the indexes under the heading Census.

In addition, Accelerated Indexing Systems has produced some consolidated microfiche indexes. Each of these consists of the census indexes of states in a certain geographical region which have been coalesced. These microfiche indexes are available in every Family History Center, one of which is close to you. Some of these published and microfiche indexes have some errors in them (omissions, misspellings, transpositions, transcription errors), so if two or more indexes are available, use all of them. And if you do not find your ancestor in them, it does not necessarily mean he/she is not in the census.

Once you have found from the indexes where in the census records your ancestor is listed (or at least your suspected ancestor), you can obtain the actual census information in several ways. First, you may borrow the census records for a small fee through your local Family History Library (locations in a later section). Second, you may personally borrow them for a small fee from the American Genealogical Lending Library, PO Box 329, Bountiful, UT 84011. Third, any library, including your local library, can borrow them for a small fee from the American Genealogical Lending Library or from the Census Microfilm Rental Program, PO Box 30, Annapolis Junction, MD 20701. Fourth, you may find them in a large genealogical library or state library (see later sections under Large genealogical libraries and State libraries), or in a Regional Branch of the National Archives, (locations and addresses in a later section), or in the National Archives in Washington, DC. Fifth, you may hire a searcher to look at them for you at the National Archives, or its Regional Branches or at the Family History Library. Instructions for hiring a searcher are given in a later section entitled Hired searchers.

22. Census of 1880

As of 01 June 1880, the 10th census of the US was taken by the federal government. The names of all persons were listed under county subdivision, then under county, then under state, with the Post Office also being shown. With each name were listed the age, sex, color (white, black, mulatto, Chinese, Indian), occupation or profession or trade, place of birth (state, territory, or country), places of birth of father (state, territory, or country), place of birth of mother (state, territory, country), if married within the previous year, if attended school within the previous year, if cannot read, if cannot write, if deaf or dumb or blind or insane or idiotic, month of birth if born within previous year, relationship to head of household, if single or married or widowed or divorced, number of months unemployed in previous year, if sick or temporarily disabled, if maimed or crippled or bedridden, or otherwise disabled. The microfilm copies of the records are as follows, along with a list of the states and territories for which the census is available:

_1880 Census [National Archives Microfilm T9, 1454 rolls]: AL, AZ, AR, CA, CO, CT, Dakota Territory, DE, DC, FL, GA, ID Territory, IL, IN, IA, KS, KY, LA, ME, MD MA, MI, MN, MS, MO, MT Territory, NE, NV, NH, NJ, NM, NY, NC, OH, OR, PA, RI, SC, TN, TX, VT, VA, WA, WV, WI, WY Territory.

To facilitate your searches of these census records there are some published indexes and a special partial microfilm index. The records of most of the states have been indexed and the indexes have been published both in book, microfiche, and CD forms. They are widely available in large libraries, especially those with good genealogical collections (large city libraries, state libraries, the larger genealogical libraries, some state archives, the Family History Library, larger Family History Centers). For listings of these published indexes, see:

_P. W. Filby, AMERICAN AND BRITISH GENEALOGY AND HERALDRY, The New England Historic Genealogical Society, Boston, MA, 1983, and periodic supplements. Be sure to examine all supplements. Look in the indexes under the heading census.

_V. N. Chambers, editor, GENEALOGICAL HELPER, Everton Publishers, Logan, UT, recent issues. Look in the index under Census for reviews and ads relating to recent and forthcoming census indexes.

In addition to the above indexes, there are partial indexed abstracts from the 1880 census records. These microfilms are separate publications for each state and territory. Unfortunately, only households in which there was at least one child 10 or under are included. The cards give the names, ages, and birth places of all members of such households. These indexed abstracts are:

_1880 Census Index-Partial [National Archives Microfilms, separate index for each state - microfilm numbers given in parentheses]: AL(T734), AZ(T735), AR(T736), CA(T737), CO(T738), CT(T739), Dakota Territory(T740), DE(T741), DC(T742), FL(T743), GA(T744), ID Territory (T745), IL(T746), IN(T747), IA(T748), KS(T749), KY(T750), LA(T751), ME(T752), MD(T753), MA(T754), MI(T755), MN(T756), MS(T757), MO(T758), MT Territory (T759), NE(T760), NV(T761), NH(T762), NJ(T763), NM(T764), NY(T765), NC(T766), OH(T767), OR(T768), PA(T769), RI(T770), SC(T771), TN(T772), TX(T773), UT(T774), VT (T775), VA(T776), WA(T777), WV(T778), WI(T779), WY Territory(T780).

These abstracts are indexed according to a special phonetic code for the surname, then according to first name. This code is called Soundex and instructions for the use are given in a later section under that title. The above microfilms are available in large genealogical libraries, in Regional branches of the National Archives, in the National Archives, in the Family History Library, on loan from Family History Centers, the American Genealogical Lending Library, and the Census Microfilm Rental Program (see below).

Once you have found from the indexes where in the census records your ancestor is listed (or at least your suspected ancestor), you can obtain the actual census information in several ways. First, you may borrow the census records for a small fee through your local Family History Library (locations in a later section). Second, you may personally borrow them for a small fee from the American Genealogical Lending Library, PO Box 329, Bountiful, UT 84011. Third, any library, including your local library, can borrow them for a small fee from the American Genealogical Lending Library or from the Census Microfilm Rental Program, PO Box 30, Annapolis Junction, MD 20701. Fourth, you may find them in a large genealogical library or state library (see later sections under Large genealogical libraries and State libraries), or in a Regional Branch of the National Archives, (locations and addresses in a later section), or in the National Archives in Washington, DC. Fifth, you may hire a searcher to look at them for you at the National Archives, or its Regional Branches or at the Family History Library. Instructions for hiring a searcher are given in a later section entitled Hired searchers.

23. Census of 1890 The 11th US census, the one of 1890, was taken as of 01 June of that year. Most of the records were ruined in a fire in 1921 and were thrown away. Those few that survive have been microfilmed and are available as follows:

_1890 Census, Surviving Records [National Archives Microfilm M407, 3 rolls]: AL (part of Perry County), DC (a few streets), GA (part of Muscogee County), IL (part of McDonough County), MN (Wright County-Rockford), NJ (Hudson County-Jersey City), NY (Westchester County-Eastchester and part of Suffolk County), NC (parts of Gaston and Cleveland Counties), OH (Hamilton County-Cincinnati and part of Clinton County), SD (part of Union County), TX (parts of Ellis, Hood, Rusk, Trinity, and Kaufman Counties).

The data contained included names of every person in each household, and under each name: age, street address, relationships to head of household, sex, color, birth place, occupation, if naturalized, number of years in US, whether home mortgage free, marital status, if married within the year, if suffering from disease, if crippled or maimed or deformed, time unemployed in year, if deaf or dumb or blind or insane, if pauper or prisoner or homeless child or convict, if able to speak English, if able to read and write, if attended school within the year, birth places of parents, if parents foreign born, number of living children, if Civil War veteran.

The above records are indexed in another microfilm set:
_1890 Census Index [National Archives Microfilm M496, 2 rolls].
Both the census microfilm and the census index microfilm are available in large genealogical libraries (large city libraries, state libraries, the larger genealogical libraries, some state archives, the Family History Library,

larger Family History Centers), Regional Branches of the National Archives, the National Archives. They may also be borrowed from Family History Centers, the American Genealogical Lending Library, and the Census Microfilm Rental Program. See the last paragraph in the section entitled Census of 1850 for addresses.

24. Census of 1900

The census of 1900, the 12th that the US had taken, was recorded as of 01 June 1900. This census listed the names of all persons in each household. They appeared in enumeration districts in counties or wards in cities. For each person, these items are given: address, relationship to head of household, color or race, sex, month and year of birth, age, marital status, number of years married if a wife is listed, number of children born to that marriage, number of children living, place of birth, places of birth or parents, citizenship, if foreign born the year of immigration and number of years in US, citizenship if foreign born the year of immigration and number of years in US, citizenship if foreign born and over 21, occupation, if can read and write and speak English, if home is owned or rented, if home is a farm, if home is mortgaged. The microfilm copies of the records are as follows, along with a list of the states and territories for which the census is available:

_1900 Census [National Archives Microfilm T623, 1854 rolls]: AL, AK, AZ, AR, CA, CO, CT, DE, DC, FL, GA, HI, ID, IL, IN, IA, KS, KY, LA, ME, MD, MA, MI, MN, MS, MO, MT, NE, NV, NH, NJ, NM, NY, NC, ND, OH, OK, OR, PA, RI, SC, SD, TN, TX, UT, VT, VA, WA, WV, WI, WY, Military, Indian Territory.

There are microfilms of card abstracts from the 1900 census which serve as indexes. The cards give name, race, month and year of birth, age, citizenship, county of residence, civil division, and in cities, the address. They are indexed by the Soundex system which is described in a section in this handbook under that name. The microfilms are:

_1900 Census Indexes [National Archives Microfilms, a separate microfilm set for each state, microfilm numbers given in parentheses]: AL(T1030), AK(T1031), AZ(T1032), AR(T1033), CA(T1034), CO (T1035), CT(T1036), DE(T1037), DC(T1038), FL(T1039), GA(T1040), HI(T1041), ID(T1042), IL(T1043), IN(T1044), IA(T1045), KS(T1046), KY(T1047), LA(T1048), ME(T1049), MD(T1050), MA(T1051), MI (T1052), MN(T1053), MS(T1054), MO(T1055), MT(T1056), NE (T1057), NV(T1058), NH(T1059), NJ(T1060), NM(T1061), NY(T1062), NC(T1063), ND(T1064),

OH(T1065), OK(T1066), OR(T1067), PA (T1068), RI(T1069), SC(T1070), SD(T1071), TN(T1072), TX(T1073), UT(T1074), VT(T1075), VA(T1076), WA(T1077), WV(T1078), WI (T1079), WY(T1080), Military(T1081), Indian Territory(T1082), Institutions(T1083).

Both the census index microfilms (T1030-T1083) and the census microfilms (T623) are available to you from many places:
_Borrow the census index microfilms and the census microfilms for a small fee through your local Family History Center (locations in later section entitled Family History Centers).
_Personally borrow the census microfilms for a small fee from the American Genealogical Lending Library, PO Box 329, Bountiful, UT 84011.
_Any library, including your local library, can borrow them for a small fee from the American Genealogical Lending Library or from the Census Microfilm Rental Program, PO Box 30, Annapolis Junction, MD 20701.
_You may find them in a large genealogical library (see later sections entitled Large genealogical libraries and State libraries), or in a Regional Branch of the National Archives (locations and addresses in a later section under that name), or in the National Archives, Washington, DC.
_You may hire a searcher to look at the microfilm records at the National Archives, at a National Archives Regional Branch, or at the Family History Library. Instructions for hiring a researcher are given in a later section entitled Hired searchers.

---

25. Census of 1910

As of 01 April 1910, the 13th census collection for the US was made. The date 01 April 1910 does not mean that all data were taken on that day, but that the information was requested as of that day. These census records appear under the state or territory, then under the county, and sometimes under large cities, then in enumeration districts. The name of every individual in a household is given, then the age, street address, relationship to head of household, sex, color, birth place, occupation, if naturalized, number of years in US, if home mortgage free, marital status, time unemployed during year, if deaf or dumb or blind or insane, if able to speak English, if able to read and write, if attended school within the year, birth places of parents, if parents foreign born, number of children if a mother, if Civil War veteran, number of years in present marriage, number of children born, native tongue. The microfilm copies of the records are as follows, along with a list of the states and territories for which the census is available:

_1910 Census [National Archives Microfilm T624, 1784 rolls]: AL, AK, AZ, AR, CA, CO, CT, DE, DC, FL, GA, HI, ID, IL, IN, IA, KS, KY, LA, ME, MD, MA, MI, MN, MS, MO, MT, NE, NV, NH, NJ, NM, NY, NC, ND, OH, OK, OR, PA, Puerto Rico, RI, SC, SD, TN, TX, UT, VT, VA, WA, WV, WI, WY, Military.

There are microfilms abstracts from the 1910 census for 21 states, and since the abstract cards are arranged in a special alphabetical order they serve as excellent indexes. Each entry gives last name, first name, county of residence, city if pertinent, race, age, birth place, and reference to the exact location in the census records. The indexes are arranged by either Soundex or Miracode, two slightly different systems which are explained in a section of this handbook entitled Soundex. The microfilms and the states to which they apply are:

_1910 Census Indexes [National Archives Microfilms, a separate microfilm set for each state, microfilm numbers given in parentheses, Soundex indicated by S, Miracode by M]: AL(T1259-S), AR(T1260-M), CA(T1261-M), FL(T1262-M), GA(T1263-S), IL(T1264-M), KS (T1265-M), KY(T1266-M), LA(T1267-S), MI(1268-M), MS(T1269-S), MO (T1270-M), NC(T1271-M), OH(T1272-M), OK(T1273-M), PA(T1274-M), SC(T1275-S), TN(T1276-S), TX(1277-S), VA(T1278-M), WV (T1279-M).

Care must be exercised in the use of the indexes for AL, GA, LA, PA, and TN, because the microfilms for each consist of two different indexes: one for one or more major cities in the state, and another for the rest of the state. There are a few published indexes for other states, and more are scheduled to appear soon, so you should seek them out. The above microfilm and the published indexes are available in large libraries, especially those with good genealogical collections (large city libraries, state libraries, the larger genealogical libraries, some state archives, the Family History Library, larger Family HIstory Centers).

Both the census index microfilms (T1259-T1279) and the census microfilms (T624) are available to you from many places:

_Borrow the census index microfilms and the census microfilms for a small fee through your local Family History Center (locations in later section entitled Family History Centers).

_Personally borrow the census microfilms for a small fee from the American Genealogical Lending Library, PO Box 329, Bountiful, UT 84011.

_Any library, including your local library, can borrow them for a small fee from the American Genealogical Lending Library or from the Census Microfilm Rental Program, PO Box 30, Annapolis Junction, MD 20701.

_You may find them in a large genealogical library (see later sections entitled Large genealogical libraries and State libraries), or in a Regional Branch of the National Archives (locations and addresses in a later section under that name), or in the National Archives, Washington, DC.

_You may hire a searcher to look at the microfilm records at the National Archives, at a National Archives Regional Branch, or at the Family History Library. Instructions for hiring a researcher are given in a later section entitled Hired searchers.

The 1910 census records for a number of states remain unindexed. In such instances, your search can be limited to fewer rolls of film if you have some prior idea of the county or city and even of the place in the county or city. City directories, county tax lists, county landowner maps, and land descriptions in deeds can often provide such data. There are cases, however, in which you may have to make a page-by-page, roll-by-roll search.

26. Census of 1920

As of 01 January 1920, the 13th census collection for the US was made. The date 01 January 1920 does not mean that all data were taken on that day, but that the information was requested as of that day. These census records appear under the state or territory, then under the county, and sometimes under large cities, then in enumeration districts. The name of every individual in a household is given, then the age, street address, relationship to head of household, sex, color, birth place, native tongue, occupation, if naturalized, year of naturalization, year of immigration, if home mortgage free, marital status, if deaf or dumb or blind or insane, if able to speak English, if able to read and write, if attended school within the year, birth places of parents, if parents foreign born, native tongues of parents. The microfilm copies of the records are as follows, along with a list of the states and territories for which the census is available:

_1920 Census [National Archives Microfilm T625, 2076 rolls]: AL, AK, AZ, AR, CA, Canal Zone, CO, CT, DE, DC, FL, GA, Guam, HI, ID, IL, IN, IA, KS, KY, LA, ME, MD, MA, MI, MN, MS, MO, MT, NE, NV, NH, NJ, NM, NY, NC, ND, OH, OK, OR, PA, Puerto Rico, RI,

Samoa, SC, SD, TN, TX, UT, VT, Virgin Islands, VA, WA, WV, WI, WY, Overseas Military.

There are microfilm abstracts from the 1920 census for all states, and since the abstract cards are arranged in a special alphabetical order they serve as excellent indexes. Each entry gives last name, first name, county of residence, city if pertinent, race, age, birth place, and reference to the exact location in the census records. The indexes are arranged by Soundex, which is explained in a section of this handbook entitled Soundex. The microfilms and the states to which they apply are:

_1920 Census Indexes [National Archives Microfilms, a separate microfilm set for each state, microfilm numbers given in parentheses]: AL(M1548), AK(M1597), AZ(M1549), AR(M1550), CA(M1551), Canal Zone(M1599), CO(M1552), CT(M1553), DE(M1554), DC(M1555), FL(M1556), GA(M1557), Guam(M1602), HI(M1598), ID(M1558), IL(M1559), IN(M1560), IA(M1561), KS(M1562), KY(M1563), LA(M1564), ME(M1565), MD(M1566), MA(M1567), MI(M1568), MN(M1569), MS(1570), MO(M1571), MT(M1572), NE(M1573), NV(M1574), NH(M1575), NJ(M1576), NM(M1577), NY(M1578), NC(M1579), ND(M1580), OH(M1581), OK(M1582), OR(M1583), PA(M1584), Puerto Rico(M1601), RI(M1585), Samoa(M1603), SC(M1586), SD(M1587), TN(M1588), TX(M1589), UT(M1590), VT(M1591), Virgin Islands(M1604), VA(M1592), WA(M1593), WV(M1594), WI(M1595), WY(M1596), Overseas Military (M1600), Various Institutions(M1605).

Both the census index microfilms (M1548-M1605) and the census microfilms (T625) are available to you from many places:

_Borrow the census index microfilms and the census microfilms for a small fee through your local Family History Center (locations in later section entitled Family History Centers).

_Personally borrow the census microfilms for a small fee from the American Genealogical Lending Library, PO Box 329, Bountiful, UT 84011.

_Any library, including your local library, can borrow them for a small fee from the American Genealogical Lending Library or from the Census Microfilm Rental Program, PO Box 30, Annapolis Junction, MD 20701.

_You may find them in a large genealogical library (see later sections entitled Large genealogical libraries and State libraries), or in a Regional Branch of the National Archives (locations and addresses in a later section under that name), or in the National Archives, Washington, DC.

_You may hire a searcher to look at the microfilm records at the National Archives, at a National Archives Regional Branch, or at the Family History Library. Instructions for hiring a researcher are given in a later section entitled Hired searchers.

---

27. Census integrated indexes

As the previous sections have indicated, many state indexes for many of the census years have been published. A sizable number of these have been put out by Accelerated Indexing Systems International, a firm located in North Salt Lake City, UT. Since their data are computerized, they have the facility to combine them in various ways and to produce overall integrated indexes. This they have done, and hence there are now available a number of these. For example, they have taken all their separate 1790, 1800, and 1810 census indexes for the various states, have added numerous other state-level records, and have combined them into one large index which they call Search 1: early-1819. They have likewise combined all the 1820 census indexes for the states with other state-level records to produce another integrated index called Search 2: 1820-1829.

The complete list of their integrated indexes which contain census records is as follows:
_Search 1: early-1819 (all states).
_Search 2: 1820-1829 (all states).
_Search 3: 1830-1839 (all states).
_Search 4: 1840-1849 (all states).
_Search 5: 1850-1859 North (CT, DE, ME, MA, NH, NJ, NY, OH, PA, RI, VT).
_Search 6: 1850-1859 South (AL, AR, DC, FL, GA, KY, LA, MD, MS, NC, SC, TN, VA).
_Search 7: 1850-1899 West (AK, AZ, CA, CO, ID, IL, IN, IA, KS, MN, MI, MD, MT, NE, NV, MN, ND, OH, OK, OR, SD, TX, UT, WA, WI, WY).
_Search 7A: Searches 5, 6, and 7 all in one alphabet.
_Search 8: 1850-1885 Mortality Censuses (see later section for description of what these records are like).

These microfiche census integrated indexes are available in a few larger genealogical libraries and in every Family History Center. The information given in the regular census indexes (Searches 1-7A) includes name, county, state, page number in census, census year. Data provided in the mortality census integrated index (Search 8) includes name, county, state, age at death, sex, month of death, place of birth, cause of death. The census integrated indexes can be of immense help to you when you have lost an ancestor, since they frequently permit you to quickly identify all people of a given name appearing in all of the indexes for a given census year.

28. Church archives

Even though the majority of church records remain in the individual churches, many of them, especially early ones and those for extinct churches, have been deposited in special church archives which various denominations maintain. Many of these archives have microfilmed some or all of their holdings, thus fostering preservation and simultaneously making them lendable. In addition, the Family History Library in Salt Lake City, UT, has microfilmed an enormous number of church records, and is therefore an unofficial super-denominational church archives. Their microfilms are available through their branch Family History Centers, at each of which you will find a catalog which lists those available:

_Family History Library Catalog, Locality Section, in every Family History Center. Look under state, then under Church records, then under denomination. Look under state, then under County, then under Church records.

After you have inquired at the local level, at the state level, and searched in the above catalog, your quest for church records of your progenitors may lead you to one or more church archives. Some of the major ones follow:

_(Adventist) General Conference of Seventh-Day Adventists, 12501 Old Columbia Pike, Silver Spring, MD 20904.

_(Baptist) American Baptist Historical Society, 1106 South Goodman Street, Rochester, NY 14620; Southern Baptist Historical Society and Archives, 901 Commerce, St., Suite 400, Nashville, TN 37203.

_(Brethren) Archives of the Brethren in Christ Church, Messiah College, Grantham, PA 17027.

_(Church of Jesus Christ of Latter Day Saints) Latter Day Saints Church Archives, Historical Department, 50 East North Temple Street, Salt Lake City, UT 84150.

_(Church of the Brethren) Brethren Historical Library and Archives, 1451 Dundee Avenue, Elgin, IL 60120.

_(Church of Christ) Harding Graduate School of Religion, Library, 1000 Cherry Road, Memphis, TN 38117; Center for Restoration Studies,

Brown Library, Abilene Christian University, Abilene, TX 79699; The Gospel Advocate Archives and Library, 1006 Elm Hill Park, Nashville, TN 37210.

_(Congregational) Congregational Christian Historical Society, 14 Beacon Street, Boston, MA 02108. See also Unitarian-Universalist and United Church of Christ entries in this list, since many former Congregational churches are now in these denominations.

_(Disciples of Christ) The Disciples of Christ Historical Society, Library Archives, 1101 Nineteenth Avenue, South, Nashville, TN 37212.

_(Evangelical United Brethren) Historical Society, Evangelical United Brethren Church, 1810 Harvard Blvd., Dayton, OH 45406.

_(Greek Orthodox) Ortodox Church in America, PO Box 675, Syosset, NY 11791.

_(Huguenot Reformed Church) Huguenot Historical Society, PO Box 339, New Paltz, NY 12561; The Huguenot Society of America Library, 122 East 58th St., New York, NY 10022.

_(Jewish) American Jewish Archives, 3101 Clifton Avenue, Cincinnati, OH 45220; American Jewish Historical Society, 2 Thornton Road, Waltham, MA 02154.

_(Lutheran) Library, Wartburg Theoogical Seminary, 333 Wartburg Place, Dubuque, IA 52001; Lutheran Archives Center, 7301 German-town Avenue, Philadelphia, PA 19119; Wentz Library, Lutheran Theological Seminary, Gettysburg, PA 17325; Lutheran Southern Seminary Library, 4201 Main Street, Columbia, SC 29203; Archives of the Evangelical Lutheran Church of America, 8765 West Higgins Road, Chicago, IL 60731; Department of Archives and History, The Lutheran Church-Missouri Synod, 801 DeMun Avenue, St. Louis, MO 63105.

_(Mennonite) Archives of the Mennonite Church and Mennonite Historical Library, Goshen College, Goshen, IN 46526.

_(Methodist) General Commission on Archives and History, United Methodist Church, Drew University, Madison, NJ 07940.

_(Moravian) The Archives of the Moravian Church, 41 West Locust St., Bethlehem, PA 18018; Moravian Archives, Southern Provinces, 4 East Bank St., Winston-Salem, NC 27101.

_(Presbyterian) Presbyterian Historical Society, 425 Lombard Street, Philadelphia, PA 19147; Presbyterian Church Department of History, PO Box 849, Montreat, NC 28757.

_(Protestant Episcopal) No overall repository nor any large regional repository. Try diocesan offices.

_(Quakers or Friends) Friends Historical Library, Swarthmore College, Swarthmore, PA 19081; Friends Historical Society and Quaker

Collection, Haverford College, Haverford, PA 19041; Heiss Genealogical Collection, Earlham College Library, Richmond, IN 47375; Friends Historical Collection, Guilford College Library, Guilford, NC 27410.

_(Reformed Church) Archives of the Reformed Church in America, New Brunswick Theological Seminary, 21 Seminary Place, New Brunswick, NY 08901.

_(Roman Catholic Church) Catholic Archives of America, Notre Dame University, South Bend, IN 46556; Department of Archives and Manuscripts, Catholic University of America, Washington, DC 20064. Contact diocesan and archdiocesan offices.

_(Unitarian-Universalist) Archives of the Unitarian-Universalist Association, 25 Beacon Street, Boston, MA 02108.

_(United Church of Christ, a merger of Evangelical and Reformed with some Congregational Churches) Congregational Library, 14 Beacon Street, Boston, MA 02108; Eden Archives, Evangelical and Reformed Churches, 475 East Lockwood Avenue, Webster Grove, MO 63119; Evangelical and Reformed Historical Society, 555 West James Street, Lancaster, PA 17603.

If the denomination you are concerned with does not appear above, take a look in the following volumes, from which many of the above listings were taken, and which contain much more church archival and headquarters information:

_National Council of Churches, YEARBOOK OF AMERICAN AND CANADIAN CHURCHES, Abingdon Press, Nashville, TN, latest annual issue.

_F. S. Mead, HANDBOOK OF AMERICAN DENOMINATIONS, Abingdon Press, Nashville, TN, latest edition.

_J. G. Melton, ENCYCLOPEDIA OF AMERICAN RELIGIONS, Gale Research Co., Detroit, MI, latest edition.

In addition to national church archives such as those listed in the previous paragraph, there are often state church archives, especially for denominations which have large memberships in the state being considered. National church archives can and will often refer you to these. Also, many of them will be found listed under the pertinent state chapter in:

_A. Eichholz, ANCESTRY'S REDBOOK, Ancestry Publishing, Salt Lake City, UT, 1992.

29. Church records

Church records often contain information regarding baptisms, christenings, confirmations, marriages, deaths, funerals, and burials. Sometimes they contain admissions, transfers, dismissals, lists of members, communion attendance records, church minutes, church histories, and contribution records. Church records of these denominations usually contain sizable genealogical information: Brethren, Church of Jesus Christ of Latter Day Saints, Congregational, Evangelical United Brethren, Greek Orthodox, Huguenot, Jewish, Lutheran, Moravian, Protestant Episcopal, Quakers, Reformed, Roman Catholic, older Unitarian-Universalist, and United Church of Christ. Presbyterian records carry somewhat less but are still very valuable. And Baptist, Methodist, later Unitarian, Mennonite, Amish, Adventist, Disciples, Church of God, Church of Christ, Christian, and Pentecostal records often contain less useful data, but must by no means be overlooked. Church records in the US are usually found in local churches, although many are now being placed in state, regional, or national church archives or repositories. Church records are among the more important genealogical sources, but unfortunately they are often among the more difficult to locate. This is largely because they are so widespread and therefore no comprehensive finding aids are available. This means that you may have to try numerous routes in order to locate your ancestor's church records. It is also well to remember that even though practically all early Americans were religious, many of them were not members of an organized church, especially those on the frontiers.

Most of the earliest settlers to the colonies up to about 1660 were Episcopalians (in the south) or Congregationalists (in the north), with Dutch Reformed coming into NY and NJ, Catholics into MD, and with New England dissenters becoming Baptist and settling RI. The Congregationalists and Episcopalians remained the major groups until about 1700. In the late 1600s, Quakers began arriving especially in PA, with many subsequently moving into NC. Sizable numbers of Presbyterians and numerous German religious groups (Amish, Brethren, Dunkards, Evangelicals, Lutherans, Mennonites, Moravians, Reformed, Schwenkfelders) began coming in the early 1700s, chiefly into PA, then migrating into the colonies to the south. By about 1740, the three major religious groups were Congregational, Episcopalian, and Presbyterian. During 1725-65 there occurred the First Great Awakening, a widespread revival in which multitudes were converted to the Baptist, the new light Presbyterian, and a little later the Methodist denominations. By the early 1800s, the Baptists had become the largest group in the US, with the

Methodists gaining on them rapidly. Catholics in large numbers, mainly from Ireland, began entering the northern and middle coastal states in the early 1800s, many remaining, and many migrating west. Also, during 1795-1835, the Second Great Awakening occurred with further conversions to Baptist, Methodist, and other smaller evangelical faiths. By 1850, the Catholics constituted the largest denomination in the US, with the Methodists being predominant among the Protestants. Just before, and continuing after the Civil War (1861-1865), many Catholics from Ireland and many Lutherans from Germany and Scandinavia entered the US, large numbers of them settling in the mid-west. Then beginning about 1880, Catholics, Orthodox, and Jewish people from southern and eastern Europe came. It is very important for you to remember that as Protestants went to the frontier, there is a tendency for them to become Baptist or Methodist, these being the most active groups on much of the frontier. For details on American religious history, consult

_J. G. Melton, ENCYCLOPEDIA OF AMERICAN RELIGIONS, Gale Research Co., Detroit, MI, latest edition.

_E. S. Gaustadt, HISTORICAL ATLAS OF RELIGIONS IN AMERICA, Harper and Row, New York, NY, 1962.

Church records are to be found in many places in many forms. Original records are located in the local churches, in churches that have superseded previous ones, in churches that have inherited records of nearly defunct congregations, in state denominational archives, in national denominational archives, in denominational colleges, in large universities in the state, and in the state archives and/or libraries. Transcribed records, both hand-written and typescript, are most likely to be found in local libraries, in state libraries, in state and national denominational archives, and in the DAR Library in Washington, DC. The DAR chapters in many states have copied very large numbers of church records. Published transcribed records, both books and genealogical periodical articles, are chiefly to be found in local libraries and state libraries. Microfilmed copies of church records are stored in state and national denominational archives, and in the Family History Library in Salt Lake City, UT. Those in the Family History Library may be borrowed through its numerous branch Family History Centers. Microfilmed abstracts from church records are available in every Family History Center in the International Genealogical Index.

In order to successfully search for your progenitor's church records, it is ordinarily necessary to know the county, city, or town. Then, with this information, you should follow three steps: (1) find the denomination, (2) find the church, and (3) find the records. We will treat these items in order. First, to ascertain the denomination to which your ancestor belonged, there are numerous clues which you can exploit and a number of records that can indicate it directly. It may be that you already know the denomination from previous ethnic origin. For immigrants, and often several generations afterwards: if English (Episcopalian, Congregational, Quaker, Baptist), if Scots or Ulster-Irish (Presbyterian), if northern German (Lutheran, Reformed, the Pietist sects named above), Irish (Catholic), southern German (Catholic), France and Italy and Austria (Catholic), Swiss (Reformed, Lutheran, Catholic), eastern Europe (Catholic, Orthodox), Scandinavia (Lutheran). Then a careful look into family Bibles, marriage records, obituaries, mortuary records, cemetery records, the ownership of the cemetery, and local histories may tell you. Another important indicator is to find out exactly what denominations had churches in your ancestor's area (county, town, city) at the time he/she lived there. This will often narrow the possibilities down, since your progenitor may very well have attended a church of a denomination different than his/her own if none of his/hers was nearby.

Second, to ascertain what churches were in the area at your forebear's time, write the local library, the local genealogical society, or the local historical society. State libraries, state denominational headquarters, state church archives, nearby denominational colleges, National church headquarters, and national church archives are other places to contact for this information. Or take a look at detailed county maps which show churches, such as those published by the US Geological Survey, those published by county and state highway departments, and those in county atlases. County, town, and city histories also often carry the names, locations, and dates of formation of local churches. For addresses and map details, look in other sections of this handbook: Atlases, County atlases, County histories, Genealogical societies, Historical societies, Libraries, Maps. In attempting to ascertain the possible churches in your ancestor's area, do not confine your quest only to his county or town. It is possible that his affiliation was with a church in a neighboring county or town.

Third, you need to seek the records of the church or churches you have identified as the more likely possibilities. Your first action is to go to your nearest Family History Center (see later section) and look in the locality section of the Family History Catalog. Under the state, you will find the county or town, and then under that look for microfilmed church records. If you find possibilities, have the microfilms borrowed for you.

For churches whose records you do not find, write essentially the same brief letter of inquiry to the church itself, the county or town library, the state library, and the state and/or national denominational headquarters. Be sure to enclose an SASE in each letter. These letters will probably locate the records for you. If the church does not have them, they may know where they are. If they do not know the location of the records, one or more of the other agencies can usually tell you. These same agencies can also often tell you if the records have been published (book, typescript, periodical) or microfilmed. And if the church is defunct, one or another of the agencies can usually indicate to you who inherited the records. In some cases, you will find that the agencies will refer you to another repository where the records or copies of them are located, or to some organization which knows.

In order to make the numerous contacts mentioned above, you will need some addresses. Those for state, county, and town libraries are given in a volume held by most libraries:
_American Library Association, AMERICAN LIBRARY DIRECTORY, R. R. Bowker, New York, NY, latest issue.
Genealogical societies and historical societies (state, county, town) are listed in
_V. N. Chambers, editor, THE GENEALOGICAL HELPER, Everton Publishers, Logan, UT, latest Jul-Aug issue, for genealogical societies and libraries.
_M. K. Meyer, DIRECTORY OF GENEALOGICAL SOCIETIES IN THE USA AND CANADA, The Author, Pasadena, MD, latest edition.
_E. P. Bentley, GENEALOGIST'S ADDRESS BOOK, Genealogical Publishing Co., Baltimore, MD, latest edition.
_American Association for State and Local History, HISTORICAL SOCIETIES AND AGENCIES IN THE US AND CANADA, The Association, Nashville, TN, latest issue.
State libraries can supply you with addresses of state denominational headquarters, state church archives, and denominational colleges in the region of your progenitor's residence. Many, but not all, are also listed under the pertinent state chapters or sections in
_A. Eichholz, ANCESTRY'S REDBOOK, Ancestry Publishing, Salt Lake City, UT, 1989.
_YEARBOOK OF AMERICAN AND CANADIAN CHURCHES, Abingdon Press, Nashville, TN, latest annual edition.
National church archives and/or headquarters are given for major denominations in the section preceding this one. You will also find instructions

there for locating the headquarters and archives of other denominations. The locations of the numerous Family History Centers are given in a later section under that title. Some larger denominations have published guides to their churches. Among them are the following:

_LUTHERAN CHURCH DIRECTORY FOR THE US, Lutheran Council in the US, New York, NY, latest issue.

_EPISCOPAL CHURCH ANNUAL, New York, NY, latest issue.

_OFFICIAL CATHOLIC DIRECTORY, Kenedy and Sons, Wilmette, IL, latest annual issue.

_YEARBOOK UNITED CHURCH OF CHRIST, The Church, New York, NY, latest annual issue.

_DIRECTORY OF SOUTHERN BAPTIST CHURCHES, Sunday School Board, Nashville, TN, latest annual issue.

30. City directories

Some early directory-like lists of city inhabitants were compiled in colonial times, but the first city directories appeared in 1782 and 1785 for Charleston as parts of almanacs. Two different city directories, which constituted individual volumes, were printed in Philadelphia in 1785. Since then many US cities, some towns, and a few counties have issued directories of inhabitants. The city directories usually contain the names of all heads-of-households and workers plus their addresses, their occupations, and sometimes the addresses of their work places. Later ones also contain listings of at least some of the following: businesses, churches, organizations, cemeteries, ward maps, street locations, and persons belonging to certain professions and occupations. Ordinarily, once city directory publication is started in a city, one is published every year or every other year with fair regularity. City directories are exceptionally useful for locating urban ancestors, for following them year-by-year, and for correlating their appearances in and disappearances from the directories with coming of age, arrival in the city, departure from the city, and death. The appearance of a widow is often very helpful, and church listings sometimes indicate those for which records should be sought.

City directories should first be sought among the very large number which have been microfilmed by Research Publications and which are listed in detail in:

_CITY DIRECTORIES OF THE US, 1752-1901, GUIDE TO THE MICROFILM COLLECTION, Research Publications, Woodbridge, CT, 1983.

The city directories in this microfilm collection and the approximate dates for which they are available include: Akron, OH (1859-60), Albany, NY (1813-1901), Alton, IL (1858), Ann Arbor, MI (1850), Atchison, KS (1859-61), Atlanta, GA (1859-1901), Auburn, NY (1857/59), Augusta, GA (1841/59), Austin, TX (1857), Baltimore, MD (1752, 1796-1901), Bangor, ME (1834, 1843-59), Belleville, IL (1860), Beloit, WI (1857-58), Biddeford, ME (1849/56), Binghamton (1857-60), Boston, MA (1789, 1796-1901), Bradford, MA (1853/57/59), Bridgeport, CT (1855-57), Brighton, MA (1848-50), Brooklyn, NY (1796/1801/11/ 1822-1901), Buffalo, NY (1828-1901), Burlington, IA (1856/59), Burlington, VT (1865/1901), Cambridge, MA (1847-60), Camden, NJ (1818/22/1853-60), Camden, SC (1816/24), Canton, OH (1856/60), Charleston, SC (1782-1901), Charlestown, MA (1831-60), Chattanooga, TN (1871-81), Chelsea, MA (1847-60), Chester, PA (1859), Chicago, IL 1839-1901), Chillicothe, OH (1855-60), Cincinnati, OH (1819/25/ 1829-1901), Circleville, OH (1859), Clarksville, TN (1859), Cleveland, OH (1837/45/1848-1901), Clinton, MA (1856), Columbia, SC (1859-60), Columbus, GA (1859), Columbus, OH (1843-1901), Concord, NH (1830/34/44/1848-61), Dallas, TX (1875-1901), Davenport, IA (1853-81), Dayton, OH (1850/1856-61), Delaware, OH (1859-1901), Denver, CO (1859-1901), Des Moines, IA (1866-1901), Detroit, MI (1837, 1845-1901), Dorchester, MA (1848-50), Dover, NH (1830-48, 1859), Dubuque, IA (1856-60), East Boston, MA (1848-52), Elmira, NY (1857/ 60), Erie, PA (1853-1900), Evansville, IN (1858-1901), Fall River, MA (1853-1901), Fitchburg, MA (1846-60), Fond du Lac, WI (1857), Fort Wayne, IN (1858-80), Fort Worth, TX (1877-79), Frederick, MD (1859), Galena, IL (1847-59), Galveston, TX (1856-1901), Geneva, NY (1857), Gloucester, MA (1860), Grand Rapids, MI (1856-1901), Great Falls, NH (1848), Hamilton, OH (1858),

Harrisburg, PA (1839-45, 1863-1901), Hartford, CT (1799, 1825-1901), Haverhill, MA (1853-61), Hudson, NY (1851-57), Indianapolis, IN (1855-1901), Iowa City, IA (1857), Jackson, MS (1860), Janesville, WI (1857-60), Jeffersonville, IN (1845/60), Jersey City, NJ (1849-1901), Joliet, IL (1872-1901), Kansas City, MO (1859-1901), Keene, NH (1827-31), Kenosha, WI (1858), Keokuk, IA (1854-60), Kingston, NY (1857-8), Lafayette, IN (1858), Lancaster, PA (1843/53/ 57/60), Lawrence, MA (1847-61), Lawrenceburg, IN (1859), Leavenworth, KS (1859-60), Lexington, KY (1806/18/38/59), Little Rock, AR (1871-1901), Loganport, IN (1859), Los Angeles, CA (1873-1901), Louisville, KY (1832-1901), Lowell, MA (1832-1901), Lunenburg, MA (1834), Lynn, MA (1832/41, 1851-60), Madison, IN (1859-60), Madison, WI (1851-58), Manchester, NH (1844-98), Mansfield, OH (1858), Marietta, OH (1860), Marysville, CA (1850-59), Medford, MA (1849), Memphis, TN (1849, 1855-1901),

Middletown, KY (1857), Milford, MA (1856), Milwaukee, WI (1847-1901), Mineral Point, WI (1859), Minneapolis, MN (1865-1901), Mobile, AL (1836-1901), Moline, IL (1855-60), Morrisania, NY (1853), Mount Vernon, OH (1858), Muscatine, IA (1856/ 59), Muscatine, IA (1856/59), Nashua, NH (1841-58), Nashville, TN (1853-1901), Nevada City, CA (1856-81), New Albany, IN (1836, 1845-60), Newark, NJ (1835-1901), New Bedford, MA (1836-59), New Brunswick, NJ (1955), Newburgh, NY (1856-60), Newburyport, MA (1849-60), New Haven, CT (1840-1901), New Ipswich, NH (1858), New London, CT (1855/59), New Orleans, LA (1805-1901), Newport, RI (1844, 1855-58), New York, NY (1665, 1786-1901), Norfolk, VA (1801/06/51, 1859-1901), Norristown, PA (1860), Norwich, CT (1846/ 57/60), Oakland, CA (1869-80), Ogdenburg, NY (1857), Omaha, NE (1866-1901), Oshkosh, WI (1857), Oswego, NY (1852-59), Paterson, NJ (1855-1901), Pawtucket, RI (1844/57), Peoria, IL (1844/50, 1856-1901), Peterborough, NH (1830), Philadelphia, PA (1785, 1791-1901), Pittsburg, PA (1813/15/19/26, 1837-1901),

Pittsfield, MA (1859), Plymouth, MA (1846/60), Portland, ME (1823-1901), Portland, OR (1863-1901), Portsmouth, NH (1817/21/ 27/34/39/50/56/60), Portsmouth, OH (1859), Poughkeepsie, NY (1843-6, 1848-60), Providence, RI (1824-32, 1836-1901), Quincy, IL (1848, 1855-9), Racine, WI (1850/58), Reading, PA (1806, 1856-1901), Richmond, IN (1857/60), Richmond, VA (1818/19/45, 1850-1901), Rochester, NY (1827/-34/38, 1841-1901), Rockford, IL (1857/59), Rock Island, IL (1855-59), Rome, NY (1857-59), Roxbury, MA (1847-60), Saco, ME (1849/56), Sacramento, CA (1850-81), St. Anthony, MN (1859), St. Louis, MO (1821, 1836-1901), St. Paul, MN 1856-1901), Salem, MA (1837-59), Salt Lake City, UT (1867-1901), Sandusky, OH (1855/58), San Antonio, TX (1877-1901), San Francisco, CA (1850-1901), Savannah, GA (1848-1901), Schenectady, NY (1841/57/60), Scranton, PA (1861-1901), Seattle,WA (1872-1901), Shelbyville, IN (1860), Somerville, MA (1849-51), South Boston, MA (1852), Southbridge, MA (1854), Springfield, IL (1855-60), Springfield, MA (1845-60), Springfield, OH (1852/59), Steubenville, OH (1856), Stockton, CA (1852/56), Syracuse, NY (1844, 1851-1901), Taunton, MA (1850/55/57/59), Terre Haute, IN (1858/60), Toledo, OH (1858-1901), Topeka, KS (1868-80), Trenton, NJ (1844/45/54/57/59), Troy, NY (1829-1901), Utica, NY (1817, 1828-1901), Vicksburg, MS (1860), Washington, DC (1822/27/30/34, 1843-1901), Watertown, NY (1840/55/56/59), Waukesha, WI (1858), West Chester, PA (1857), Wheeling, WV (1856/59), Williamsburgh, NY (1847-54), Wilmington, DE (1814/45, 1853-1901), Worcester, MA (1828-29, 1841-1901), Yonkers, NY (1859-60), Zanesville, OH (1851/56/60).

In addition to the city directories, the above microfilm collection cotains a number of county directories and some business directories for states: Bureau County, IL (1858), CT (1849/51/56/57), Erie County, PA (1859), Essex County, NJ (1859), Greene County, AL (1855), Henry County, IA (1859), IL (1847/54/58/60), IL-Northern (1855), IN (1858/ 60), IA (1846), Jefferson County, IN (1859), Kane County, IL (1855-60), KY (1859), ME (1849/55/56), MA (1835/49), 1850-59), MI (1838-40, 1856/60), MS Valley (1837/44), MO (1854/60), Monongahela Valley (1859), New England (1849/56/60), NH (1849), NJ (1950), NY (1842/ 50/59), OH (1835/57/59/60), PA (1844/54/60), Randolph County, IL (1859), RI (1849), Rock County, WI (1857-8), TN (1860), Tuolumne County, CA (1856), Vt (1849, 1855-60), VA (1852), Westchester County, NY (1860), Western Reserve (1852), WI (1857-59), Wythe County, VA (1857). All the above microfilms are available at the Family History Library (and obtainable through its branch Family History Centers), at some large genealogical libraries, at some state libraries, and at some large university libraries.

The city directories listed above are by no means all that are in existence. There are many more. They are available in local libraries, in various town and city libraries, in state libraries, and in some large gene-alogical and historical libraries, as well as in the Library of Congress. If you have an ancestor in any sizable town or city after about 1800, you should write the above institutions to find out if town or city directories are in their collections. Be sure and enclose an SASE and ask about charges for having them searched for your progenitor.

31. City histories   Histories of many towns, townships, and cities have been written. They often contain much information on inhabitants and they are some-times indexed. Quite often they also contain biographies of leading citizens, lists of city officers, brief histories of churches, businesses, industries, and organizations, names of early settlers, and rosters of physicians, lawyers, clergymen, teachers, and other professional groups. To discover if such histories are available for your forebear's town or city, consult:

_M. J. Kaminkow, US LOCAL HISTORIES IN THE LIBRARY OF CONGRESS, Magna Carta Book Co., Baltimore, MD, 1975, 5 volumes, index in the 5th volume.

_FAMILY HISTORY LIBRARY CATALOG, LOCALITY SECTION, nearest Family History Center (see later section). Look under state, then county, then town or township or city.

If you find no volume listed, dispatch letters (with SASEs) to the pertinent town or city library and the state library asking about both published and manuscript histories. Be sure and inquire regarding periodical articles, also. When you locate an appropriate volume, ask your local 4library to borrow it for you on interlibrary loan. Most repositories will not lend their genealogical materials, but historical books can generally be borrowed.

---

32. City panoramic views

There are available well over 1000 beautiful panoramic views of US cities which were done mostly during the years 1860-1910, although there are a fair number for earlier years. These map-like paintings depict the city as it looked if viewed from an airplane. Details are usually superb: streets, waterways, churches, public buildings, even private homes are all rendered accurately. You can often pick out the house of your ancestor. The panoramas are usually of such a size that they can be framed for hanging in your home. To discover if such panoramic maps are available for your forebear's city during the dates he/she was there, consult:

_J. R. Hebert, PANORAMIC MAPS OF ANGLO-AMERICAN CITIES, Library of Congress, Washington, DC, 1974.
_CATALOG OF HISTORIC CITY PLANS AND VIEWS, Historic Urban Plans, Ithaca, NY, latest edition.

Should you locate panoramic maps that you want, instructions for ordering are contained in the above volumes.

---

33. City research

City research in general follows genealogical research elsewhere, but there are some special aspects of it that you need to recognize. From its early settlement in 1607 until the present, the area which is now the US has moved from being a predominantly rural society to being a predominantly urban or city society (75%). In 1790 there were only four cities in the US with populations over 10,000. They were, in order of decreasing size: New York City, Philadelphia, Boston, Baltimore. As of 1850, there were seven cities with populations over 50,000 (listed in order): New York City, Baltimore, Boston, Brooklyn, Philadelphia, Cincinnati, St. Louis. By 1900, the major cities, that is, those with more than 500,000 people were: New York City, Chicago, Philadelphia, St. Louis, Boston, Baltimore. In general, this has given genealogists an advantage because cities generally collect more information on their inhabitants than do rural counties and towns.

Among the most important of the genealogical sources for cities are city directories, which were discussed in the section just before this one. You will recall that city directories give you the potential to follow your urban ancestor year-by-year. In addition, they often contain excellent contemporary maps, ward boundaries, and church and cemetery listings. Cities also keep more detailed land records than rural jurisdictions, often including maps of land owners, property tax assessment and collection lists, building permits, assessment records for street and sewer improvements, and utility (water, gas, light, garbage) installation and payment records. School records in urban areas are more likely to have been saved for earlier years than elsewhere. And vital records were often kept earlier in cities than in the state in general. Mortuaries were operating earlier in cities than elsewhere. Further, local libraries and archives, both public and private, are better financed in cities, and thus have preserved more material. It may also be noted that city newspapers, especially valuable for obituaries, are better and earlier in cities. The possibility of large ethnic groups in the highly populated cities gives rise to the publication of special ethnic newspapers, which are likely to carry more data on members of the ethnic community than regular newspapers do. Likewise, cities afford concentrations of professionals (attorneys, physicians, dentists, engineers, teachers), which gives rise to professional directories which list them. Cities sometimes function independently of counties (as in VA), but more often their jurisdictions overlap, yet in both cases, the cities may have courts which have no counterparts outside the urban areas. These city courts are called by various names, so you must be careful to identify them, and to use their records.

Cities with concentrated populations, and with better facilities for record preservation, also often have repositories which have saved business records, corporation records, employment records, professional association records, union records, maritime records, railroad records, and city employee records. All the above special record types and others may be sought in city halls, city offices, city archives, city libraries, and private libraries in the city (especially historical and genealogical libraries). The names and addresses of many of these will be found under the appropriate state in:

_A. Eichholz, ANCESTRY'S REDBOOK, Ancestry Publishing, Salt Lake City, UT, 1992.

There are several important volumes which are useful in city research. For references to city historical data, which are always of value to city researchers, see:

_J. D. Buenker, G. M. Greenfield, and W. J. Murin, URBAN HISTORY: A GUIDE TO INFORMATION SOURCES, Gale Research Co., Detroit, MI, 1981.

For maps and references to many useful maps, see:

_E. K. Kirkham, A HANDY GUIDE TO RECORD SEARCHING IN THE LARGER CITIES OF THE US, Everton Publishers, Logan, UT, 1974.

_Library of Congress, FIRE INSURANCE MAPS IN THE LIBRARY OF CONGRESS, The Library, Washington, DC, 1981. Very detailed maps for over 12000 towns and cities from 1867 forward. Also consult the separate section in this volume entitled Maps.

Some valuable city research guides are in print. They should be consulted before you attempt research in the indicated cities.

_E. M. Guzik, GENEALOGICAL RESOURCES IN THE NEW YORK METROPOLITAN AREA, Jewish Genealogical Society, New York, NY, 1989.

_R. F. Bailey, GUIDE TO GENEALOGICAL AND BIOGRAPHICAL SOURCES FOR NEW YORK CITY (MANHATTAN), The Author, New York, 1954.

_J. D. Scuzs, CHICAGO AND COOK COUNTY SOURCES: A GENEALOGICAL AND HISTORICAL GUIDE, Ancestry Publishing, Salt Lake City, UT, 1986.

_D. S. Provine, PRELIMINARY INVENTORY OF THE RECORDS OF THE GOVERNMENT OF THE DISTRICT OF COLUMBIA, National Archives, Washington, DC, 1976.

_K. A. Garner-Wescott, MA SOURCES, PART I: BOSTON, NEW BEDFORD, SPRINGFIELD, WORCESTER, MA Society of Genealogists, Boston, MA, 1988.

_J. Daly, DESCRIPTIVE INVENTORY OF THE ARCHIVES OF THE CITY OF PHILADELPHIA, Department of Records, Philadelphia, PA, 1970.

34. Civil War records

The Civil War was fought 1861-65 between a group of southern states (AL, AR, FL, GA, MS, NC, SC, TN, TX, VA) called the Confederacy and the remainder of the states of the US. Every Confederate state except SC fielded at least one Union regiment, and the Union states KY, MD, MO, and WV fielded sizable numbers of Confederates. About 1.5 million Union men served, and about 1.1 million Confederate men. Approximately one out of every eight men in the country entered the military. There are three main types of records which the war generated and which are of use to genealogists: (1) service records, (2) pension records, and (3) regimental histories. Service records include rolls and rosters (enlistment, muster in, muster out, monthly, pay), and lists (description, wounded, death, deserter, casualty, court martial, promotion). Among the items which may be found in service records are birth place and date, enlistment place and date, age, physical description, occupation, residence, and details of events during the period of service. Pension records consist of application papers, authenticating documents, and payment records, sometimes for both a veteran and his wife. Information may include birth place and date, maiden name of wife, residence, age, summary of service, marriage place and date, minor children, death place and date, and migrations. Regimental histories are accounts of the events and men of a given regiment during the war. They may be in the form of periodical articles, pamphlets, newspaper accounts, sections in books, or books, and they often mention or list a large number of their men and their activities.

The first step that you should take is to discover your ancestor's state (which you probably already know) and his exact regiment. You need this information in order to obtain the records. To obtain it, use some microfilm indexes, and then write some letters if they fail you. If your forebear was a Confederate, you should look for him in a large overall microfilm Confederate index or in the proper microfilm state index:
_National Archives, CONSOLIDATED INDEX TO COMPILED SERVICE RECORDS OF CONFEDERATE SOLDIERS, Microfilm M253, The Archives, Washington, DC.
_National Archives, INDEXES TO COMPILED SERVICE RECORDS OF CONFEDERATE SOLDIERS WHO SERVED FROM AL (M374), AZ Territory (M375), AR (M376), FL (M225), GA (M226), KY (M377), LA (M378), MD (M379), MS (M232), MO (M380), NC (M230), SC (M381), TN (M231), TX (M227), VA (M382), Confederate National Government (M818), National Archives, Washington, DC. Microfilm numbers in parentheses.
If your veteran was in the Union forces, look for him in both the separate state microfilm indexes and the microfilm pension index:
_National Archives, INDEXES TO COMPILED SERVICE RECORDS OF UNION SOLDIERS WHO SERVED FROM AL (M263), AZ Territory (M532), AR (M383), CA (M533), CO Territory (M534), CT (M535), Dakota Territory (M536), DE (M537), DC (M538), FL (M264), GA (M385), IL (M539), IN (M540), IA (M541), KS (M542), KY (M386), LA (M387), ME (M543), MD (M388), MA (M544), MI

(M545), MN (M546), MS (M389), MO (M390), NE Territory (M547), NV (M548), NH (M549), NJ (M550), NM Territory (M242), NY (M551), NC (M391), OH (M552), OR (M553), PA (M554), RI (M555), TN (M392), TX (M393), UT Territory (M556), VT (M557), VA (M394), WA Territory (M558), WV (M507), WI (M559), US Colored Troops (M589), Veterans Reserve Corps (M636), National Archives, Washington, DC. Microfilm numbers in parentheses.

_National Archives, GENERAL INDEX TO PENSION FILES, 1761-1934, Microfilm T288, National Archives, Washington, DC.

These microfilm indexes are available in the National Archives, Regional Branches of the National Archives, the Family History Library (and its branch Family History Centers), large genealogical libraries, and state libraries. They may also be borrowed from the American Genealogical Lending Library. If you fail to find your progenitor in these indexes, write the appropriate state library, state archives, and state adjutant general.

Once you have found your forebear's state and regiment, you can obtain the service records on him and the pension records on him and/or his wife. Confederate service records have all been put on microfilms:

_COMPILED MILITARY SERVICE RECORDS OF CONFEDERATE SOLDIERS FROM AL (M311), AZ Territory (M318), AR (M317), FL (M251), GA (M266), KY (M319), LA (M320), MD (M321), MS (M269), MO (M322), NC (M270), SC (M267), TN (M268), TX (M323), VA (M324), Confederate National Government (M258), General and Staff Officers (M331), National Archives, Washington, DC. Microfilm numbers in parentheses.

These microfilms are in the same places mentioned in the previous paragraph. Confederate pension applications and records are available in the state archives of the Confederate States and the border states OK, KY, and MO. The dates on which the states began giving general Confederate pensions are: AL (1867), AR (1891), FL (1885), GA (1870), KY (1902), LA (1898), MS (1888), MO (1913), NC (1885), OK (1915), SC (1898), TN (1891). Write the state archives, enclosing an SASE, and inquiring about their records and fees.

Some Union service records have been microfilmed, but most are only in their original form. Those on microfilm are:

_COMPILED MILITARY SERVICE RECORDS OF UNION SOL-DIERS FROM AL (M276), AR (M399), FL (M400), GA (M403), KY (M397), LA (M396), MD (M384), MS (M404), MO (M405), NM Territory (M427), NC (M401), TN (M395), TX (M402), UT Territory

(M692), VA (M398), WV (M508), US Volunteers (M1017), National Archives, Washington, DC. Microfilm numbers in parentheses.

These microfilms may be found in the same places as those above. Service records for men from all other Union States and pension records for men and their wives from all Union States are in the National Archives in Washington, DC. To obtain them, write the National Archives and request order forms, fill them out, and return them. An alternate route which is often faster is to hire a searcher in Washington, DC to copy the records for you. (See the sections on Hired researchers and the National Archives.)

Histories of the regiments in the Civil War can be useful for understanding your ancestor's military experience. There are a number of works which present historical data or lead you to them:

_COMPILED RECORDS OF MILITARY UNITS IN UNION ORGA-NIZATIONS, Microfilm M594, National Archives, Washington, DC.

_COMPILED RECORDS OF MILITARY UNITS IN CONFEDER-ATE ORGANIZATIONS, Microfilm M861, National Archives, Washington, DC.

_THE WAR OF THE REBELLION, A COMPILATION OF OFFI-CIAL RECORDS OF THE UNION AND CONFEDERATE ARMIES, Government Printing Office, Washington, DC, 1901, 128 volumes, index in last volume.

_THE WAR OF THE REBELLION, A COMPILATION OF THE OFFICIAL RECORDS OF THE UNION AND CONFEDERATE NAVIES, Government Printing Office, Washington, DC, 1897-1927, 31 volumes, index in last volume.

_C. E. Dornbusch, MILITARY BIBLIOGRAPHY OF THE CIVIL WAR, NY Public Library, New York, NY, 1961-72, 3 volumes. Refers you to regimental histories.

Do not fail to check with the pertinent state library, state adjutant general, and state archives, even if you have already obtained considerable material on your Civil War veteran. They quite often can provide you with further information. Ask about rosters, lists, histories, bounties, claims, graves, hospitals, and prisons. It is also well to investigate records in the localities where your ancestor enlisted, lived after the war, and died. The local library is a good place to start, with the local genealogical and historical societies not being overlooked. Many other Civil War records are available: graves, prison, casualty, medical, amnesty, chaplains, deserters, GAR, UCV, home guard, hospital, militia, oath of allegiance, pardon, substitutes, wounded, draft, cemetery. Details on these and other records are found in:

_National Archives, GUIDE TO GENEALOGICAL RESEARCH IN THE NATIONAL ARCHIVES, The Archives, Washington, DC, 1985, Chapters 4-9.

_Geo. K. Schweitzer, CIVIL WAR GENEALOGY, The Author, Knoxville, TN, 1991.

_J. C. Neagles, CONFEDERATE RESEARCH SOURCES, Ancestry Publishing, Salt Lake City, UT, 1986.

__J. C. Neagles, US MILITARY RECORDS, Ancestry, Salt Lake City, UT, 1994.

35. Claims From its very beginnings, the US has permitted its citizens to petition for settlement of injustices against its citizens. Most claims have involved payment for materials or services rendered the government, for damages sustained because of the action or the failure to act of governmental officials, for damages by foreign powers and Indian tribes, and for governmental recognition of land ownership of property owned by people in areas taken from foreign powers by the US. Before 1855, a Court of Claims was established to investigate claims and to report their results to Congress, then in 1863, the court was given the authority to reject or settle claims.

Among the many claims records, the following often turn out to be of genealogical relevance:

_PRIVATE CLAIMS SUBMITTED TO THE CONTINENTAL CONGRESS, 1774-89, indexed in INDEX TO JOURNALS OF THE CONTINENTAL CONGRESS, National Archives, Washington, DC, 1976, and INDEX TO THE PAPERS OF THE CONTINENTAL CONGRESS, National Archives, Washington, DC, 1978, these lead to the JOURNALS which have been printed and the PAPERS which are on National Archives Microfilm M247.

_PRIVATE CLAIMS BROUGHT BEFORE THE US SENATE, 1815-1909, Senate Miscellaneous Documents, Serial Nos. 1945-6, 3175, 3881, 4433, 4917, 6165. These lead to claims files in National Archives Record Group 46.

_PRIVATE CLAIMS BROUGHT BEFORE THE US HOUSE OF REPRESENTATIVES, 1789-1891, House Miscellaneous Documents, Serial Nos. 653-5, 1574, 2036, 3268. Documents 653-5 published as ALPHABETICAL LIST OF PRIVATE CLAIMS, 1789-1851, Genealogical Publishing Co., Baltimore, MD, 1970. These all lead to claims files in National Archives Record Group 233.

_CLAIMS AGAINST THE US ARMY PRESENTED TO THE QUARTERMASTER GENERAL'S OFFICE, 1839-1914, National Archives Record Group 92, name indexes included. Claims, both military and civilian, relate chiefly to Mexican War and Civil War.

_INDEX TO CIVIL WAR SOUTHERN CLAIMS COMMISSION RECORDS, Aegean Park Press, Laguna Hills, CA, 1980. Leads to claims in National Archives Record Groups 217 and 233. Claims were made by Southerners who alleged they remained loyal and assisted the Union.

_INDIAN DEPREDATION CASE FILES, 1814-91, US COURT OF CLAIMS, National Archives Record Group 123, and CLAIMANT INDEX AND CASE FILES, National Archives Record Group 205.

_CASES DECIDED IN THE COURT OF CLAIMS OF THE US, 1863-, many volumes, cumulative indexes in volumes 30, 54, and 62, separate index in each volume thereafter.

_PRIVATE LAND CLAIMS, 1789-1908 (for AL, AZ, AR, CA, CO, FL, IL, IN, IA, LA, MI, MS, MO, NM, WI lands claimed by settlers who claimed they received it before the US acquired the land from some other government), in AMERICAN STATE PAPERS, PUBLIC LANDS, Gales and Seaton, Washington, DC, 1832-61, with indexes; also indexed in P. W. McMullin, GRASSROOTS OF AMERICA, Gendex Corp., Salt Lake City, UT, 1972. Original records in National Archives Record Groups 46, 49, and 233, and in House Miscellaneous Document 81, Serial No. 1836.

Some other claims records and much further information on the above can be found in:

_National Archives, GUIDE TO GENEALOGICAL RESEARCH IN THE NATIONAL ARCHIVES, The Archives, Washington, DC, 1985, Chapters 10, 15, 16, and 20.

The publications referred to above will be found in the federal records section of large libraries, especially state and state university libraries. And the National Archives materials will be found in the National Archives.

In doing research in claims records, you should by no means neglect the records in state archives. Claims were also lodged with various states for redress of grievances similar to those mentioned above. The legislative journals and reports of these states should also be examined.

36. Colonial families

There are numerous older and a few recent volumes and sets which provide genealogical information on families which came to America in pre-Revolutionary or colonial times. Some of these volumes must be used with discretion and caution since all of the data are not always amenable to independent substantiation. Even so, used with care they can be of value. With some exceptions noted below, these works are to be used only to provide clues or leads to research in the original documents. All data must be verified with careful investigations into primary source materials. If you know or suspect that your ancestor arrived here before 1775, consult:

_F. A. Virkus, THE ABRIDGED COMPENDIUM OF AMERICAN GENEALOGY, Genealogical Publishing Co., Baltimore, MD, 1968, 7 volumes. (54,000 lineages, 425,000 names)

_G. M. Mackenzie and N. O. Rhoades, COLONIAL FAMILIES OF THE USA, Genealogical Publishing Co., Baltimore, MD, 1966, 7 volumes. (125,000 names)

_D. Baird, LINEAGE BOOK, NATIONAL SOCIETY COLONIAL DAMES OF THE 17TH CENTURY, The Society, Rotan, TX, 1980. (20,000 names)

_National Society Daughters of the Colonial Wars, BICENTENNIAL ANCESTOR INDEX FOR LINEAGE VOLUMES, The Society, Clifton, VA, 1984. (16,000 lineages)

_T. P. Hughes, AMERICAN ANCESTRY, Genealogical Publishing Co., Baltimore, MD, 1968, 12 volumes. (7500 persons)

_Order of Founders and Patriots of America, REGISTER OF LINEAGES OF ASSOCIATES, 1896-1993, Genealogical Publishing Co., Baltimore, MD, 1994, 4 volumes. (100,000 lineage links)

_J. Savage, A GENEALOGICAL DICTIONARY OF THE FIRST SETTLERS OF NEW ENGLAND, Genealogical Publishing Co., Baltimore, MD, 1981, 4 volumes. Very good.

_G. R. Crowther, III, SURNAME INDEX TO 65 VOLUMES OF COLONIAL AND REVOLUTIONARY PEDIGREES, National Genealogical Society, Washington, DC, 1964.

_H. Whittemore, GENEALOGICAL GUIDE TO EARLY SETTLERS OF AMERICA, Genealogical Publishing Co., Baltimore, MD, 1967.

_R. Lawrence, COLONIAL FAMILIES OF AMERICA, The Author, New York, NY, 1928-48, 27 volumes.

_C. K. Bolton, THE FOUNDERS, PERSONS WHO CAME TO THE COLONIES BEFORE 1701, Genealogical Publishing Co., Baltimore, MD, 1976, 2 volumes.

_BURKE'S DISTINGUISHED FAMILIES OF AMERICA, Burke's Peerage, London, England, 1948.
_H. D. Pittman, AMERICANS OF GENTLE BIRTH AND THEIR ANCESTORS, Genealogical Publishing Co., Baltimore, MD, 1970, 2 volumes.
_C. E. Banks, THE PLANTERS OF THE COMMONWEALTH, Genealogical Publishing Co., Baltimore, MD, 1972.
_W. A. Crozier, A KEY TO SOUTHERN PEDIGREES, Southern Book Co., Baltimore, MD, 1953. (7000 names)

Other volumes of this sort for the US, plus many more for specific regions and states, are listed in the very important reference works:
_P. W. Filby, AMERICAN & BRITISH GENEALOGY & HERALDRY, The New England Historic Genealogical Society, Boston, MA, 1983, plus 1982-5 SUPPLEMENT, and succeeding SUPPLEMENTS.

37. Colonial war records

The colonies which later became the US engaged in a number of colonial wars which were usually American expressions of large conflicts among the nations of Europe. There were the Dutch-Swedish hostilities (1640-55) ending in 1655 with the Dutch out of their colony of New Amsterdam (NY) defeating the Swedes in the DE area. The Second Anglo-Dutch War (1664-67) was manifested in America by the English capture of New Amsterdam (NY), then in the Third Anglo-Dutch War (1672-78), the Dutch retook NY (1673), then relost it (1674). King William's War (1689-99) involved hostilities between the French and the English, chiefly on the NY and New England frontiers. Soon after, during Queen Anne's War (1702-13), the English clashed with the Spanish and French in and around SC and with the French in New England. Spanish-English conflicts in the back country and south of the Carolinas characterized the Anglo-Spanish War (1727-28), and the War of Jenkin's Ear (1739-42) continued English-Spanish engagements, mainly on the GA-FL border and south of there. King George's War (1744-48) saw extensive hostilities between the English and the French on the NY and New England boundaries and north and west of them. The last of the major colonial wars, the French and Indian War (1754-63), was fought along and beyond the borders of VA, MD, PA, NY, and New England. The war ended in the decisive defeat of the French, and the cession to the English of French Canada, Spanish FL, and all the country back of the colonies to the MS River.

In addition to the above wars, which generally involved Indians on one or both sides, there were many small and several major Indian wars. Among the major ones were the Pequot War (1636-37) in New England, the Mohawk War (1642-45) in New Amsterdam (NY), the Opechancanough War (1644-46) in VA, King Philip's [the Indian chief Metacomet's] War (1675-76) in New England, the Tuscarora War (1711-13) in the Carolinas, the Yamassee Conflicts (1715-16) in SC, Lovewell's or Dummer's [Abenaki] War (1722-25) in the ME area, and Pontiac's War (1763-66) in the old northwest.

The original records of the above conflicts are largely in the state archives of the states which were among the 13 colonies, but some are also in local and regional libraries and archives. For the most part, the materials consist of lists of participants with very little additional information except the identity of the military group and the approximate or precise dates of service. Even so, they are very valuable because they allow you to locate your ancestor in a particular place at a particular time. For most of the wars, no veterans' benefits (pensions or bounty lands) were given, but in some cases in the later wars, bounty land was awarded.

A large proportion of these colonial war records have been published, and the books are available at large genealogical libraries, state libraries, and the Family History Library (Family History Centers). Among the more important of these volumes are:
_(CT) F. D. W. Andrews, CT SOLDIERS IN THE FRENCH AND INDIAN WAR, The Author, Vineland, NJ, 1925; T. Buckingham, ROLL AND JOURNAL OF CT SERVICE IN QUEEN ANNE'S WAR, 1710-11, Acorn Club, New Haven, CT, 1916; CT Adjutant General's Office, LIST OF CT MEN WHO SERVED IN THE PEQUOT WAR, The Office, New Haven, CT, 1939; CT Historical Society, ROLLS OF CT MEN IN THE FRENCH AND INDIAN WARS, 1755-62, The Society, Hartford, CT, 1903-5; D. L. Jacobus, LIST OF OFFICIALS, CIVIL, MILITARY, AND ECCLESIASTICAL OF CT COLONY, 1636-77, ALSO SOLDIERS IN THE PEQUOT WAR, The Author, New Haven, CT, 1935; J. Shepard, CT SOLDIERS IN THE PEQUOT WAR OF 1637, The Author, Meriden, CT, 1913.
_(DE) Public Archives Commission of DE, DE ARCHIVES, The Commission, Wilmington, DE, 1911-16, Vol. 1.
_(GA) M. J. Clark, COLONIAL SOLDIERS OF THE SOUTH, 1732-74, Genealogical Publishing Co., Baltimore, MD, 1983. Soldiers from GA, MD, NC, SC, VA.

_(MD) M. J. Clark, COLONIAL SOLDIERS OF THE SOUTH, 1732-74, Genealogical Publishing Co., Baltimore, MD, 1983. Soldiers from GA, MD, NC, SC, VA. E. F. Stormont and B. D. Aul, MD COLONIAL MILITARY SERVICE INDEX, 1637-1776, FL Daughters of Colonial Wars, Tallahassee, FL, 1988.

_(MA) G. M. Bodge, SOLDIERS IN KING PHILIP'S WAR, Genealogical Publishing Co., Baltimore, MD, 1976; M. E. Donahue, MA OFFICERS AND SOLDIERS, 1702-22, QUEEN ANNE'S WAR TO DUMMER'S WAR, Society of Colonial Wars in MA, Boston, MA, 1980; C. Doreski, MA OFFICERS AND SOLDIERS IN THE 17TH CENTURY CONFLICTS, Society of Colonial Wars in MA, Boston, MA, 1982; K. D. Goss and D. Zarowin, MA OFFICERS AND SOLDIERS IN THE FRENCH AND INDIAN WARS, 1755-56, New England Historic Genealogical Society, Boston, MA, 1985; R. E. Mackay, MA SOLDIERS IN THE FRENCH AND INDIAN WARS, 1744-55, Society of Colonial Wars in MA, Boston, MA, 1978; M. O. Stachiw, MA OFFICERS AND SOLDIERS, 1723-43, DUMMER'S WAR TO THE WAR OF JENKIN'S EAR, Society of Colonial Wars in MA, Boston, MA, 1980; N. E. Voye, MA OFFICERS IN THE FRENCH AND INDIAN WARS, 1748-63, Society of Colonial Wars in MA, Boston, MA, 1975.

_(New England) G. M. Bodge, SOLDIERS IN KING PHILIP'S WAR, Genealogical Publishing Co., Baltimore, MD, 1976, soldiers from CT, MA, ME, NH; E. L. Coleman, NEW ENGLAND CAPTIVES CARRIED TO CANADA, 1677-1760, DURING THE FRENCH AND INDIAN WARS, Southworth Press, Portland, ME, 1925; S. G. Drake, A PARTICULAR HISTORY OF THE FIVE YEARS FRENCH AND INDIAN WARS IN NEW ENGLAND AND PARTS ADJACENT, Heritage Books, Bowie, MD, 1984.

_(NH) CEMETERY RECORDS OF NH VETERANS, VOL. 1, FRENCH AND INDIAN WARS, Typescript, NH Veterans Council; I. W. Hammond, NH STATE AND PROVINCIAL PAPERS, No. 16, FRENCH AND INDIAN WAR ROLLS, 1712-55, Manchester, NH, 1885-89; NH STATE PAPERS, WITH FRENCH AND INDIAN WAR LISTS, Vols. 5-6, 14, 16, Concord, NH; C. E. Potter, THE MILITARY HISTORY OF THE STATE OF NH, 1623-1861, Genealogical Publishing Co., Baltimore, MD, 1972; G. C. Gilmore, ROLL OF NH MEN AT LOUISBURG, Pearson, Concord, NH, 1896; NH Adjutant General's Office, ANNUAL REPORTS, The Office, Concord, NH, 1858/9-1915/6, passim.

83

_(NJ) NJ State Library, NJ WARS: INDEXES TO COLONIAL PERIOD, 1665-1774, Genealogical Society of UT, Salt Lake City, UT, 1969.
_(NY) NY Historical Society, MUSTER ROLLS OF NY PROVINCIAL TROOPS, 1755-64, The Society, New York, NY, 1891; NY State Historian, SECOND AND THIRD ANNUAL REPORTS OF THE NY STATE HISTORIAN, The Historian, Albany, NY 1897-98; C. M. Meyers, EARLY MILITARY RECORDS OF NY, 1689-1738, The Author, Saugus, CA, 1967; E. B. O'Callaghan and B. Fernow, THE DOCUMENTARY HISTORY OF THE STATE OF NY, Weed, Parsons, and Co., Albany, NY, 1849-81, 4 volumes, passim; INHAB-ITANTS OF COLONIAL NY, Genealogical Publishing Co., Baltimore, MD, 1979.
_(NC) M. J. Clark, COLONIAL SOLDIERS OF THE SOUTH, 1732-74, Genealogical Publishing Co., Baltimore, MD, 1983. Soldiers from GA, MD, NC, SC, VA. Treasurer and Comptroller, FRENCH AND INDIAN WAR PENSIONS, NC State Archives, Raleigh, NC.
_(PA) B. Laverty, COLONIAL MUSTER ROLLS AT THE HISTORI-CAL SOCIETY OF PA, The Society, Philadelphia, PA, 1983; THE PUBLISHED PA ARCHIVES, Colonial Series Volumes 4-5, First Series Volumes 1-2, 4-5, Second Series Index in each volume, Fourth Series Index in Volume 12, Fifth Series Index in Volume 15 of the Sixth Series; H. M. Richards, THE PA-GERMAN IN THE FRENCH AND INDIAN WAR, PA German Society, Lancaster, PA, 1905.
_(RI) H. M. Chapin, RI IN THE COLONIAL WARS, KING GEOR-GE'S WAR, 1740-48, The Author, Providence, RI, 1920; H. M. Chapin, RI IN THE COLONIAL WARS, THE OLD FRENCH AND INDIAN WARS, 1755-62, The Author, Providence, RI, 1918; H. M. Chapin, RI PRIVATEERS IN KING GEORGE'S WAR, 1739-48, RI Historical Society, Providence, RI, 1926; J. J. Smith, CIVIL AND MILITARY LIST OF RI, 1647-1850, Preston and Rounds, Providence, RI, 1900-07; Society of Colonial Wars, NINE MUSTER ROLLS OF RI TROOPS ENLISTED DURING THE OLD FRENCH WAR, The Society, Providence, RI, 1915.
_(SC) L. O. Andrea, SC COLONIAL SOLDIERS AND PATRIOTS, SC Daughters of Colonial Wars, Columbia, SC, 1952; M. J. Clark, COLONIAL SOLDIERS OF THE SOUTH, 1732-74, Genealogical Publishing Co., Baltimore, MD, 1983, soldiers from GA, MD, NC, SC, VA; T. Draine and J. Skinner, SC SOLDIERS AND INDIAN TRADERS, 1725-30, Congaree Publns., Columbia, SC, 1986.
_(VA) L. D. Bockstruck, VA'S COLONIAL SOLDIERS, Genealogical Publishing Co., Baltimore, 1988; W. A. Crozier, VA COLONIAL

MILITIA, 1651-1776, Genealogical Publishing Co., Baltimore, MD, 1982; H. J. Eckenrode, LIST OF COLONIAL SOLDIERS OF VA, Genealogical Publishing Co., Baltimore, MD, 1974; V. A. Lewis, SOLDIERY OF WV IN THE FRENCH AND INDIAN WAR, LORD DUNMORE'S WAR, THE REVOLUTION, AND THE LATER INDIAN WARS, Genealogical Publishing Co., Baltimore, MD, 1967; P. F. Taylor, A CALENDAR OF WARRANTS FOR LAND IN KY GRANTED FOR SERVICE IN THE FRENCH AND INDIAN WAR, Genealogical Publishing Co., Baltimore, MD, 1967; E. P. Bentley, VA MILITARY RECORDS FROM THE VA MAGAZINE OF HISTORY AND BIOGRAPHY, THE WILLIAM AND MARY COLLEGE QUARTERLY, AND TYLER'S QUARTERLY, Genealogical Publishing Co., Baltimore, MD, 1983; VA State Library, LIST OF THE COLONIAL SOLDIERS OF VA, Genealogical Publishing Co., Baltimore, MD, 1961.

In addition for the above published records, each state archives has additional manuscript materials relating to colonial wars. Many of them have numerous records, others only a few. A sizable number of these records have been put on microfilm and are at the Family History Library. Check the indexes at your nearest Family History Center and borrow those you need. Or you can write the appropriate state archives, enclosing an SASE, and inquiring as to whether your progenitor is listed. Addresses of state archives are given in a later section, as are locations of Family History Centers.

38. Computer indexes

One of the most important benefits to the genealogical community of computer technology has been the production of indexes. Automated alphabetization, scanning entry, and astonishingly rapid recall from large data assemblages are among the advantages of computerized indexes. In addition, vast amounts of data can be stored on extremely small devices (disks), which can be marketed inexpensively, and thus can be made available for use by persons owning a personal computer. Further, those owning a personal computer can use communication devices (modems) to gain access to indexes residing in large data banks in central locations.

You will encounter a number of these computer-generated indexes as you go about your research, and you will discover that many of them can also be computer-accessed. Others of them are accessed by print outs or microfiche, but as time goes on, computer access will increase. Among the computer indexes now available, several examples will now be mentioned. Of international coverage is the following:

_INTERNATIONAL GENEALOGICAL INDEX (IGI), Family History Library, Salt Lake City, UT. On compact disks, several hundreds of millions of entries, chiefly birth and marriage records. Available at Family History Centers on microfiche and/or computer. See section on the IGI.

Largely of US interest are these:

__MASTER NAME INDEX TO AUTOMATED ARCHIVES CD-ROMs, Automated Archives, Salt Lake City, UT. An overall index to the 40 million name entries on over 50 CDROMs.

_BIOBASE, Gale Research, Detroit, MI. A master index to hundreds of older and current biographical compilations. Also available on microfiche. See section on Biography.

_AISI COMPUTERIZED DATABASE, Accelerated Indexing Systems, North Salt Lake City, UT. Well over 80 million indexed names largely from 1790-1850 censuses, with many entries from later censuses and other state and federal records. See section on Census integrated indexes.

_COMPUTERIZED ROOTS CELLAR and COMPUTERIZED FAMILY FILE, Everton Publishers, Genealogical Helper, Logan, UT. Indexes of hundreds of thousands of names being researched by genealogists. See section on Surname indexes.

_ANCESTRAL FILE, Family History Library, Salt Lake City, UT. On CDROMs at Family History Centers.

Other examples selected from some regional and state indexes are:

_IL COMPUTERIZED CENSUS PROJECT, Newberry Library, Chicago, IL. Index to the 1860-70 censuses of IL.

_KY CEMETERY RECORDS PROJECT, KY Historical Society, Frankfort, KY. An index of KY cemetery data.

_VA SETTLERS RESEARCH PROJECT, Association for the Preservation of VA Antiquities, Richmond, VA. Index of early VA settlers, data taken from numerous sources, including county records.

_COMBINED COMPUTER OUTPUT MICROFILM INDEX, SC Department of Archives and History, Columbia, SC. A large index of many SC records, especially colonial material, alphabetical by name.

_COMPUTERIZED SOUTHERN STATE NAME INDEX, Brigham Young University, Provo, UT. Index to family histories, Bible records, DAR abstracts and compilations, and other materials relating to the southern states.

These entries are only illustrations of the types of computerized indexes which are available. You will note that many types of organizations have compiled them. The best places to inquire about such computerized indexes are the Family History Library and pertinent state libraries. The Family History Library is usually aware of all that are available, and the state libraries know of those for their states.

There are also many valuable indexes on commercially-available CDROMs and computer floppy disks. Among the CDROMs are the following:
__Census Indexes: CD136-Colonial America, [For 1790] CD137-US, [For 1800] CD138-New England-NY, CD151-Mid-Atlantic-South, [For 1810] CD149-New England-NY, CD150-Mid-Atlantic-South-Great Lakes,[For1820]CD139-Northeast,CD154-Mid-Atlantic-South-Great Lakes,[For1830]CD140-Northeast,CD148-Mid-Altantic-South-Great Lakes, [For 1840] CD141-New England-NY, CD142-Mid-Atlantic, CD152-South, CD-153-Great Lakes-Midwest, [For 1850] CD40-New England, CD41-Mid-Atlantic, CD42-NY, CD43-DC-MD-NC-VA, CD44-KY-TN, CD45-South, CD46-OH-IN, CD47-IL-IA-MI-MN-MO-WI, [For 1860] CD21-NY, CD22-DE-NJ-PA, CD24-DC-MD-NC-VA-WV. CD26-AL-AR-FL-GA-LA-SC, CD27-IL-IN, CD39-WI, CD51-MA, CD77-ME, CD-78-VT, CD80-CT, [For 1870] CD34-KY-NC-VA-WV, CD286-Eastern PA, CD291-GA, ACD0001-GA, ACD0002-NY City, ACD0003-Eastern PA, ACD-0004-St. Louis-Chicago-Baltimore, ACD0005-NC-SC, ACD0006-VA-WV, ACD0007-Western PA, [For 1880] CD20-OH, CD35-Chicago-Cook County, [For 1860-70-80-90] CD49-TX, [For Mortality Schedules 1850-80] CD164-All US.
__Marriage Records: CD1-LA, CD2-IL-IN-KY-OH-TN, CD3-AL- GA-SC-CD4-MD-NC-VA, CD5-AR-MS-MO-TX, CD6-AR, CD226-GA, CD227-AR-CA-IA-LA-MN-MO-OR-TX, CD229-KY-NC-TN-VA.
__Family Records: CD15-Computerized Family File, CD100-101-102-Family Pedigrees, CD113-Family History Series.
__Land Grant Records: CD253-AR-FL-LA, CD254-MI.
__Social Security Death Records: CD110-CD111-CD112-All US.

Some of the records available on floppy disks are the following early marriage records (state given after the hyphen):
__Marriage Records: K3M-AL1, K3M-AR1, K3M-CA1, K3M-DC1, K3M-GA1, K3M-GA2, K3M-IL1, K3M-IL2, K3M-IN1, K3M-IN2, K3M-IA1, K3M-KY1, K3M-KY2, K3M-LA1, K3M-MI1, K3M-MN1, K3M-MS1, K3M-MO1, K3M-MO2, K3M-NC1, K3M-NC2, K3M-OR1, K3M-TN1, K3M-TN2, K3M-TX1, K3M-VA1.

Also available on floppy disks are these census indexes:
__Census Records: [For 1790] ME, NH, NY, NC, RI, VT, [For 1860] CA, CT, DE, DC, FL, OR, RI, SC, [For 1870]: GA, Chicago, St. Louis, Long Island, NC, Philadlphia, Western PA, SC, VA, WV, [1890 Civil War Veterans]: KY, LA, ME, MD, MA, MI, MN, MS, MO, NY, TX, VA, WV, [Miscellaneous]: 1856 UT, 1910 NV, 1910 WY.

All of the above CDROMs and the floppy disks and many more are available from the American Genealogical Lending Library, PO Box 329, Bountiful, UT 84011-0329.

39. Computer programs

Many genealogists are finding that the use of computer programs is a very useful thing. Computers employing genealogical computer programs can assist you in organizing, managing, displaying, and printing your research data. They permit you to extract data under many different headings (names, dates, places); print out numerous forms (pedigree charts, ancestor tables, family group sheets, descendant charts); add, delete, and edit entries; incorporate references, notes, and abstracts of documents; and arrange your materials for a printed family history. And all of this can be done from one entry of each name and each piece of information. You do not have to copy names and data over and over again, since the computer system is superb at rearranging and/or duplicating your single entries. In order to do computer genealogy, you will need five items: (a) a computer, (b) a monitor, (c) a printer, (d) an operating system, and (e) a genealogy program. All of these can be had for about $2000 for a system which will be adequate for most people. Such a system might consist of (a) an IBM clone with a 440MB hard disk, (b) a color monitor, (c) a 24-pin dot-matrix printer, (d) an MS-DOS set of diskettes, and (e) a genealogy program on a set of diskettes.

A genealogical computer system is useful for many people, but it is not for everyone. You should guard carefully against the idea that you cannot do genealogy without a computer. It is simply not true. Second, please don't think for one minute that having a computer will make you a better researcher. Computer or not, every serious genealogist must exercise patience, persistence, diligence, thoroughness, and critical care in locating, examining, and recording data. Just remember that the computer substitutes for none of these. In other words, if you put bad data in a computer, you'll get bad data out, even though it may be organized. Thirdly, people differ in their computer adaptability. You should not be afraid of computers, simply because most genealogists are smart enough to learn them. The reason is that you don't need to know how they work in order to operate them, no more than you need to know how an internal combustion engine functions in order to drive a car. But, as in the case of driving, you do need to go through a learning period, and there will be some mistakes and some frustrations. However, excellent instructions usually accompany genealogical programs, and they resemble recipes, even though they may be longer. So if you can follow recipes, you can operate a computer. However, please do not spend $2000 or more for a genealogical computer system until you have done several of these: talked with some people who own them, spent several hours in genealogical computing seminars, gone to at least a few meetings of a local genealogical computing group, have had some hands-on experience with a borrowed or rented computer, and have used a friend's computer.

Among the better genealogical computer programs are the following:
_FAMILY ORIGINS, Parsons Technology, PO Box 100, Hiawatha, IA 52233.
_FAMILY ROOTS, Quinsept, Inc., PO Box 216, Lexington, MA 02173.
_FAMILY TREE MAKER, Banner Blue Software, 39500 Stevenson Place, Suite 204, Fremont, CA 94539.
_THE MASTER GENEALOGIST, Kent Supply Co., PO Box 4136, Chatsworth, CA 91313.
_MY FAMILY RECORD, Everton Publishers, PO Box 368, Logan, UT 84323.
_PERSONAL ANCESTRAL FILE, Distribution Center, 1999 West 1700 South, Salt Lake City, UT 84104.
_REUNION, Leister Products, PO Box 289, Mechanicsburg, PA 17055.
_ROOTS IV, Commsoft, Inc., PO Box 310, Windsor, CA 95492.
You may write these organizations and request information on their programs. Do not purchase any program which does not contain GEDCOM, which allows data transfer from program to program. If you care to read further about genealogical computing, three items may be recommended:
_P. A. Andereck and R. A. Pence, COMPUTER GENEALOGY, Ancestry, Inc., Salt Lake City, UT, latest edition.
_K. C. Clifford, GENEALOGY AND COMPUTERS FOR THE COMPLETE, DETERMINED, AND ADVANCED RE-SEARCHER, Clearfield Co., Baltimore, MD, 1995, 3 volumes. Almost completely Personal Ancestral File oriented.
_G. W. Archer, ARCHER'S DIRECTORY OF GENEALOGICAL SOFTWARE, Heritage Books, Bowie, MD, latest edition.

In addition, there is an excellent genealogical periodical which you may want to look at and perhaps subscribe to:
_GENEALOGICAL COMPUTING, Ancestry, Salt Lake City, UT, 1981-.

40. Computer/modem facilities

A computer can be equipped with a device called a modem. Such a device permits the connection of the computer to your telephone line. There are available at various telephone numbers numerous genealogically-oriented data bases and communication media. These include genealogy information sources supplied by (1) commercial on-line providers, (2) commercial Internet connections, and (3) commercial dedicated genealogical information providers. Some agencies provide both of the first two. Each of the first two charges an installation fee and then a monthly access fee, and sometimes a per-minute usage fee.

The major commercial on-line providers now operating are as follows:
_AMERICA ON-LINE, call 1-800-227-6364. Access their Genealogy Club by typing KEYWORD:ROOTS. Research methods, sources, surname lists, messages to/from other genealogists. Includes Internet access.
_COMPUSERVE, call 1-800-554-4079. Access their Genealogy Forum by typing GO ROOTS. Surname lists, software, library files, genealogy information from the US, Europe, Canada, Latin America. Includes Internet access.
_DELPHI, call 1-800-695-4005. Access their genealogy forum by typing GO CUST 68, then select Searching for Roots. Service includes Internet access.
_GENIE, call 1-800-638-9636. Access their Genealogy Roundtable by typing GO GENEALOGY. Much genealogical information plus a question-and-answer bulletin board.
_PRODIGY, call 1-800-776-3449. Access their genealogical information section by typing JUMP:GENEALOGYBB. Sources, data lists, advice from an expert genealogist.
_MICROSOFT NETWORK. Contact them for detailed information on their genealogical materials.

The best overall information on the numerous Internet providers and internet facilities is:

_H. Hahn and R. Stout, THE INTERNET YELLOW PAGES, Osborne
  McGraw Hill, New York, NY, latest edition. See the GENEALOGY
  SECTION.
In this volume and in the yellow pages of your telephone directory, you
will find addresses and telephone numbers of Internet providers. It is
usually well to purchase the services of a provider in your local area since
this saves telephone line costs. Once you have an internet connection,
you can access hundred of things, such as the following:
_UNIVERSITY OF MI GENEALOGY COLLECTION, gopher access
  by typing mlink.hh.lib.umich.edu, then selecting Entertain-
  ment/Recreation, then selecting Genealogy. Software, advice, books,
  computer files.
_UNIVERSITY OF TOLEDO GENEALOGY COLLECTION, gopher
  access by typing alpha.cc.utoledo.edu, then selecting Genealogy.
  Leads to Usenet groups such as soc.roots, soc.genealogy.methods,
  soc.genealogy.computing, and soc.genealogy.misc.
_INDIVIDUAL'S BULLETIN BOARDS. Many persons have estab-
  lished bulletin boards dealing with numerous genealogy topics. Each
  has an individual telephone number. Recent listing of hundred of
  them available on National Genealogical Society's Bulletin Board.
_WORLD WIDE WEB GENEALOGY, browser access by pointing to
  http://www.ftp.cac.psu.edu^saw/genealogy.html. The Genealogy
  Home Page which you will get will lead you to many data bases and
  information collections. Important internet sources include soc.roots
  and Roots-L.

  Several societies and commercial firms have set up genealogical
informaton access lines. These include:
_EVERTON'S ON-LINE SEARCH, Everton Publishers, PO Box 368,
  Logan, UT 84323. Many genealogical databases.
_AGLL BULLETIN BOARD, American Genealogy Lending Library,
  PO Box 329, Bountiful, UT. Over 45 different genealogical data
  bases and services.
_NATIONAL GENEALOGICAL SOCIETY BULLETIN BOARD, c/o
  Donald K. Wilson, NGS-BBS System Operator, 6177 Hardy Drive,
  McLean, VA.

  A very useful book describing in detail the many genealogical
items available through a computer/modem is:
_E. P. Crowe, GENEALOGY ONLINE, RESEARCHING YOUR
  ROOTS, Windcrest/McGraw-Hill, New York, NY, latest edition.

41. County atlases

Shortly before the Civil War atlases of US counties began to be published. These books contain maps, township plats, sometimes city plans, sometimes names of property owners, land boundaries, roads, railroads, lakes, streams, rivers, sometimes cemeteries, and sometimes churches. Some have historical sketches of the counties, biographies of inhabitants, directories of patrons, pictures of businesses, farms, and homes, and portraits of leading citizens and their families. As a genealogist, you will find in them many clues to family relationships. To discover if atlases were available for the county in which your ancestor lived, consult the volumes below. Once you have found that there is a relevant atlas, it can usually be found in the local library or the pertinent state library.

_C. E. LeGear, US ATLASES, Library of Congress, Washington, DC, Vol. 1, 1950, Vol. 2, 1953.

Microfilm copies of numerous early county atlases are also available. These are listed in:

_J. J. Walsh, MICROFORMS IN PRINT, Microform Review, Westport, CT, latest edition, classifications 240 and 280.

The best sources for county atlases (in addition to local and state libraries) are state university libraries, large genealogical libraries, and the Family History Library. Those in the Family History Library can be borrowed through its many branch Family History Centers.

42. County courthouses

In most of the over 5000 counties of the US, the major repository for original records of genealogical value is the county court house. These records usually include many of the following: adoption, birth, bonds, civil court, criminal court, death, deed, divorce, equity court, guardian, marriage, mortgage, land, license, naturalization, probate, tax, and will. When you enter a court house, you will usually find a number of offices in which these records are located. Generally there will be a few offices in smaller counties, several offices in larger ones. These offices will bear signs resembling some of the following: assessor, auditor, board of commissioners, board of freeholders, chancery court, circuit court, clerk of court(s), commissioner(-ers), county clerk, county court, county judge, county recorder, county surrogate, court administrator, court clerk, court of common please, court of ordinary, court of quarter sessions, deed office, district court, family court, health department, orphans' court, probate court, prothonotary, recorder of deeds, regist(er, -rar, -ry) of deeds, regist(-er, -rar, -ry) of probate, regist(-er, -rar-, -ry) of vital records, regist(-er, -rar, -ry) of wills, superior court, tax assessor, treasurer, trial court clerk. All offices should be visited, and the records in each should be examined. It is well to remember that in New England (CT, ME, MA, NH, RI, VT) the towns have jurisdiction over some of the above-mentioned records. Also, please recognize that parishes substitute for counties in LA, and districts in AK.

Details on the record types mentioned above are given in other sections in this handbook. Addresses of county court houses are available in:

_A. Eichholz, ANCESTRY'S REDBOOK, Ancestry Publishing, Salt Lake City, UT, latest edition.

_NAME AND NUMBERS, Wiley and Sons, New York, NY, latest edition.

_L. K. Meitzler, THE US COUNTY COURTHOUSE ADDRESS BOOK, Heritage Quest, Orting, WA, 1988.

_E. P. Bentley, COUNTY COURTHOUSE BOOK, Genealogical Publishing Co., Baltimore, MD, latest edition.

County record office personnel are generally very busy people, doing what they are paid to do, namely, to manage the records of the county. They seldom have time to do any research for genealogists, and thus you should ask them for a very minimum of assistance, because they are not paid to do family tracing. Hence, letters to them should be very brief, to the point, asking only a single question, and enclosing an SASE. Further, before visiting a county court house or dispatching a hired researcher to go there, you should first examine all the records that have been published or microfilmed. Such copied materials are available at the state library, state archives, large genealogical libraries, and the Family History Library. The holdings of the Family History Library, which are extensive for many counties, can be borrowed through its numerous Family History Centers, at least one of which will be near you. In many cases, this will permit you to look at most of the more important records without going to the county. Then, if you need to do further research, you can continue with the county. Detailed listings of county records are provided in some of the guidebooks listed in the section entitled State source guides, and brief listings are presented in the book edited by Eichholz which is listed above.

43. County histories

Histories of the large majority of US counties have been published. These volumes often contain a great deal of information on former and present inhabitants. They include biog-

raphies of leading citizens, details about early settlers, histories of
organizations, churches, lodges, businesses, buildings, schools, physicians,
teachers, government officials, farmers, and other groups. To discover if
such histories are available for your progenitor's county, consult:
_M. J. Kaminkow, US LOCAL HISTORIES IN THE LIBRARY OF
    CONGRESS, Magna Carta Book Co., Baltimore, MD, 1975, 5
    volumes, index in the 5th volume.
_P. W. Filby, A BIBLIOGRAPHY OF AMERICAN COUNTY
    HISTORIES, Genealogical Publishing Co., Baltimore, MD, 1985.
It is also well to inquire at the local library in the county of your interest,
since they sometimes have county histories which were published in a
limited edition, ones which are only in typescript, or ones which are in
manuscript. Microfilm copies of many early county histories have been
made by commercial organizations. They are listed in:
_J. J. Walsh, MICROFORMS IN PRINT, Microform Review, Westport,
    CT, latest edition, classifications 240 and 480.
The best places to find county histories are in local libraries, state libraries, state university libraries, large genealogical libraries, and the
Family History Library. The latter institution has microfilmed many of
them, and has made them available through its numerous branch Family
History Centers.

44. County landowner maps

During the past century (1800-99),
detailed maps of many US counties
were prepared to show the names of
the landowners printed on the pieces
of property they owned. These maps were produced by several agencies,
one of the more important being the county tax authority. Such maps
should be sought in county tax and assessor offices, county libraries, state
libraries, state archives, state university geography libraries, the US
Geological Survey Library, the NY City Public Library, the National
Archives, the Library of Congress, and the Family History Library. Many
of the records of the last library can be accessed through its numerous
branch Family History Centers. The over 1400 landowner maps in the
Library of Congress are listed in:
_R. W. Stephenson, LANDOWNERSHIP MAPS, A CHECKLIST,
    Library of Congress, Washington, DC, 1967.
The book may be checked to see if a landowner map of your ancestor's
county was issued while he or she was there. If you find a relevant map,
you may write the Library of Congress for a quote on providing you with
a copy.

---

45. County records

In most states, the county governments are the institutions which have generated the most valuable and the most abundant genealogical records. In the New England states, this is shared by the town governments. The major types of records that may be found in the counties are adoption, birth, bonds, court (civil, criminal, equity), death, deed, divorce, guardian, marriage, land, license, naturalization, probate, tax, and will. Among the records found in the New England towns might be those of baptism, birth, burial, cemetery, church, death, land grant, marriage, and military. In most cases, the original records of counties and towns remain in the counties and towns, but in some states, the earlier ones have been transferred to the state archives. In the counties, original records are usually stored in the appropriate offices in the court house. Sometimes, especially in larger counties, there are separate county archives for storage and management of older records. The pertinent offices are generally those of the county clerk, the clerks of the various courts, the registrar of deeds, the registrar of vital records (births, deaths, marriages), and in appropriate cases, the county archivist. In the towns, original records are usually in the office of the town clerk in the town hall. A survey of US counties and some notes about the more important of their records are given in:

_E. P. Bentley. COUNTY COURTHOUSE BOOK, Genealogical Publishing Co., Baltimore, MD, latest edition.

Because of the importance of the county and towns records, many of them have been transcribed and published, as books, as typescripts, and as articles in genealogical periodicals. These will be found in local libraries (county and town), in state libraries, and in large genealogical libraries, especially those in the region. In addition, many of the records have been microfilmed or reproduced on microfiche, some by private organizations, but most by the Family History Library. Listings of these latter records will be found in:

_Family History Library, FAMILY HISTORY LIBRARY CATALOG, LOCALITY SECTION, on microfiche and CDROM at the Library and every branch Family History Center.

The microfilms of the Family History Library may be borrowed through its numerous Family History Center branches, which are located all over the US. Unless you are near, it is best to seek county or town records last in the county or town. It is ordinarily far better to first use the facilities of your nearest Family History Center, second to go to or hire a researcher for the state library and archives, and third to go to or hire a researcher for the largest genealogical library in the region. Only then should you go to or write to a researcher to go to the county or town. The reason is that the county or town employees are not paid to help you; their job is to manage the records for the administration of the county or town. Hence, you should examine as many records as you possibly can before you call upon their good graces. And this means making prior use of all the copied records available in the other places mentioned above. Separate sections in this handbook are devoted to most of the record types named in the previous paragraph.

46. Court records

The records of courts are exceptionally important genealogical source materials. No genealogist should overlook them in spite of the fact that they are often incompletely indexed and sometimes difficult to access and use. The reason they are so useful is that practically no citizen of the colonies and/or the US failed to be involved in at least one court action, quite likely many. The law is the basis of society and courts are the governmental means by which the law is administered. The county courts are especially important because they were wrapped up with your ancestors' everyday lives. These courts not only administered the law, but they also ran practically every detail of governmental structure of the county. And the majority of these actions generated records. Separate sections in this handbook deal with some particular types of court records: adoption, birth, death, deed, divorce, estate, guardian, land, legal appeals, marriage, naturalization, orphan, probate, tax, will. However, there are many, many more records of numerous sorts. In addition to some special courts and court agencies which keep the types of records just mentioned, all these additional records are kept by three major kinds of courts: (1) civil courts, (2) equity courts, and (3) criminal courts.

In civil court actions, one individual or organization brings action against another individual or organization. Such actions usually involve alleged damage to the rights, person, property, or reputation of an individual or group. Examples of such cases are property damage, trespass, slander, assault, libel, fraud, nuisance, and negligence. In equity court actions, disagreements and disputes over matters which are not violations of any particular laws are involved. The purpose of the court is to settle the matter with a maximum fairness and justice to both parties. Examples of such cases are distributions of estates, divorce, adoption, and property rights. In criminal court actions, the government brings suit against an individual or organization alleging a violation of law. Examples include theft, murder, larceny, burglary, robbery, and rape. The most serious crimes are called felonies, those of minor character are called misdemeanors. In some instances, there are separate courts for these actions, but more usually one court acts in all three capacities.

There is an amazing variety of courts, but it will help your understanding to recognize a couple of distinctions. The first of these has to do with courts of origin and appeals courts. Courts of origin are those in which an action can be started, and where the matter is decided by a trial involving judges and/or a jury. Appeal courts are available to losing parties for requesting that the decisions of courts of origin be reconsidered. The second distinction is for you to know that three main court systems are important: (1) the colonial courts, (2) the federal courts, and (3) the state courts. In general, colonial courts in the 13 original colonies (1607-1776) had somewhat similar structures. There were at the bottom of the structure the inferior courts which handled minor cases, then superior courts just above them for the handling of major cases, then sometimes courts of appeal, and at the top the governor and his council or the colonial assembly or both. There were also some special courts. The colonial courts carried a wide variety of names, so the safest research procedure is to be sure to seek your ancestors in all available records of all courts. During and shortly after the Revolution, modified colonial systems were employed in the newly formed states. Then, beginning in 1789, the courts in the US came to be divided into separate federal and state systems. The federal courts, which deal with matters of federal law, are on three levels. At the lower level are the US District Courts. At first there was one per state, but some states now have more. Just above them, US Circuit Courts were established, they having broader jurisdiction than the district courts, plus some appeals function. At the top of the structure is the US supreme court. In 1891, US Courts of Appeals were put in place just below the Supreme Court, and in 1911 the US Circuit Courts were abolished. There are also some special federal courts, but not many (claims, customs, freedmen's bureau, martial, military appeals, patent appeals).

The state court systems, which concern themselves with state law, are distinct for each state, but generally function on four levels. At the bottom are the inferior courts which deal with restricted and/or minor matters (examples are city courts, small claims courts, magistrates' courts). Above them are the superior courts which deal with more serious cases, quite often with a jury. These courts carry a wide variety of names in various states, including the following examples: county court, superior court, circuit court, chancery court, court of common pleas, quarterly

court, court of general sessions, civil court, and county district court (not to be confused with federal District Court). Then there are often courts of appeals, and finally a state supreme court. There are also special courts designated to handle particular sorts of matters (land, probate, surrogate, claims). Many of the courts in the state system are county based, and these are the ones that will most likely be of genealogical importance to you, although the others must not be overlooked. Brief descriptions of the courts in each state are provided in:
_A. Eichholz, ANCESTRY'S REDBOOK, Ancestry Publishing, Salt Lake City, UT, 1992, see sections under each state.
_J. Cerny and W. Elliott, THE LIBRARY, Ancestry Publishing, Salt Lake City, UT, 1988, see sections under each state.
_Family History Library, STATE RESEARCH OUTLINES, An outline for each state, The Library, Salt Lake City, UT, latest edition.
As you delve into the voluminous court records, you will probably need to look up many of the legal terms you will encounter. Two very good volumes for this are:
_H. C. Black, BLACK'S LAW DICTIONARY, West Publishing Co., St. Paul, MN, any edition.
_W. C. Burton, LEGAL THESAURUS, Macmillan and Co., New York, NY, 1981.

Now, we will discuss the forms in which you are likely to find court records. These include: (1) indexes, (2) dockets, (3) minutes, (4) orders, (5) judgments, and (6) case packets or case files. Indexes to court records are ofttimes available, but they are sometimes non-existent or incomplete. They should be the first thing you ask for since they greatly simplify your search. The indexes usually list the names of the plaintiffs (the persons bringing suit) and defendants (the persons being accused), the date(s), and case numbers and/or case packet numbers. Dockets are volumes which list in chronological order brief entries indicating every time the court acts on each case. Be careful in seeking these out, because there may be different docket books for different kinds of cases. Sometimes dockets are indexed, but if they are not, and if case indexes (as mentioned above) are unavailable, the dockets must be scanned page-by-page for your ancestor. References in dockets will lead you to the other materials now to be described. Minutes are brief recordings of exactly what actions the court took. Dockets only indicate that action has been taken, but minutes tell you what the action was. Minutes are generally not indexed, so it is best if you first have case information from the above-indicated indexes or dockets. Orders of the court are recorded in separate volumes. They ordinarily give a summary of the case. The above indexes and/or dockets and/or minutes will lead you to them. Judgments represent the closing of cases with the final decision of the court. These judgments usually give a condensed version of the case and the verdict. The case files or packets or jackets are collections or packages of all the documents in given cases: evidence, depositions, testimonies, bonds, petitions, correspondence, subpoenas, and writs. These files often contain abundant genealogical data. They are accessed by requesting them using a case file number, which has been obtained from the index, docket, or minutes. There are also some other court records which might help you in certain situations: witness lists, jury lists, attorney records, coroner's records, sheriffs' records, and jail records.

Finally, we will indicate to you where court records may be found. Colonial court records, at least some of them, have been published for all of the 13 original colonies. These publications will be found in the appropriate state libraries, large genealogical libraries, and large law libraries, such as those in the law colleges of large universities. Many, but not all, are also at the Family History Library. Federal court records of the US Supreme Court and the US Courts of Appeals are well indexed in volumes available at large law libraries. The records of US District and Circuit Courts prior to about 1950 are stored in the eleven Field Branches of the National Archives, those for any given state being in the Branch which serves that state. Most include indexes. A later section will discuss these Branches and give you their addresses. Good listings of available federal court records will be found in:

_National Archives, FEDERAL COURT RECORDS: A SELECT CATALOG OF NATIONAL ARCHIVES MICROFILM PUBLICATIONS, The Archives, Washington, DC, 1987.

_National Archives, GUIDE TO GENEALOGICAL RESEARCH IN THE NATIONAL ARCHIVES, The Archives, Washington, DC, 1985. See the chapter on Court Records.

_L. D. Szucs and S. H. Luebking, THE ARCHIVES, A GUIDE TO THE NATIONAL ARCHIVES FIELD BRANCHES, Ancestry, Salt Lake City, UT, 1988.

_The Public Record Research Library, THE SOURCEBOOK OF FEDERAL COURTS, BRB Publications, Clearfield Company, Baltimore, MD, 1993.

State court records of the higher courts (state supreme courts, state appeals courts) for the earlier years are to be found in state archives, where they are usually indexed. However, most original court records of the county-based courts remain in the county courthouses. A few of these have been published and can be found in state libraries and at the Family History Library. Many have been microfilmed and are located at the state archives and the Family History Library. Not too many of the exceedingly valuable case files have been microfilmed because of their tremendous volume, so they usually must be sought in the courthouses. A good guide to where county courthouse records may be obtained is:

_The Public Record Research Library, THE SOURCEBOOK OF COUNTY COURT RECORDS, BRB Publications, Clearfield Company, Baltimore, MD, 1993.

Many court cases have been appealed to a higher court. There is a series of volumes which index by plaintiff most of these appealed cases during 1658-1906:

_AMERICAN DIGEST, 1906 DECENNIAL EDITION, West Publishing Co., St. Paul, MN, 1911, volumes 21-25.

There is also a series of similar indexes for each state of the US, except that they are indexed by both plaintiff and defendant. These indexes will be found in large law libraries.

---

47. DAR records

The National Society, Daughters of the American Revolution (DAR) has collected, transcribed, and indexed many records as part of their predominant interest in ancestors who participated in the Revolutionary War (1775-1783). Practically all of this work has been done by members of their local and state chapters. In addition to Revolutionary War records, the DAR chapters have collected many records of these types: Bible, cemetery, church, court, family, marriage, newspaper, and tax. The many hundreds of volumes that they have compiled and their extensive manuscript collection of genealogies are in their national library: Library of the DAR, 1776D Street, NW, Washington, DC 20006-5392. There are four keys to their materials:

_National Society, DAR, DAR PATRIOT INDEX, The Society, Washington, DC, 1966/79, 2 volumes.

_National Society, DAR, DAR LIBRARY INDEX OF THE ROLLS OF HONOR, The Society, Washington, DC, 1980, 4 volumes.

_National Society, DAR, DAR LIBRARY CATALOG, VOLUME ONE: FAMILY HISTORIES AND GENEALOGIES, The Society, Washington, DC, 1982.

_National Society, DAR, DAR LIBRARY CATALOG, VOLUME TWO: STATE AND LOCAL HISTORIES AND RECORDS, The Society, Washington, DC, 1986.

Typescript copies of many of the DAR record compilations will be found in pertinent county and state libraries, and many are available on microfilm at the Family History Library. These records should not be overlooked by any genealogist, because they can often save you much time by leading you directly to widely-scattered and otherwise unindexed original records.

48. Death records Official death records have been kept by colony, state, territory, district, county, city, and town agencies. These records at their best include name, date, place, sex, birthdate, birthplace, hospital, marital status, name of spouse, names of parents, mortician, burial or cremation place, and reporting physician. As the records get earlier, the amount of information usually gets less. Every state initiated death registration at some date between 1841 and 1920. For records after this date, you should write to either the state registration agency or the state archives. Below are listed these dates for the various states and the names and addresses of the agencies that should be contacted for the records. The date appears [in brackets] and the agency follows. Then information regarding the source of official death records before this date is given.

_In AL [1908] AL Department of Public Health, Montgomery, AL 36130. From 1881-1908, very incomplete registration in counties. Before 1881, a few records in county probate courts.

_In AK [1913] AK Bureau of Vital Statistics, PO Box H-02G, Juneau, AK 99811-0675. Before 1913, church records are the best source.

_In AZ [1909] AZ Vital Records Section, PO Box 3887, Phoenix, AZ 85030-3887. They also have abstracts of some county records before 1909.

_In AR [1914] AR Division of Vital Records, 4815 West Markham Street, Little Rock, AR 72201. They also have some Little Rock and Fort Smith deaths from 1881.

_In CA [1905] CA Vital Statistics Branch, 410 N Street, Sacramento, CA 95814. For 1850-1905, records are in counties, in most for only part of this period.

_In CO [1900] CO Vital Records Section, 4210 E. 11th Avenue, Denver, CO 80220. For 1872-1910, some counties have some records, mostly for only part of this time.

_In CT [1897] CT Vital Records Section, 79 Elm Street, Hartford, CT 06115. For 1640-1897, contact town or city clerk, or CT State Library.

_In DE [1861-3, 1881] For records after 1930 DE Bureau of Vital Statistics, State Health Building, PO Box 637, Dover, DE 19901-0637.

For records 1861-3 and 1881-1930 DE State Archives, Dover, DE 19901.

_In DC [1855] DC Vital Records Section, Room 3007, 425 I Street, Washington, DC 20001. Earlier records very poor.

_In FL [1917] FL Office of Vital Statistics, PO Box 210, Jacksonville, FL 32231. Also some records 1865-1917. A few counties have records 1875-1917, mostly for only part of this time.

_In GA [1919] GA Vital Records Unit, Room 217-H, 47 Trinity Avenue, SW, Atlanta, GA 30334. Atlanta 1896-1919, Savannah 1803-1919, Macon 1882-1919 from county health departments. A few counties have earlier records.

_In HI [1853] HI State Health Department, 1250 Punchbowl Street, Honolulu, HI 96813. Early records incomplete. Records 1853-1896 also at HI State Archives.

_In ID [1911] ID Vital Statistics Unit, Statehouse Mall, Boise, ID 83720-9990. For 1907-1911 county recorder.

_In IL [1916] IL Division of Vital Records, 535 West Jefferson Street, Springfield, IL 62761. For 1877-1916, contact counties. For Chicago 1871-1916, contact county. A few counties have earlier records.

_In IN [1900] IN Division of Vital Records, PO Box 1964, Indianapolis, IN 46206. For 1882-1907, contact counties. A few counties have earlier records.

_In IA [1880] IA Vital Records Section, Lucas State Office Building, Des Moines, IA 50319.

_In KS [1911] KS Department of Health, 900 South Jackson, Topeka, KS 66612. For 1880-1911, some counties have some records, mostly for a part of this time.

_In KY [1911] KY Office of Vital Statistics, 275 East Main Street, Frankfort, KY 40621. For 1852-1911 KY Department for Libraries and Archives, 300 Coffee Tree Road, Frankfort, KY 40601, or contact counties.

_In LA [1914] LA Division of Vital Records, PO Box 60630, New Orleans, LA 70160. New Orleans 1790-1914 very incomplete, available from city.

_In ME [1892] ME Office of Vital Records, State House, Augusta, ME 04333. For 1892-1955 also at ME State Archives, State House, Augusta, ME 04333. For 1635-1892, records incomplete, contact towns.

_In MD [1898] MD Division of Vital Records, PO Box 13146, Baltimore, MD 21203. For 1898-1982 and Baltimore 1875-1982 also at MD State Archives, 350 Rowe Boulevard, Annapolis, MD 21401. For earlier records, contact MD State Archives.

_In MA [1841] For 1896 and later, MA Registry of Vital Records and Statistics, 150 Tremont Street, Boston, MA 02111. For 1841-1896 MA State Archives, 220 Morrissey Boulevard, Boston, MA 02125. For 1620-1896, consult town or city. Most records published.

_In MI [1867] MI Office of the State Registrar, PO Box 30035, Lansing, MI 48909.

_In MN [1908] MN Section of Vital Statistics, 717 Delaware Street, SE, Minneapolis, MN 55440. For 1870-1908, contact county or health departments in St. Paul and Minneapolis.

_In MS [1912] MS Bureau of Vital Statistics, PO Box 1700, Jackson, MS 39205.

_In MO [1909] MO Bureau of Vital Records, Jefferson City, MO 65101. For 1863-1909, contact counties. For St. Louis 1870-1910 or Kansas City before 1909, write city vital records departments.

_In MT [1907] MT Bureau of Records and Statistics, Helena, MT 59601. For 1878-1907, some counties have some records, usually only for a part of this time.

_In NE [1904] NE Bureau of Vital Statistics, PO Box 95007, LIncoln, NE 68509.

_In NV [1911] NV Section of Vital Statistics, 505 East King Street, Carson City, NV 89710. For 1887-1911, contact counties.

_In NH [1901] NH Bureau of Vital Records, 6 Hazel Drive, Concord, NH 03301. Also has some records since 1640. For 1640-1901, contact towns. Also NH State Library, 20 Park Street, Concord, NH 03301.

_In NJ [1848] For 1848-1923 NJ State Archives, 185 West State Street, Trenton, NJ 08625-0307. For after 1923, NJ State Registrar, Trenton, NJ 08625-0360.

_In NM [1920] NM Vital Statistics Office, PO Box 968, Santa Fe, NM 87504-0968.

_In NY [1880] NY Vital Records Section, Room 244, Corning Tower Building, Albany, NY 12237. For records before 1914 in Albany, Buffalo, and Yonkers, and for records before 1880 for Rochester, Syracuse, and Utica, contact city registrar. For New York City records since 1920, contact Bureau of Vital Records, 125 Worth Street, New York, NY 10013. For Manhattan records 1865-1919, contact Municipal Archives, 31 Chambers Street, New York, NY 10007.

_In NC [1913] For 1913-1929, contact State Records Center, 215 North Blount St., Raleigh, NC 27602. For 1930 and after, contact NC Vital Records Branch, PO Box 2091, Raleigh, NC 27602. A few counties have a few records prior to 1913.

_In ND [1907] ND Division of Vital Records, First Floor, Judicial Wing, Bismarck, ND. Also have some incomplete records 1893-1907. For before 1907, also consult counties.

_In OH [1908] OH Department of Health, 65 South Front Street, Columbus, OH 43215. For 1867-1908, consult probate court offices in counties.

_In OK [1908] OK Vital Records Section, PO Box 53551, Oklahoma City, OK 73152. A few counties have incomplete records before 1908.

_In OR [1903] OR Vital Records Unit, PO Box 116, Portland, OR 97207. For Portland records 1864-1903 contact OR State Archives, 1005 Broadway, NE, Salem, OR 97130.

_In PA [1906] PA Division of Vital Records, PO Box 1528, New Castle, PA 16103. For 1860-1915 Philadelphia records contact Vital Statistics, City Hall Annex, Philadelphia, PA 19107. For 1870-1906 incomplete records of Allegheny City, Easton, Harrisburg, Pottsville, Pittsburgh, and Williamsport, contact cities. Some early records also with county registers of wills.

_In RI [1853] RI Division of Vital Statistics, 75 Davis Street, Providence, RI 02908. For 1636-1853, consult town clerks. Also 1636-1850 mostly in book by J. N. Arnold.

_In SC [1915] SC Office of Vital Records, 2600 Bull Street, Columbia, SC 29201. For 1821-1915 Charleston, 1895-1915 Florence, and 1895-1915 Newberry records, contact county health departments.

_In SD [1905] SD Health Statistics Program, Joe Foss Building, Pierre, SC 57501. Some incomplete earlier records available in counties.

_In TN [1914] TN Division of Vital Records, Cordell Hull Building, Nashville, TN 37219. Also have 1908-1912 records, and 1874-1914 for Nashville, 1887-1914 for Knoxville, and 1872-1914 for Chattanooga. For 1848-1914 Memphis records, contact city health department. For 1881-1914 some counties and larger cities have incomplete records.

_In TX [1903] TX Bureau of Vital Statistics, 1100 West 49th Street, Austin, TX 78756. A few counties have incomplete earlier records.

_In UT (1905) UT Bureau of Health Statistics, PO Box 16700, Salt Lake City, UT 84116. Some counties have incomplete records 1887-1905. For Salt Lake City and Ogden 1890-1904, contact city health departments.

_In VT [effectively 1857] VT Public Records Division, 6 Baldwin Place, Montpelier, VT 05602 for index, abstracts, and microfilm copies for 1760-1954. But original record must be obtained from town clerk.

_In VA [effectively 1853] VA Division of Vital Records, PO Box 1000, Richmond, VA 23208. There is a gap of no records 1896-1912. For the few records before 1853, contact VA State Archives, 11th and

Capitol Streets, Richmond, VA 23219. For 1869-1912, inquire at VA State Archives, county, and city.
_In WV [1917] WV Division of Vital Statistics, Charleston, WV 25305. For 1853-1900, contact WV Archives and History Library, Charleston, WV 25305, or clerk of county court.
_In WI [1907] WI Bureau of Health Statistics, PO Box 309, Madison, WI 53701. For 1852-1907, contact county register of deeds and State Historical Society of WI. Earlier records incomplete.
_In WY [1909] WY Vital Records Services, State Office Building West, Cheyenne, WY 82002.

Many microfilm copies of the records before the state registration dates are available at the Family History Library, and therefore can be borrowed through its many branch Family History Centers. There are also microfilm copies of county death records (as well as the state records) in the relevant state archives and state libraries, and sometimes in the state historical or genealogical libraries. State libraries also often hold published copies of the records, and local libraries (county, city, town) may have their own death records in published or typescript form.

The addresses of county court houses, county officials, town halls, and town clerks will be found in:
_A. Eichholz, ANCESTRY'S REDBOOK, Ancestry Publishing, Salt Lake City, UT, 1992.
_NAMES AND NUMBERS, Wiley and Sons, New York, NY, latest edition.
_L. K. Meitzler, THE US COUNTY COURTHOUSE ADDRESS BOOK, Heritage Quest, Orting, WA, 1988.
_E. P. Bentley, COUNTY COURTHOUSE BOOK, Genealogical Publishing Co., Baltimore, MD, latest edition.
More detail on death records in the various states will also be found in the first volume. Please remember that death records can often extend your research data back as many as 70 more years. For example, if you obtain a death record in 1893 for a forebear who was 79 years old, then his /her birth goes back to 1813/14, and quite often you will find the birth date and birth place on the death record. As can be seen from the above listings, official (governmental) death records cease to be available in most states at some time during their histories. Before these dates, you will need to seek death information in other sorts of records. The most likely sources include records of the following types: Bible, biography, cemetery, church, city directories, county and city history, directories, family records, fraternal organizations, gravestone, hereditary societies,

military, mortality census, mortuary, <u>newspaper</u>, <u>pension</u>, <u>probate</u>, published genealogy, tax, <u>will</u>. All of these are discussed in detail in other sections of this Handbook. Those that are usually the most helpful have been underlined.

49. Deed records

Land in the colonies and in the US was acquired by the first owners from the crown or colonies (CT, DE, GA, MD, MA, NH, NJ, NY, NC, PA, RI, SC, VA), from the states (CT, DE, GA, HI, KY, ME, MD, MA, NH, NJ, NY, NC, PA, RI, SC, TN, TX, VT, VA, WV), or from the federal government (for land in the other 30 states). The New England colonies and states (CT, ME, MA, NH, RI, VT) described their land by blocks called towns, within which there were divisions, and within the divisions lots. The other colonies and state-land states (DE, GA, HI, KY, MD, NJ, NY, NC, PA, SC, TN, TX, VA, WV) described their land in terms of metes and bounds. This method employed geographical locations such as streams, stones, trees, neighboring boundaries, and compass directions. There were also some very large original tracts which were subdivided various ways by the first or subsequent owners. The federal land (of the other 30 states) was described by a strict geometric survey pattern of townships (six miles square) containing 36 numbered one-mile square sections, each section containing 640 acres, with precise rules for describing land locations within the section.

The acquisition of land from the government by its first private owner was certified by a grant or patent which constituted the first-title deed. Records of these grants or patents are discussed in a later section called Land grants. The person receiving the land usually registered this first deed (grant or patent) with the county (or the town in CT, RI, VT), but this was not always done, especially in the early years. Most subsequent transfers of land were done by deeds which were copied into the county (or town) records by the clerk, recorder, registrar, or other official. The major exceptions to this were lands that passed by will or by probate action, in which cases records should be sought in the probate offices. Other land records were also kept by county (or town) land officials, chief being mortgage, lease, and tax.

Original deed, mortgage, and lease record books, along with indexes are usually found in the counties (towns in CT, RI, VT). They date from the origin of the county (or town), unless some destruction of records has occurred. The indexes are generally of two types: by the grantor (seller), and by the grantee (buyer). Some deed books and indexes have been published and are available in the relevant county libraries, state libraries, large genealogical libraries, and the Family History Center. In addition, deed records and indexes have been microfilmed for almost 2000 counties. These microfilms are available at the state libraries, at the Family History Library, and through Family History Centers all over the US. As mentioned before, large tracts of land were sometimes granted to companies who subsequently distributed the land as smaller tracts. The records of these companies may be sought in state libraries, state archives, university archives, and local archives. The best place to inquire is at the state library since, if they do not have them, they usually can tell you who does.

County (or town) deed records usually list the names of the grantor and grantee, their residences, a description of the land, the amount of money or other commodity exchanged for the land, any conditions to the transaction, the date of the exchange, witnesses, and the date and place when the deed was recorded. Please note that the date of the deed and the date of the recording may be quite different. One valuable use of deed records is to locate a person in time and in place. Further, deeds often tell from where a person has come and to where a person has gone. Sometimes several people are listed as grantors or grantees, and these relationships may be important. The relation of the grantor and grantee are often very meaningful, and the amount of money or other consideration can sometimes indicate family connections. The location of the land on a map should be ascertained, and the owners of property on the various sides should be discovered. These neighbors are usually relatives, associates, or friends and often married into your family. Another important point to recognize is that deed books often contain records of the transfer of property other than real estate: slaves, indentured servants, goods, merchandise, personal labor, a business or company.

50. Directories

A directory is a published compilation of alphabetically arranged names and addresses. Directories of greatest interest to genealogists are those in which the names are names of persons. The major directories of this sort are city directories which have been treated in a previous section of this Handbook. There are also a few county directories and a few regional directories. However, there are many directories of another sort, namely, directories of persons with a common connection: occupational, ethnic, or organizational. These directories got their start in the late 1700s or early 1800s in the larger cities of the US, then some began to appear on the state, regional, and national levels.

Among the various directories are ones of accountants, alumni, architects, attorneys, bankers, clergy, dentists, engineers, governmental officials, leaders (Who's Who volumes), manufacturers, mariners, merchants, military, physicians, professors, scientists, teachers, and union members. Also there are directories of members of various types of societies: agricultural, benevolent, dental, educational, ethnic, fraternal, hereditary, historical, literary, medical, musical, patriotic, scientific, service. Especially notable are telephone directories. Early telephone directories are useful mainly for locating people, and current ones can be valuable for locating distant cousins, if the surname you are seeking is not too common. Distant cousins may have inherited family records that have data on your common progenitors.

The above directories and other similar ones may be sought in local, regional, and state libraries, in the offices and archives of relevant organizations, and in state, state university, and regional archives. Many current directories are listed in:
_DIRECTORY OF DIRECTORIES, Gale Research Co., Detroit, MI, latest edition.
These current directories can often lead you to earlier counterparts. Many large libraries have microfiche or computer copies of current telephone directories of numerous cities. In addition, they usually have good collections of telephone directories.

51. Divorce records

Divorce records can be very valuable genealogically because of the important family place and date information they carry. At their best, such records include the couple's birth dates and places, their current residences, children's birth dates and places, history of the marriage, an inventory of property, claims and counterclaims, custody decisions, the grounds, and sometimes other family members. Divorce was rare early in the counties, but as time passed, it became easier to obtain and more frequent. In colonial times, the means was to petition the governor/council and/or the legislature. As the number of petitions increased, the courts were also authorized to handle divorce matters, at first concurrently with the above agencies, then later they were given exclusive jurisdiction. In the various colonies, the governor/councils could grant divorce during these dates: CT(to 1711), DE(to 1773), GA(never), MD(never), MA(1760-86), NH(to 1776), NJ(to

1773), NY(1655-75), NC(never), PA(to 1773), RI(never), SC(never), VA(never). The legislature could grant divorce during these dates: CT(1655-1849), DE (to 1866), GA(1798-1835), MD(to 1851), MA(1639-1786), NH(1766-91), NJ(to 1844), NY(to 1827), NC(to 1835), PA(to 1847), RI(1650-1851), SC(never), VA(to 1848). Dates on which courts begin to grant at least some of the divorces in these colonies/states were: CT(1711), DE(1832), GA(1798), MD(1842), MA(1786), NH(1791), NJ(1794), NY(1787), NC(1814), PA(1785), RI(1747), SC(1949), VA(1827). Most of the early divorce records of the governors/councils and the legislatures have been published as books or journal articles. The best place to locate them is in the respective state libraries. Those that have not been published are generally available in the appropriate state archives. Be sure to contact both if you are seeking divorce records.

The large majority of divorce records have been accumulated by the county and town clerks. Various courts in the different states have these records, but the most common courts are the district, circuit, superior, probate, and chancery. In seeking divorce records, be sure you ask for both the records written in books and the case file (package of loose papers). Listed below are the agencies in each state to contact in your search for divorce records (remember an SASE):

_AL: After 1950, Bureau of Vital Statistics, Department of Public Health, Montgomery, AL 36130. Before 1950, in equity records of county Circuit Court. Published state index up through 1865.

_AK: After 1950, Bureau of Vital Statistics, Pouch H-02G, Juneau, AK 99811. Before 1950, contact Clerk of Superior Court in Judicial District.

_AZ: Clerk of Superior Court in county.

_AR: Circuit or Chancery Court in county. Coupons turned in to state since 1923 available at Division of Vital Records, 4815 West Markham Street, Little Rock, AR 72201.

_CA: Index at Vital Statistics Branch, 410 N. Street, Sacramento, CA 95814. Records from Clerk of Superior Court in county.

_CO: Records from Clerk of District Court in county. Index at Vital Records Section, 4210 East 11th Avenue, Denver, CO 80220.

_CT: Recent records in county Superior Courts. Earlier records at CT State Library and Archives, 231 Capitol Avenue, Hartford, CT 06106.

_DE: Records before 1975 from County Prothonotary, after 1975 from county Family Court.

_DC: Records 1803-1956 from Clerk of US District Court, Constitution Avenue and John Marshall Place, NW, Washington, DC 20001. After

1956 from Clerk of Superior Court, 500 Indiana Avenue, NW, Washington, DC 20001.

_FL: After 1927, Bureau of Vital Statistics, PO Box 210, Jacksonville, FL 32231. Before 1927 from Clerk of Circuit Court in county. Many divorces 1822-45 in published volume.

_GA: Clerk of County Superior Court in county. Index of early divorces at GA Department of Archives and History, 330 Capitol Avenue, SE, Atlanta, GA 30334.

_HI: After 1951, State Department of Health, PO Box 3378, Honolulu, HI 96801. Earlier records in Circuit Court in county. Records 1849-1915 also at HI State Archives, 478 South King Street, Honolulu, HI 96813.

_ID: After 1947, Vital Statistics Unit, 450 West State Street, Boise, ID 83720. Before 1947 from county Recorder.

_IL: Clerk of Circuit Court of County. Index from 1962 at Office of Vital Records, 535 West Jefferson Street, Springfield, IL 62761.

_IN: Clerk of Circuit Court in county.

_IA: Clerk of District Court in county.

_KS: After 1951, Bureau of Registration, 6700 South Topeka Avenue, Topeka, KS 66620. Before 1951 from Clerk of District Court in county.

_KY: After 1958, Office of Vital Statistics, 275 East Main Street, Frankfort, KY 40621. For 1809-1958, from Clerk of Circuit Court in county. Before 1850 in published Acts of General Assembly.

_LA: Clerk of Court in parish. For Orleans Parish, contact Division of Vital Records, PO Box 60630, New Orleans, LA 70160.

_ME: After 1892, Office of Vital Records, State House, Augusta, ME 04333. Before 1892, Clerk of District Court in judicial division.

_MD: After 1961, Division of Vital Records, PO Box 13146, 201 West Preston Street, Baltimore, MD 21203. For 1842-1961, contact Clerk of Circuit Court in county. Before 1842, consult published divorce records abstracted from legislative acts.

_MA: Registrar of Probate Court or Superior Court in county. Also for 1692-1922, check Supreme Judicial Court. Before 1692, records in MA State Archives, 220 Morrissey Boulevard, Boston, MA 02125.

_MI: After 1897, Office of Vital Statistics, 3500 North Logan Street, Lansing, MI 48914. Before 1897, County Clerk in county.

_MN: Clerk of District Court in county. Index since 1970 at Section of Vital Statistics, 717 Delaware Street, SE, Minneapolis, MN 55440.

_MS: Chancery Clerk in county. Index since 1926 at Vital Records, PO Box 1700, Jackson, MS 39205.

_MO: Clerk of Circuit Court in county, except in St. Louis (City Circuit Court Clerk) and Kansas City (Judicial Records Department).

_MT: Clerk of District Court in county.

_NE: After 1909, Bureau of Vital Statistics, PO Box 95007, Lincoln, NE 68509. Before 1909, from Clerk of District Court in county.

_NV: County clerk. Index since 1968 from Vital Statistics, Capitol Complex, Carson City, NV 89710. Territorial divorce index at DAR, 1776 D Street, NW, Washington, DC 20006.

_NH: AFter 1808, Bureau of Vital Records, Hazen Drive, Concord, NH 03301. Before 1808, from Clerk of Superior Court.

_NJ: Superior Court, Chancery Division, State House Annex, Trenton, NJ 08625 for records after 1850. Before 1850, contact NJ Division of Archives, State Library Building, 185 West State Street, Trenton, NJ 08625.

_NM: Clerk of District Court in county.

_NY: After 1963, Bureau of Vital Records, Empire State Plaza, Tower Building, Albany, NY 12237. For 1847-1963, County Clerk. Before 1847, contact NY State Archives, Empire State plaza, Albany, NY 12230.

_NC: After 1958, Vital Records Branch, PO Box 291, Raleigh, NC 27602. For 1814-1958, Clerk of Superior Court in county. For earlier records, contact NC Division of Archives, 109 East Jones Street, Raleigh, NC 27611.

_ND: Clerk of District Court in county. Index for after 1949 at Division of Vital Records, State Department of Health, Bismarck, ND 58505.

_OH: Clerk of Court of Common Pleas in county. Also legislature records before 1846.

_OK: Clerk of Court in county.

_OR: After 1925, Vital Statistics Section, PO Box 116, Portland, OR 97207. Before 1925, County Clerk in county.

_PA: Prothonotary in county back to 1804. Before 1804, contact State Library of PA, PO Box 1601, Harrisburg, PA 17105, and Bureau of Archives and History, PO Box 1026, Harrisburg, PA 17108.

_RI: After 1962, Clerk of Family Court, 1 Dorrance Plaza, Providence, RI 02903. Before 1962, Office of Superior Court, Providence City Courthouse, Providence, RI 02901.

_SC: After 1962, Office of Vital Records, 2600 Bull Street, Columbia, SC 29201. For 1949-62, County Clerk. Divorce illegal in SC until 1949.

_SD: After 1905, Health Statistics Program, Joe Foss Office Building, Pierre, SC 57501. Before 1905, Clerk of Court in county.

_TN: After 1945, Division of Vital Records, Cordell Hull Building, Nashville, TN 37219. Before 1945, Circuit Court in county. Early records 1797-1858 published.
_TX: Clerk of District Court in county.
_UT: County Clerk. Since 1968, brief abstracts available from Bureau of Health Statistics, PO Box 2500, Salt Lake City, UT 84110.
_VT: Town or city clerk.
_VA: After 1853, Division of Vital Records, PO Box 1000, Richmond, VA 23208. Before 1853, Clerk of Circuit Court in county or city.
_WA: After 1968, Vital Records, PO Box 9709, Olympia, WA 98504. Before 1968, County Clerk.
_WV: Clerk of Circuit Court in county. Index since 1968 at Division of Vital Statistics, State Office Building No. 3, Charleston, WV 25305.
_WI: After 1907, Bureau of Health Statistics, PO Box 309, Madison, WI 53701. Before 1907, from county.
_WY: After 1941, Vital Records Services, Hathaway Building, Cheyenne, WY 82002. Before 1941, Clerk of District Court.

Addresses of county and town offices will be found in the following volumes:
_A. Eichholz, ANCESTRY'S REDBOOK, Ancestry Publishing, Salt Lake City, UT, 1989.
_R. Nordland, NAMES AND NUMBERS, Wiley and Sons, New York, NY, latest edition.
_L. K. Meitzler, THE US COUNTY COURTHOUSE ADDRESS BOOK, Heritage Quest, Orting, WA, 1988.
_E. P. Bentley, COUNTY COURTHOUSE BOOK, Genealogical Publishing Co., Baltimore, MD, latest edition.
More detail on divorce records in the various states will be found in the first-mentioned volume. It may be that you will encounter some restraining regulations on the availability of more recent divorce records. A contact with a local genealogical society and/or a local researcher can often be helpful in such instances.

52. Encyclopedias

Invaluable in the research of any developing genealogist is the use of one or more good encyclopedias. An encyclopedia is a work giving alphabetically-arranged introductory information on the major items of knowledge. Among those that are recommended are:
_WORLD BOOK ENCYCLOPEDIA, World Book, Chicago, IL, latest edition.

_COLLIER'S ENCYCLOPEDIA, Macmillan, New York, NY, latest
    edition.
_ENCYCLOPEDIA AMERICANA, Grolier, Danbury, CT, latest
    edition.
_ENCYCLOPEDIA BRITANNICA, Encyclopedia Britannica, Chicago,
    IL, 1973.
Encyclopedias are particularly useful for geographies, histories, governments, and the people of the US, the individual states of the US, and the
various countries from which immigrants came. They also give you good
introductory articles on cities, religious groups, wars, large geographical
features (Mississippi River, Appalachian Mountains), ethnic groups
(American Indians, Afro-Americans), immigration, the westward
migration, colonial life, frontier life, the development of technologies
which changed your progenitors' lives (steam boat, railroad), economic
and political occurrences which changed their circumstances, and many
other items. The articles are generally accompanied by lists of books
which will give you expanded data on the topics.

Of special importance are encyclopedias which were published
contemporary with the dates of your forebears. These older reference
works often give more concrete detail on items which are of interest to
genealogists. Among those which you can seek in large libraries are:
_ENCYCLOPEDIA AMERICANA, Carey, Lea, and Carey, Philadel-
    phia, 1st edition, 13 volumes, 1833, and later editions.
_THE (NEW) AMERICAN CYCLOPEDIA, Appleton, New York, NY,
    16 volumes, 1863, new edition, 16 volumes, 1876.
_(NEW) UNIVERSAL CYCLOPEDIA, Johnson, New York, NY, 4
    volumes, 1877, new edition, 8 volumes, 1895.
_ENCYCLOPEDIA BRITANNICA, Encyclopedia Britannica, Adam
    Black, Edinburgh, Scotland, 1842, and later editions.

53. Emigration records

Most people who came from foreign
countries to the US in the 1800s came
from Europe. They embarked from
numerous ports in many countries.
Fortunately, records of some of these ports have survived and are
available for searching. There are also some records which come from
governmental centers which recorded departures. In some cases, the
records reveal the exact place from which the emigrant came, in other
cases, this detail is not included. The easiest way to access many of these
departure records is in the microfilm collection of the Family History
Library in Salt Lake City, UT. The microfilms may be borrowed through

the numerous branches of this library known as Family History Centers. One is probably within easy reach of where you live.

Following are the chief ones of these emigration (departure) records which the Family History Library holds:
__Austria, Vienna, passports, 1792-1918
__Denmark, Copenhagen, emigration, 1867-1910
__Denmark, passports, 1780-1920
__Finland, emigration, 1818-1922
__France, Alsace, departures, 1817-66
__Germany, Bremen, some emigration for 1847-1880
__Germany, Hamburg, emigration, 1850-1934
__Germany, Wuerttemberg, departure, 1700s-1915
__Netherlands, emigration, 1820-80
__Norway, Alesund, emigration, 1852-1923
__Norway, Bergen, emigration, 1874-1924
__Norway, Christiana or Oslo, emigration, 1867-1902
__Norway, Kristiansund, emigration, 1873-1959
__Norway, Stavanger, emigration, 1814-1910
__Norway, Trondheim, emigration, 1867-1925
__Sweden, Gothenburg, emigration, 1869-1951
__Sweden, Malmo, emigration, 1874-1939
__Sweden, Norrkoping, emigration, 1869-1921
__Sweden, Stockholm, emigration, 1869-1920

54. English and Welsh genealogy

The countries of England and Wales are very important to US genealogists because most of us trace one or more ancestral lines back there. The early settlement of the Atlantic Coast of what is now the US was very largely English, and these progenitors of ours set the major cultural patterns which persist today. Succeeding immigrants entered into this English matrix and in a large measure adapted to it by adopting much of it. England and Wales make up the southern two-thirds of the island of Great Britain. When the Romans invaded the island in the 1st century BC, they found several tribes: Britons, Celts (who had come from Central Europe), Belgae (who had come from around modern Belgium). When the Romans withdrew about 400, further invaders entered: Angles (from area now NW Germany), Saxons (from same area), Jutes (area around mouth of Rhine River). They drove the older Celtic population into what is now Wales. Then for about a century (787-878), many Danes invaded and settled. During the middle 900s, the

Saxons, Angles, Jutes, and Danes united and came to be called Anglo-Saxons, with the Danish leader Canute coming to rule all England in 1017. Normans from NW France conquered England in 1066 and invaded Wales several times thereafter in the face of repeated Welsh revolts. The Normans introduced Norman law, feudalism, and societal order which fostered trade and set England on the road to becoming a major European power. Church order was strengthened, the jury system was introduced, education was improved, and a country-wide census was taken. In 1215, the king signed the Magna Carta, which gave the people some basic freedoms, and sowed the seed for a constitutional government. By 1284, Wales had been conquered, and gains had been made in Scotland and Ireland. Scotland was defeated in 1296, just a year after a parliament was established. From 1337-1453, the Hundred Years War raged between England and France over matters of territory, tax, and kingship. The warfare resulted in the loss of all the sizable English territory in France. During this period there were devastating episodes of the black plague, English became the official language, and better conditions for feudal workers and the abolition of serfdom were worked out. Two groups of contenders for the British throne joined battle in the War of the Roses (1455-85), which ended in victory for Henry Tudor (Henry VII). The English exploration of North America was started in 1497, as England continued to grow in influence.

The reign of Henry VIII (1509-47) brought the split of the Church of England from the Roman Catholic Church (1529), the alliance between England and Wales (1536), the order from the Crown that parish registers be kept (1538), and persecution of other religious denominations. After a brief period of re-established Catholicism (1554-8), under Elizabeth I (1558-1603) the Church of England was re-made official. In 1584, an English settlement on Roanoke Island (now NC) was made (but did not endure), and in 1588, the Spanish Armada was defeated by the English, effectively opening North America up for the victors, and England became a world power. Permanent settlements in what came to be the 13 colonies followed: VA(1607), MA(1620, 1628-30), MD(1631-34), PA(1682); and in 1664, the English seized DE, NJ, and NY from the Dutch. During 1642-49 there was a civil war in England between the monarchy and parliament, the latter winning, and a Puritan common-wealth was set up in 1649, lasting only 11 years. During the 1650s, the Quakers were founded and increased in numbers rapidly, many subsequently going to the colonies. The year 1707 saw political union between England and Scotland, and for 70 years the British Empire expanded all over the earth. In the American colonies, the age-long English-French conflicts manifested themselves as a series of French-English wars called the French and Indian Wars. These ended in the English driving the French out of North America (1763). The successful revolt of the American colonies in 1775-83 resulted in the establishment of an independent US. In the century following the British-US War of 1812, about nine million persons came to the US from Great Britain.

If you have an English or Welsh ancestor, every possible effort must be made to find the exact place of origin (town or parish) in American records. No record whatsoever should be overlooked, because if you know the place or origin, your research efforts in English/Welsh records are massively simplified. Many English/Welsh records are on microfilm at the Family History Library and are available through its branch Family History Centers. At every Family History Center there is also a microfiche copy of the exceedingly large International Genealogical Index (IGI) which lists English/Welsh births and marriages. Now let's talk about the records which give the best genealogical data on English/Welsh ancestors. These are, in order of importance: church (parish) records, civil registrations, censuses, probate, and military. <u>Church</u> (parish) records begin to be available in 1538 and gradually get better, considerable improvement occurring in 1558. The records in the parish registers include baptisms, marriages, and burials. There are also separate marriage record books which list licenses, banns, allegations, and/or bonds. Between 1597-1837, parishes were required to forward copies (bishop's transcripts) of their records to the office of the local bishop. In addition to the IGI, there are two other large indexes which list many marriages 1538-1837, these being Boyd's and Phillimore's. Both are available at the Family History Library. Most non-Anglicans (not members of the Church of England) kept few records, except Quakers and Jews. These groups (called non-conformists) sent many of their records in and they are now in the Public Record Office (microfilm copies at the Family History Library). <u>Civil</u> registrations of births, marriages, and deaths began in 1837. There are overall quarterly (every 3 months) indexes for 1837-1980. Microfilm copies are at the Family History Library (borrowable from Family History Centers), but the certificates to which they refer must be obtained from England. <u>Censuses</u> of use to genealogists are available for 1841, 1851, 1861, 1871, 1887, and 1891. Microfilm copies are available at the Family History Library along with indexes for many parishes. <u>Probate</u> records were kept in church courts before 1858, and after 1858 in the Probate Registry in London. Indexes and microfilm abstracts of many of these records are available at the Family History Library. <u>Military</u> records can be helpful, but for those before 1855, you need to know the precise regiment in which your progenitor served. There are, of course, other records in addition to these major ones. They include biographies, cemetery records, court records, guild records, and tax records. You should also not overlook the many genealogical compilations and periodicals for England and/or Wales or parts of them.

Before you do English/Welsh genealogical research, you should study very thoroughly several of the following:
_J. Cerny and W. Elliott, THE LIBRARY, Ancestry Publishing, Salt Lake City, UT, 1988, pages 385-473.
_A. Baxter, IN SEARCH OF YOUR BRITISH AND IRISH ROOTS, Genealogical Publishing Co., Baltimore, MD, latest edition.
_G. K. S. Hamilton-Edwards, IN SEARCH OF BRITISH ANCESTRY, Genealogical Publishing Co., Baltimore, MD, 1983.
_G. K. S. Hamilton-Edwards, IN SEARCH OF WELSH ANCESTRY, Genealogical Publishing Co., Baltimore, MD, 1986.
_S. Irvine, YOUR ENGLISH ANCESTRY, Ancestry, Salt Lake City, UT, 1993.
_C. D. Rogers, TRACING YOUR ENGLISH ANCESTORS, Manchester University Press, Manchester, England, 1989.
_Association of Family History Societies of Wales, WELSH FAMILY HISTORY, The Association, Aberystwyth, Wales, 1993.
_P. A. Saul and F. C. Markwell, THE A-Z GUIDE TO TRACING ANCESTORS IN BRITAIN, Genealogical Publishing Co., Baltimore, MD, 1991.
_J. Cox and T. Padfield, TRACING YOUR ANCESTORS IN THE PUBLIC RECORD OFFICE, Her Majesty's Stationery Office, London, England, 1983.
_R. Mellen, THE HANDY BOOK TO ENGLISH GENEALOGY, Heritage Books, Bowie, MD, 1992.
_J. Rowlands, WELSH FAMILY HISTORY: A GUIDE TO RESEARCH, Genealogical Publishing Co., Baltimore, MD latest edition.

55. Ethnic genealogy

The major minority groups in the US today are Black Americans (12%), Hispanic Americans (8%), Jewish Americans (3%), Asian Americans (2%), and American Indians (1%). These groups are specifically mentioned here because special techniques or resources are required to do thorough genealogical research on their members. Excellent introductory articles on research involving these five groups will be found in:

_A. Eakle and J. Cerny, THE SOURCE, Ancestry Publishing, Salt Lake
    City, UT, 1984, Black (579-85), Hispanic (559-77), Jewish (603-49),
    Asian (597-601), American Indian (535-57).
_J. C. Smith, ETHNIC GENEALOGY, Greenwood Press, Westport, CT,
    1983, sections: American Indian (209-38), Asian (239-308), Black
    (309-63), Hispanic (365-401).
Separate sections in this Handbook are devoted to Black genealogy,
Indian genealogy, and Jewish genealogy. Hence the remainder of this
section will treat the remaining two (Hispanic, Asian).

Hispanic Americans, the second largest ethnic group in the US, a
group of over 20 million people, trace their ancestry back to Spain, the
majority of their ancestral lines coming through Mexico, Puerto Rico,
Cuba, Central America, or South America. The major states in which
they live are NM, TX, CA, AZ, NY, and FL. Spanish explorers entered
the southeast and the southwest portions of what is now the US in the
1500s, and sparse settlements of the areas followed. Except for 1763-83,
the rule of Spain in the southeast persisted until 1821, when the US took
over. The southwest passed to Mexico in 1821, then to the US in
1845/48. Before 1900, Hispanic immigration to the US was quite small,
but 1910-30 saw almost 700,000 Mexicans entering the southwest. In the
1950s, Hispanic immigration surged again, with Mexicans, Puerto Ricans,
and Cubans coming. New York City has the largest number of Puerto
Ricans of any US city, and Miami has the largest number of Cubans.
Since 1970, many Hispanics from Central America have entered the US.

The most important special resources that Hispanic-ancestor
searchers need are the Spanish and Mexican records for the Spanish/
Mexican areas that later became US territory. These materials are
broadly spread, but in almost all instances, the best places to start are in
the respective state archives and libraries. They hold a number of original
land, court, probate, and vital record materials plus many copies of such
documents. In addition, since the Roman Catholic Church represented
the predominant Spanish religious institution, church repositories in the
appropriate states are also important, since they hold many records. Other
places which hold Spanish/Mexican records for these areas, and which
may be consulted next, are: the National Archives and its Denver Branch,
the US Bureau of Land Management, university collections, and the
Mexican and Spanish Archives. A good collection of microfilm copies of
records is at the Family History Library. Guide books which will describe
these resources in further detail and will tell you how to use them are as
follows:

_H. P. Beers, SPANISH AND MEXICAN RECORDS OF THE
AMERICAN SOUTHWEST, University of AZ Press, Tucson, AZ,
1979.
_G. R. Ryskamp, TRACING YOUR HISPANIC HERITAGE, Hispanic
Family History Research, Riverside, CA, 1984.

Asians began entering the US in sizable numbers in the middle
1800s. The Chinese came first, then Japanese, then Koreans, Filipinos,
Indians (from India), and Southeast Asians (from Viet Nam, Laos,
Cambodia). Most of these, except the Chinese and Japanese, have come
very recently. And many family lines proceed through Hawaii, then to the
mainland. Apart from the regular US genealogical sources, important
specialized records are to be found in the Hawaii State Archives, various
Asian ethnic associations in the US, ethnic newspapers, ethnic cemeteries,
Buddhist temples, Shinto shrines, Confucian shrines, and west-coast
passenger arrival lists. In addition to the two volumes mentioned in the
first paragraph of this section, the following will be helpful as you pursue
your Asian ancestry:
_S. J. Palmer, STUDIES IN ASIAN GENEALOGY, Brigham Young
University Press, Provo, UT, 1972.

---

56. Family History Centers

The Family History Library in Salt
Lake City, UT, the largest genealogical library in the world, is sponsored and supported by The Church
of Jesus Christ of Latter-Day Saints (LDS), often referred to as
Mormons. Their collection contains over 1.7 million reels of microfilm
and microfiche, about 200,000 books, and a large collection of compiled
data. These materials are copies of original genealogical records,
compilations of genealogical data, genealogical reference works, and
indexes to many of these. Every type of record mentioned in this
Handbook is represented in the collection, and the collection is international in extent. Chances are extremely high that they have numerous
records on many, possibly even most, of your forebears. In fact, this
massive collection is of supreme value to most genealogists.

The vast microfilm and microfiche resources of the Family History
Library are available to you through its over 1400 branches. These
branches are called Family History Centers, and are maintained by LDS
members in or near their local meetinghouses all over the US (in fact, all
over the world). These Family History Centers are open to all people,
and are staffed by knowledgeable genealogical researchers. One of them

is most certainly located within 50-100 miles of you. The way you use the Family History Center is quite straightforward. You call them, ascertain their open hours, then you go. The attendants will show you a series of indexes, you will look for your ancestors in some them, and you will look at other indexes showing records from the places your progenitors lived. Then you will ask the attendant to order the microfilms and microfiche that you want. A small postage and handling fee is charged. The micro--films and microfiche will be ordered from the Family History Library in Salt Lake City, and when they arrive, you will be notified. You can then return to the Family History Center to read the microfilms and microfiche on the machines which they have. Below, we will list for you all the cities which have a Family History Center, and you will be given instructions for finding the telephone numbers. But, for now, a detailed outline of exactly what you do when you go to a Family History Center will be set out.

When you arrive at a Family History Center, sign the register, then look for the name or names you are working on in the following indexes, which the attendant will hand to you and show you how to use:
_THE INTERNATIONAL GENEALOGICAL INDEX, Family History Library, Salt Lake City, UT, latest microfiche or CDROM edition; over 200 million entries; mainly birth, marriage, church, probate, census, and family records; names listed alphabetically under US state, or subdivisions of foreign countries usually.
_THE FAMILY HISTORY LIBRARY CATALOG, SURNAME SECTION, Family History Library, Salt Lake City, UT, latest microfiche or CDROM edition. Leads you to family histories, genealogies, research collections, previous work.
_ANCESTRAL FILE, Family History Library, Salt Lake City, UT, latest CDROM edition. Over 20 million listings of ancestral lineages, ancestors, and persons who are doing research on them.
_ACCELERATED INDEXING SYSTEMS INTEGRATED CENSUS INDEXES, Search 1 (early-1819), Search 2 (1820-29), Search 3 (1830-39), Search 4 (1840-49), Search 5 (North 1850-99), Search 6 (South 1850-99), Search 7 (West 1850-99), Search 7A (Searches 5, 6, and 7 combined), Search 8 (1850-85 Mortality Censuses), Search 9 (1900-10), Search 10 (Canadian Censuses), Accelerated Indexing Systems, North Salt Lake City, UT.
The references in all these indexes are coded so that the attendant can order for you the records to which they refer.

After searching the above indexes for your ancestral names, you should next make a search of records available in your forebears' county

and/or town. These records are listed under the state, then under the county, then under the town in this reference work:
_THE FAMILY HISTORY LIBRARY CATALOG, LOCALITY SECTION, Family History Library, Salt Lake City, UT, latest microfiche or CDROM edition. Leads you to many, many types of county and city records, especially birth, marriage, death, and probate records, which are likely to include your ancestry.
When you find records which you believe are pertinent to your progenitor, and you will probably locate quite a few, you may ask the attendant to order them from the Family History Library. You then should examine all the listings in this index under the state. Some of these will also be relevant to your investigation, and they may likewise be ordered.

Before concluding your visit to the Family History center, ask the attendant for the following CDROM index if you are seeking ancestors who lived from late in the last century up until the present:
_SOCIAL SECURITY DEATH INDEX, 1937-present. Lists persons and death dates as recorded by the Social Security Administration. Over 44 million names.

Listed below are cities in which Family History Centers are located. Look under CHURCHES-LATTER-DAY SAINTS in the yellow pages of the telephone directory for addressees and telephone numbers. Call for information on open times and directions.
___In AL: Bessemer, Birmingham, Dothan, Huntsville, Mobile, Montgomery, Tuscaloosa, in AK: Anchorage, Fairbanks, Juneau, Ketchikan, Kotzebue, Sitka, Sodotna, Wasilla, in AZ: Benson, Buckeye, Camp Verde, Casa Grande, Cottonwood, Eagar, Flagstaff, Glendale, Globe, Holbrook, Kingman, Mesa, Nogales, Page, Payson, Peoria, Phoenix, Prescott, Safford, Scottsdale, Show Low, Sierra Vista, Snowflake, St. David, St. Johns, Tucson, Winslow, Yuma, in AR: Fort Smith, Jacksonville, Little Rock, Rogers,
___In CA (Bay Area): Antioch, Concord, Fairfield, Los Altos, Menlo Park, Napa, Oakland, San Bruno, San Jose, Santa Clara, Santa Cruz, Santa Rosa, In CA (Central): Auburn, Clovis, Davis (Woodland), El Dorado (Placerville), Fresno, Hanford, Merced, Modesto, Monterey (Seaside), Placerville, Sacramento, Seaside, Stockton, Turlock, Visalia, Woodland, In CA (Los Angeles County): Burbank, Canoga Park, Carson, Cerritos, Chatsworth (North Ridge), Covina, Glendale, Granada Hills, Hacienda Heights, Huntington Park, La Crescenta, Lancaster, Long Beach (Los Alamitos), Los Angeles, Monterey Park, Northridge, Norwalk, Palmdale, Palos Verdes (Rancho Palos Verdes),

Pasadena, Torrance (Carson), Valencia, Van Nuys, Whittier, In <u>CA</u> (<u>Northern</u>): Anderson, Chico, Eureka, Grass Valley, Gridley, Mt. Shasta, Quincy, Redding, Susanville, Ukiah, Yuba City, In <u>CA</u> (<u>Southern</u>, except Los Angeles): Alpine, Anaheim, Bakersfield, Barstow, Blythe, Buena Park, Camarillo, Carlsbad, Corona, Cypress (Buena Park), El Cajon (Alpine), Escondido, Fontana, Garden Grove (Westminster), Hemet, Huntington Beach, Jurupa (Riverside), Los Alamitos, Mission Viejo, Moorpark, Moreno Valley, Needles, Newbury Park, Orange, Palm Desert, Palm Springs (Palm Desert), Poway (San Diego), Redlands, Ridgecrest, Riverside, San Bernardino, San Diego, San Luis Obispo, Santa Barbara, Santa Maria, Simi Valley, Thousand Oaks (Moorpark), Upland, Ventura, Victorville, Vista, Westminster,

___<u>CO</u>: Alamosa, Arvada, Aurora, Boulder, Colorado Springs, Columbine, Cortez, Craig, Denver, Durango, Fort Collins, Frisco, Grand Junction, Greeley, La Jara, Littleton, Louisville, Manassa, Meeker, Montrose, Longmont, Northglenn, Paonia, Pueblo, in <u>CT</u>: Bloomfield, Hartford, Madison, New Canaan, New Haven, Waterford, Woodbridge, in <u>DC</u>: Kensington, MD, in <u>DE</u>: Newark, Wilmington, in <u>FL</u>: Boca Raton, Cocoa, Ft. Lauderdale, Ft. Myers, Gainesville, Hialeah, Homestead, Jacksonville, Lake City, Lake Mary, Lakeland, Miami, Orange Park, Orlando, Palm City, Panama City, Pensacola, Plantation, Rockledge, St. Petersburg, Tallahassee, Tampa, West Palm Beach, Winterhaven, in <u>GA</u>: Atlanta, Augusta, Brunswick, Columbus, Douglas, Gainesville, Jonesboro, Macon, Marietta, Powder Springs, Roswell, Savannah, Tucker, in <u>HI</u>: Hilo, Honolulu, Kaneohe, Kauai, Kona, Laie, Lihue, Miliani, Waipahu,

___In <u>ID</u>: Basalt, Blackfoot, Boise, Burley, Caldwell, Carey, Coeur D'Alene, Driggs, Emmett, Firth, Hailey, Idaho Falls, Iona, Lewiston, McCammon, Malad, Meridian, Montpelier, Moore, Mountain Home, Nampa, Pocatello, Paris, Preston, Rexburg, Rigby, Salmon, Sandpoint, Shelley, Soda Springs, Twin Falls, Weiser, in <u>IL</u>: Champaign, Chicago Heights, Fairview Heights, Nauvoo, Peoria, Rockford, Schaumburg, Wilmette, in <u>IN</u>: Bloomington, Evansville, Fort Wayne, Indianapolis, New Albany, Noblesville, South Bend, Terre Haute, West Lafayette, in <u>IA</u>: Ames, Cedar Rapids, Davenport, Sioux City, West Des Moines, in <u>KS</u>: Dodge City, Olathe, Salina, Topeka, Wichita, in <u>KY</u>: Hopkinsville, Lexington, Louisville, Martin, Paducah, in <u>LA</u>: Alexandria, Baton Rouge, Denham Springs, Monroe, Metairie, New Orleans, Shreveport, Slidell,

___In <u>ME</u>: Augusta, Bangor, Cape Elizabeth, Caribou, Farmingdale, Portland, in <u>MD</u>: Annapolis, Baltimore, Ellicott City, Frederick,

Kensington, Lutherville,in MA: Boston, Foxboro, Tyngsboro, Weston, Worcester, in MI: Ann Arbor, Bloomfield Hills, East Lansing, Escanaba, Grand Blanc, Grand Rapids, Hastings, Kalamazoo, Lansing, Ludington, Marquette, Midland, Muskegon, Traverse City, Westland, in MN: Anoka, Duluth, Minneapolis, Rochester, St. Paul, in MS: Clinton, Columbus, Gulfport, Hattiesburg, in MO: Cape Girardeau, Columbia, Farmington, Frontenac, Hazelwood, Independence, Joplin, Kansas City, Liberty, Springfield, St. Joseph, St. Louis, in MT: Billings, Bozeman, Butte, Glasgow, Glendive, Great Falls, Havre, Helena, Kalispell, Missoula, Stevensville, in NE: Grand Island, Lincoln, Omaha, Papillion,

In NV: Elko, Ely, Henderson, LaHonton Valley, Las Vegas, Logandale, Mesquite, Reno, Tonapah, Winnemucca, in NH: Concord, Exeter, Nashua, Portsmouth, in NJ: Caldwell, Dherry Hill, East Brunswick, Morristown, North Caldwell, in NM: Albuquerque, Carlsbad, Farmington, Gallup, Grants, Las Cruces, Santa Fe, Silver City, in NY: Albany, Buffalo, Ithaca, Jamestown, Lake Placid, Liverpool, Loudonville, New York City, Pittsford, Plainview, Queens, Rochester, Scarsdale, Syracuse, Vestal, Williamsville, Yorktown, in NC: Asheville, Charlotte, Durham, Fayetteville, Goldsboro, Greensboro, Hickory, Kinston, Raleigh, Skyland, Wilmington, Winston-Salem, in ND: Bismarck, Fargo, Minot, in OH: Akron, Cincinnati, Cleveland, Columbus, Dayton, Dublin, Fairborn, Kirtland, Perrysburg, Reynoldsburg, Tallmadge, Toledo, Westlake, Winterville,

In OK: Lawton, Muskogee, Norman, Oklahoma City, Stillwater, Tulsa, in OR: Beaverton, Bend, Brookings, Central Point, Coos Bay, Corvallis, Eugene, Grants Pass, Gresham, Hermiston, Hillsboro, Keizer, Klamath Falls, LaGrande, Lake Oswego, Lebanon, Minnville, Medford, Newport, Nyssa, Ontario, Oregon City, Portland, Prineville, Roseburg, Salem, Sandy, The Dallas, in RI: Providence, Warwick, in SC: Charleston, Columbia, Florence, Greenville, North Augusta, in SD: Gettysburg, Rapid City, Rosebud, Sioux Falls, in TN: Chattanooga, Franklin, Kingsport, Knoxville, Madison, Memphis, Nashville, in TX: Abilene, Amarillo, Austin, Bay City, Beaumont, Bryan, Conroe, Corpus Christi, Dallas, Denton, Duncanville, El Paso, Ft. Worth, Friendswood, Harlingen, Houston, Hurst, Katy, Kileen, Kingwood, Longview, Lubbock, McAllen, Odessa, Orange, Pasadena, Plano, Port Arthur, Richland Hills, San Antonio, Sugarland,

In UT: American Fork, Altamont, Beaver, Blanding, Bloomington, Bluffdale, Bountiful, Brigham City, Canyon Rim, Castle Dale, Cedar City, Delta, Duchesne, Escalante, Farmington, Ferron, Fillmore, Granger, Heber, Helper, Highland, Holladay, Hunter, Huntington,

Hurricane, Hyrum, Kanab, Kaysville, Kearns, Laketown, Layton, Lehi, Loa, Logan, Magna, Manti, Mapleton, Midway, Moab, Monticello, Moroni, Mt. Pleasant, Murray, Nephi, Ogden, Orem, Panguitch, Parowan, Pleasant Grove, Price, Provo, Richfield, Riverton, Roosevelt, Rose Park, Salt Lake City, Sandy, Santaquin, South Jordan, Springville, St. George, Syracuse, Tooele, Trementon, Tropic, Vernal, Wellington, Wendover, West Jordan, West Valley City, in <u>VA</u>: Annandale, Bassett, Charlottesville, Chesapeake, Dale City, Falls Church, Fredericksburg, Hamilton, Martinsville, McLean, Newport News, Norfolk, Oakton, Pembroke, Richmond, Roanoke, Salem, Virginia Beach, Waynesboro, Winchester, in <u>VT</u>: Berlin, Montpelier,

In <u>WA</u>: Auburn, Bellevue, Bellingham, Bremerton, Centralia, Colville, Edmonds, Ellensburg, Elma, Ephrata, Everett, Federal Way, Ferndale, Lake Stevens, Longview, Lynnwood, Marysville, Moses Lake, Mt. Vernon, North Bend, Olympia, Othello, Port Angeles, Pullman, Puyallup, Quincy, Renton, Richland, Seattle, Silverdale, Spokane, Sumner, Tacoma, Vancouver, Walla Walla, Wenatchee, Yakima, in <u>WV</u>: Charleston, Fairmont, Huntington, in <u>WI</u>: Appleton, Eau Clair, Hales Corner, Madison, Milwaukee, Shawano, Wausau, in <u>WY</u>: Afton, Casper, Cheyenne, Cody, Gillette, Green River, Jackson Hole, Kemmerer, Laramie, Lovell, Lyman, Rawlins, Riverton, Rock Springs, Sheridan, Urie, Worland.

The Family History Library is constantly adding new branches so this list will probably be out-of-date by the time you read it. An SASE and a $2 fee to the Family History Library (address in the next section) will bring you an up-to-date listing of Family History Centers.

57. Family History Library

The largest collection of genealogical materials in the world is in the Family History Library of the Church of Jesus Christ of Latter-Day Saints. The Family History Library is situated at 35 North West Temple, Salt Lake City, UT 84150. This massive collection is open free of charge to all persons. The hours are 7:30-6 Monday, 7:30-10 Tuesday through Friday, and 7:30-5 Saturday, except holidays.

The Family History Library has over 1,700,000 reels of microfilm, about 170,000 microfiche, and about 180,000 books. All materials except the books may be borrowed through the over 1400 branch Family History Centers, most of which are in the US. See the previous section for details on these Family History Centers, including information on borrowing the microfilms and microfiche. The major types of genealogical records represented in the microform materials are birth, cemetery, census, church, court, death, deed, land, marriage, military, naturalization, passenger lists, probate, tax, town, will. Records from every state in the US are included. The books include ones of the following types: atlases, biographies, city histories, county histories, directories, family histories, gazetteers, genealogical periodicals, historical periodicals, indexes, maps, town histories, transcripts of original records.

The key which permits you to locate records in the Family History Library is the Family History Library Catalog, which is on microfiche at both the Library and at its branch Centers. Some portions of the Catalog are on CDROM also. The Catalog is divided into four sections:
_ *FAMILY HISTORY LIBRARY CATALOG, SURNAME SECTION, latest microfiche or CDROM edition. To be searched for surnames you are interested in. Leads you to family histories, genealogies, research collections, previous work other people have done on the family.
_ *FAMILY HISTORY LIBRARY CATALOG, LOCALITY SECTION, latest microfiche or CDROM edition. To be searched for your ancestor's state, county, city, town. Leads you to the state, county, city, and town records which the Family History Library has, and which are likely to include your ancestor. Federal records which the library has will be listed under the United States. These include census, land, military, naturalization, passenger lists, and federal court records.
_ *FAMILY HISTORY LIBRARY CATALOG, SUBJECT SECTION, latest microfiche edition. To be searched for specific types of records, for example, divorce or bounty land or guardian or postal guides.
_ *FAMILY HISTORY LIBRARY CATALOG, AUTHOR/TITLE SECTION, latest microfiche edition. To be searched for particular volumes, either by their authors or their titles. Microform records can be located in this index under the name of the organization that created the records.

There are several very important ancestor locators in the Family History Library which must not be overlooked. These are:
_ *THE INTERNATIONAL GENEALOGICAL INDEX, latest microfiche or CDROM edition, over 200 million entries. To be searched for your ancestors' names. Refers you to records, mainly birth, marriage, church, probate, census, and family records.

_*ANCESTRAL FILE, latest CDROM edition. Alphabetical list of ancestors, ancestral charts, and persons who are doing research on them. Over 22 million persons listed.

_FAMILY GROUP RECORDS COLLECTION, on microfilm, over 8 million family genealogy sheets, arranged alphabetically. In three groups: Archives Section 1942-69, Patron's Section 1924-62, and Patron's Section 1962-79. To be searched for your ancestors' names. See the Subject Section of the Family History Library Catalog for microfilm access numbers.

_*ACCELERATED INDEXING SYSTEMS INTEGRATED CENSUS INDEXES, Search 1 (early-1819), Search 2 (1820-29), Search 3 (1830-39), Search 4 (1840-49), Search 5 (North 1850-99), Search 6 (South 1850-99), Search 7 (West 1850-99), Search 7A (Searches 5, 6, and 7 combined), Search 8 (1850-85 Mortality Censuses), Search 9 (1900-10), Search 10 (Canadian Censuses), Accelerated Indexing Systems, North Salt Lake City, UT.

All of the materials preceded by an asterisk * are also available at each Family History Center. Hence, if you are planning a trip to the Family History Library in Salt Lake City, all of these should be thoroughly used before you go. From them, you can compile a list of records that you want to see when you get there. Be sure and include in your list the access number for each record. This will make the best use of your time at the Library, since you will be able to immediately begin using the records.

There are several very good reference books which will prepare you for a visit to the Family History Library. Among the better ones are:

_ J. C. Parker, GOING TO SALT LAKE CITY TO DO FAMILY HISTORY RESEARCH, Marietta Publishing Co., Turlock, CA, latest edition.

_ L. R. Jaussi, GENEALOGY FUNDAMENTALS, Jaussi Publications, Orem, UT, 1994.

_ J. Cerny and W. Elliott, THE LIBRARY, A GUIDE TO THE LDS FAMILY HISTORY LIBRARY, Ancestry, Salt Lake City, UT, 1988.

_ N. E. Carlberg, RESEARCHING IN SALT LAKE CITY, Carlberg Press, Anaheim, CA, 1994.

58. Family investigations

One of the very best sources of information about your progenitors is your relatives, especially the older ones. You should make every effort to visit them or to write double-spaced typed letters to them asking about two important things. First, inquire about what they remember of their brothers and sisters, parents, aunts, uncles, cousins, grandparents, grand aunts, grand uncles, and even great-grand relatives, as well as more distant cousins. If you are visiting them, take careful notes, and/or record the session (with permission, of course). If you write them, ask carefully-composed questions, leave blanks beneath the questions, and request your relative to answer in the blanks, and then return to you. Don't ask relatives to simply tell you all they know about the family. Be specific: ask for birthdates, birthplaces, moves from one place to another, home locations, marriage dates, marriage places, childrens' names and birthplaces, occupations, religious affiliations, military participation, organizational memberships, insurance companies, home addresses, employers' names, nearest towns, schools attended, political preferences, women's maiden names, where ancestors came from to this country and when, death dates, death places, burial places, and heirs. Be sure and ask the older relatives about other farther-removed relatives that you did not realize existed. You can then extend your inquiries to them.

Second, inquire whether your relatives have any articles associated with or belonging to your ancestors which have been passed down. In particular, ask if they have personal records, legal papers, school records, religious records, government records, or health records. Personal records might include such things as diaries, letters, newspaper clippings, photographs, baby books, wedding albums, funeral notices and programs, retirement papers, books, scrapbooks, bank books, and samplers. Legal records which you should seek include contracts, deeds, tax bills, wills, mortgages, promissory notes, marriage licenses, bills, and business records. School records such as the following ought to be sought: diplomas, yearbooks, grade cards, awards, tuition receipts, and alumni organization papers. Religious records include christening certificates, baptismal certificates, marriage licenses, family Bibles, attendance awards, funeral notices, and funeral programs. Government records of the following types should be looked for: military enlistment papers, military discharge papers, naturalization papers, homestead documents, passports, business licenses, tax receipts, social security records, and income tax records. Health records include hospital records, insurance records, physicians' records, and dentists' records. Other items which might provide genealogical clues are uniforms, engraved jewelry, initialed or engraved silver items, rings with inscriptions, and lockets with pictures.

Now, a few words of warning need to be given you. The first of these is that your interviewing and letter writing must be done with tact, sensitivity, and patient persistence. The second of these is that you need to keep a healthy skepticism about what you are told in a genuine effort to separate fact and fiction. Most family traditions have elements of truth in them, but sometimes these elements of truth have been distorted, garbled, and/or confused. Further, practically every family has or has had in it at least one person whose strong desire to be a descendant of a famous individual has turned into a direct claim. Many families have also generated a fiction that there is some tremendous inheritance awaiting them if they can only establish certain genealogical connections. People generally do not deliberately fabricate false data, but things do have a way of getting glamorized, embellished, and exaggerated as they are passed down. A third and final word of warning relates to this second one. All the data you obtain from family inquiries need to be treated only as clues which will lead you to explore further for substantiation and documented proof of them in original records. Remember that the more substantiation and documentation you bring to your genealogical data, the surer and more valid the data will be.

59. Family organizations

Many organizations, associations, and societies have been established for the purpose of acting as an information center for a single family surname or for the ancestors or descendants of one or more persons. These organizations are generally known as family organizations. They set themselves to do research, to elicit information from other researchers, to organize the data, to publish the data or otherwise disseminate them (books, bulletins, newsletters, computer bulletin boards), to communicate with members and other interested parties, and to organize meetings. Early in your research on any given name, it is important for you to discover if such an organization exists, and to find out if it has material on your family line bearing that name. If so, the organization can put you in touch with the persons who are doing the research work. It is obviously important for you to share with them all information as you discover it. Names and addresses of many of these family organizations will be found in the following publications:

_THE GENEALOGICAL HELPER, Everton Publishers, Logan, UT, latest Mar-Apr issue.

_E. P. Bentley, DIRECTORY OF FAMILY ASSOCIATIONS, Genealogical Publishing Co., Baltimore, MD, latest edition.

60. Family publications

Quite a few of the numerous family organizations publish one or more books, or a newsletter, or a bulletin, or a list of members and contacts, or a periodical. Often there is information valuable to you in these publications. For each of your family names, you need to discover if such materials have been or are now being published. You may then request a sample copy (sometimes there is a small fee), and if you find it useful, subscribe. Listings of many of these publications along with their addresses can be found in:

_THE GENEALOGICAL HELPER, Everton Publishers, Logan, UT, latest Mar-Apr issue.

_E. P. Bentley, DIRECTORY OF FAMILY ASSOCIATIONS, Genealogical Publishing Co. Baltimore, MD, latest edition.

_J. Konrad, DIRECTORY OF FAMILY ONE-NAME PERIODICALS, Heritage House, Indianapolis, IN, latest edition.

_FAMILY HISTORY LIBRARY CATALOG, SURNAME SECTION, Microfiche or CDROM, Family History Library, Salt Lake City, UT, and at every Family History Center, all over the US.

_K. Cavanaugh, DIRECTORY OF FAMILY NEWSLETTERS, The Author, Fort Wayne, IN, latest edition.

_SURNAME PERIODICALS, L and H Enterprises, Sacramento, CA, latest edition.

61. Farm and ranch censuses

In several of the regular population census years, an agricultural census was taken. Practically all of the schedules (lists) for 1850-60-70-80 exist. These records show the name of the farm or ranch owner, size of the farm or ranch, value of the property, number of livestock, and quantities of produce. If you know or suspect that your forebear was a farmer or rancher, it will be worthwhile to look him up in these records which list farm and ranch owners in each county of each state. Even though the farm and ranch censuses are not indexed, your search in them can be shortened by recognition of a relationship. The regular 1850-60-70-80 population census schedules are generally indexed, allowing you to locate your ancestor there. Since the 1850-60-70-80 farm and ranch census data were usually gathered in the same order, the relative place of your progenitor's listing in the farm and ranch census will be similar to that in the regular population census. For example, if your ancestor appears about one-third of the way through his county in the regular census, he will probably appear about one-third of the way through that same county in the farm and ranch census. A very valuable use of these special censuses is that sometimes a forebear will have been missed in the regular census, but can be located in the farm and ranch schedules.

Most of the original farm and ranch censuses are now in state libraries or archives. Many of them have been microfilmed, mostly by the National Archives. The best places to start your search for them are the State Libraries and State Archives. They usually have the records or copies of them, and if they do not, they can tell you who does. Microfilm copies of some of them can also be found at the National Archives, and the Regional branches of the National Archives:

_National Archives, NON-POPULATION CENSUS SCHEDULES, on Microfilm T1137 for GA, T1133 for IL, T1156 for IA, T1130 for KS, T1136 for LA, T1204 for MA, T1164 for MI, T1128 for NE, T1159 for OH, T1157 for PA, T1135 for TN, T1134 for TX, T1132 fro VA, The Archives, Washington, DC.

Some are also available at the Family History Library. The microfilm copies at the latter repository can be borrowed through the numerous Family History Centers.

---

62. Finding aids

Every genealogical repository (library or archives) has finding aids. These are various items which are organized listings of the materials available in the repository accompanied by codes or other indicators which permit easy location of the materials. These are the first items that a researcher should seek out upon visiting any repository. In fact, many major repositories are described in guidebooks which have been specifically written to assist investigators. If such a guide book exists for a repository which you plan to visit, the guide should by all means be read beforehand. This will save you an immense amount of time after you arrive because you will already be acquainted with the contents and arrangement of the repository. Examples of such guides are as follows:

_J. Cerny and W. Elliott, THE LIBRARY, A GUIDE TO THE LDS FAMILY HISTORY LIBRARY, Ancestry Publishing, Salt Lake City, UT, 1988.

_Staff of the National Archives, GUIDE TO GENEALOGICAL RESEARCH IN THE NATIONAL ARCHIVES, National Archives and Records Service, Washington, DC, 1982.

_L. D. Szucs and S. H. Luebking, THE ARCHIVES, A GUIDE TO THE NATIONAL ARCHIVES FIELD BRANCHES, Ancestry Publishing, Salt Lake City, UT, 1988.

_A GENEALOGIST'S GUIDE TO THE ALLEN COUNTY PUBLIC LIBRARY, Watermill Publications, Fort Wayne, IN, latest edition. Guide to the 2nd largest genealogical library in the US.

_P. T. Sinko, GUIDE TO LOCAL AND FAMILY HISTORY AT THE NEWBERRY LIBRARY, Ancestry Publishing, Salt Lake City, UT, 1987.

_J. Oldenburg, A GENEALOGICAL GUIDE TO THE BURTON HISTORICAL COLLECTION, DETROIT PUBLIC LIBRARY, Ancestry Publishing, Salt Lake City, UT, 1988.

Similar guides or inventories have been published for many state archives (including DE, IL, MD, MS, NC, PA, VA) and for some state libraries (such as IN, MN, TX, WI). In short, before you go, be sure to write, inquiring about a guide.

When you arrive at a genealogical repository, look carefully for the many finding aids that they are likely to have. These finding aids will usually be listings which are arranged alphabetically by author, locality, name, subject, and/or title, or chronologically by date, or sequentially by some code number which permits the items to be located.

_Card catalogs.
_Microfilm and microfiche catalogs.
_Computer catalogs.
_Alphabetical and chronological files.
_Indexes.
_Inventories (detailed lists of items in a collection).
_Calendars (a list by date) and minutes.
_Lists, checklists, registers, schedules, and directories.
_Charts and tables of contents.

There is a final very important finding aid available in every repository. This is the personnel, that is, the librarians, archivists, and attendants. You should never fail to consult them regarding the information you are seeking.

63. Foreign genealogy

Once you have traced an ancestor back to a country other than the US, you will then need to continue your progenitor tracking in that country. The most likely countries or areas from which your ancestor will have come are Germany, Ireland, England, Africa, Scotland, France, Spain-Portugal, Italy, Poland, Holland, Sweden, Norway, the USSR, and Wales. Separate sections in this Handbook are devoted to Canadian genealogy, English-Welsh genealogy, German genealogy, Irish genealogy, Black genealogy, Scots-Irish genealogy, and Scottish genealogy. The others mentioned above and numerous other foreign countries will be treated succinctly in this section.

Once you have identified or suspect that you have identified your immigrant ancestor, you must look into every possible source here in the US in a concerted effort to locate the precise place in the foreign county from which your progenitor came. The name of the country is not good enough, neither is the name of the county or district. You need to know the city or town or village or parish. If you find this, your procedure in the foreign country becomes very easy and straight-forward. If you don't know this, your search will usually remain difficult. Instructions for discovering this precise place of origin are given in the section entitled Immigrant ancestor origins.

Having found the exact place in the foreign country, your next step is to discover what records are available in that country, where they are located, and how you may obtain them or copies of them. The chief sorts of records that you will be seeking are those which give dates and places of birth, marriage, and death, and those which name parents. Brief treatments of foreign records, with special attention to ones which are available at the Family History Center, are given in:

_Johni Cerny and W. Elliott, THE LIBRARY, Ancestry Publishing, Salt Lake City, UT, 1988. Countries included are: Canada, England and Wales, Ireland, Scotland, Scandinavia [Denmark, Finland, Greenland, Iceland, Norway, Sweden], Germany, Central Europe [Austria, Czechoslovakia, Hungary, Switzerland, Liechtenstein], Eastern Europe [Romania, Yugoslavia, Bulgaria, Albania, Poland, USSR], Southern Europe [Italy, Spain, Portugal, Greece], Western Europe [France, Netherlands, Belgium Luxembourg], South America [Argentina, Bolivia, Brazil, Chile, Colombia, Ecuador, French Guiana, Guyana, Paraguay, Peru, Surinam, Uruguay, Venezuela], Mexico, Central America [Belize, Costa Rica, El Salvador, Guatemala, Honduras, Nicaragua, Panama], South Pacific [Australia, New Zealand, South Pacific Islands, Caribbean Islands [Bermuda, Barbados, Bahamas, Puerto Rico, Dominican Republic], South Africa.

Your first action should be to read the appropriate section in this book. Then, you should order from the Family History Center (35 North West Temple, Salt Lake City, UT 84150) the appropriate research guide or outline to the country you are working on. There is a small fee. This guide or outline will give you more detail on the records, their locations, and which of them are available as microfilm copies at the Family History Center:

_RESEARCH GUIDE OR OUTLINE FOR ARGENTINA, Family History Center, Salt Lake City, UT, latest edition. Also available for Australia, Austria, Belgium, Canada, Chile, Columbia, Costa Rica, Denmark, Ecuador, El Salvador, England/Wales, France, Germany, Guatemala, Honduras, Hong Kong, Hungary, Iceland, Ireland, Isle of Man, Italy, Japan, Mexico, Netherlands, New Zealand, Nicaragua, Norway, Panama, Poland, Samoa, Scotland, South Africa, Sweden, Switzerland, Taiwan, Uruguay, Venezuela, and others.

Having read the two above treatments of the genealogical sources available to you in the country you are interested in, it is usually to your distinct advantage to carefully go through a guide book specifically written about genealogical research in that country, if one is available. Recommended volumes include:

_(Australia) D. Meadley, WRITING A FAMILY HISTORY, Family History Services, Nuawading, Australia, 1990; N. V. Hall, TRACING YOUR FAMILY HISTORY IN AUSTRALIA, Rigby Publishers, Adelaide, Australia, 1985; N. Gray, COMPILING YOUR (AUSTRALIAN) FAMILY HISTORY, Society of Australian Genealogists, Sydney, Australia, 1982; B. R. Blaze and M. E. Runting, ANCESTORS FOR AUSTRALIANS, Genealogical Society of Victoria, Melbourne, Australia, 1977.

_(Austria) D. Senekovic, HANDY GUIDE TO AUSTRIAN GENEALOGICAL RECORDS, Everton Publishers, Logan, UT, 1979.

_(Bahamas) D. G. Saunders and E. A. Carson, GUIDE TO THE RECORDS OF THE BAHAMAS, Government Printing Department, Nassau, Bahamas, 1983.

_(Barbados) M. J. Chandler, A GUIDE TO RECORDS IN BARBADOS, Blackwell, Oxford, England, 1965.

_(Belgium) E. H. Nederhand, ANCESTRAL RESEARCH IN BELGIUM, The Author, Salt Lake City, UT, 1973; M. Martens-Malengreau, MANUEL DE GENEALOGISTE, Service de Centralisation des Etudes Genealogiques, Bruxelles, Belgium, 1980.

_(Bermuda) H. Rowe, A GUIDE TO THE RECORDS OF BERMUDA, Bermuda Archives, Hamilton, Bermuda, 1980.

_(Bolivia) La Sociedad Genealogica, FUENTES PRINCIPALES DE REGISTROS GENEALOGICAS EN BOLIVIA, La Sociedad, Salt Lake City, UT, 1977.

_(Czechoslovakia) D. Schlyter, A HANDBOOK OF CZECHOSLOVAK GENEALOGICAL RESEARCH, Genun Publishers, Buffalo Grove, IL, 1985; O. Miller, GENEALOGICAL RESEARCH FOR CZECH AND SLOVAK AMERICANS, Gale Research, Detroit, MI, 1978; M.

A. Wellauer, TRACING YOUR CZECH AND SLOVAK ROOTS, The Author, Milwaukee, WI, 1980.

_(Denmark) N. E. Carlberg, BEGINNING DANISH RESEARCH, Carlberg, Anaheim, CA, 1992; F. Smith and F. A. Thomsen, GENEALOGICAL GUIDEBOOK AND ATLAS OF DENMARK, Bookcraft, Salt Lake City, UT, 1969; E. M. Poulsen and G. P. Korvallis, THE DANISH GENEALOGICAL HELPER, Everton Publishers, Logan, UT, 1969; A. Fabritius and H. Hatt, HAANDBOG I SLAEGTSFORSKNING, Schultz Forlag, Kobenhavn, Denmark, 1963.

_(Finland) C. Ross and V. M. Doby, HANDBOOK FOR DOING FINNISH AMERICAN FAMILY HISTORY, The Authors, Minneapolis, MN, 1980; M. Hypponen, SUKUTUTKIMUKSEN KASIKIRJA, Soederstroem, Porvoo, Finland, 1988; A. Brenner, SLAEKTFORSKNING: PRAKTISK HANDBOOK FOER FINLAND, Soederstroem, Helsinki, Finland, 1947.

_(France) M. F. Beauregard, LA GENEALOGIE, RETROUVER SES ANCETRES, Editions de l'Homme, Montreal, Canada, 1987; M. Audin, BARKING UP THAT FRENCH TREE, Cook-McDowell Publications, Owensboro, KY, 1980; P. Durye, GENEALOGY, AN INTRODUCTION TO CONTINENTAL CONCEPTS, Polyanthos, New Orleans, 1978; G. Bernard, GUIDE DES RECHERCHES SUR L'HISTORIE DES FAMILIES, Archives Nationales, Paris, France, 1981; H. Gilles, RECHERCHEZ VOS ANCETRES, C. Corlet, Conde-sur-Noireau, France, 1982; C. Dubourguey, LA GENEALOGIE, RMC, Monte Carlo, 1988.

_(Greece) L. C. Bywater, GREEK GENEALOGICAL RESEARCH, Family History Library, Salt Lake City, UT, 1988; M. Broadbent, STUDIES IN GREEK GENEALOGY, E. J. Brill, Leiden, 1968.

_(Hungary) J. H. Suess, HANDY GUIDE TO HUNGARIAN GENEA-LOGICAL RECORDS, Everton Publishers, Logan, UT, 1980.

_(Iceland) E. Jonasson, TRACING YOUR ICELANDIC FAMILY TREE, The Author, Winnipeg, Manitoba, 1982.

_(Italy) J. P. Colletta, FINDING ITALIAN ROOTS, Genealogical Publishing Co., Baltimore, MD, 1993; J. M. Glynn, MANUAL FOR ITALIAN GENEALOGY, Italian Family History Society, Newton, MA, 1981; F. and P. Preece, HANDY GUIDE TO ITALIAN GENEALOGICAL RECORDS, Everton Publishers, Logan, UT, 1983; G. G. Camanaji, GENEALOGY IN ITALY, Genealogico Italiana, Firenze, Italia, 1969.

_(Netherlands) C. M. Franklin, DUTCH GENEALOGICAL RE-SEARCH, Ye Olde Genealogie Shoppe, Indianapolis, IN, 1982; E. H.

Nederhand, ANCESTRAL RESEARCH IN THE NETHERLANDS, Genealogical Society of UT, Salt Lake City, UT, 1972; W. Wijnaendts von Resandt, SEARCHING FOR YOUR ANCESTORS IN THE NETHERLANDS, Centraal Bureau voor Genealogie, The Hague, Netherlands, latest issue.

_(New Zealand) A. Bromell, TRACING FAMILY HISTORY IN NEW ZEALAND, GP Books, Wellington, New Zealand, 1988; N. T. Hansen, GUIDE TO GENEALOGICAL SOURCES: AUSTRALIA AND NEW ZEALAND, Hall's Printery, Prahran, Australia, 1962.

_(Norway) N. E. Carlberg, BEGINNING NORWEGIAN RESEARCH, Carlberg Press, Anaheim, CA, 1991; F. Smith and F. A. Thomsen, GENEALOGICAL GUIDEBOOK AND ATLAS OF NORWAY, The Authors, Salt Lake City, UT, 1983; M. A. Wellauer, TRACING YOUR NORWEGIAN ROOTS, The Author, Milwaukee, WI, 1979; M. N. Longeteig, ROOTS NORWEGIAN STYLE, The Author, Craigmont, ID, 1979; E. Poulsen and G. P. Korvallis, THE SCANDI-NAVIAN GENEALOGICAL HELPER, Everton Publishers, Logan, UT, 1969-72, 3 volumes.

_(Poland) D. M. Schlyter, ESSENTIALS IN POLISH GENEAL-OGICAL RESEARCH, Polish Genealogical Society of America, Chicago, IL, 1993; R. Chorzempa, POLISH ROOTS, Genealogical Publishing Co., Baltimore, MD, 1993; J. W. Hoskins, POLISH GENEALOGY AND HERALDRY, Library of Congress, Washington, DC, 1987; J. O. R. Nuthack and A. Goertz, translators, GENEALOGICAL GUIDE TO GERMAN ANCESTORS FROM EAST GERMANY AND EASTERN EUROPE, Verlag Degener, Neustadt/Aisch, West Germany, 1984; J. and L. Gnacinski, POLISH AND PROUD, TRACING YOUR POLISH ANCESTRY, Janlen Enterprises, West Allis, WI, 1979; M. A. Wellauer, TRACING YOUR POLISH ROOTS, The Author, Milwaukee, WI, 1979.

_(Portugal) A. de Mattos, MANUAL DE GENEALOGIA PORTU-GUESE, Fernando Machado, Porto, Portugal, 1943.

_(South Africa) R. T. J. Lombard, HANDBOOK FOR GENEALOGI-CAL RESEARCH IN SOUTH AFRICA, Human Sciences Research Council, Pretoria, South Africa, 1977.

_(Spain) G. R. Ryskamp, TRACING YOUR HISPANIC HERITAGE, Hispanic Family History Research, Riverside, CA, 1984; L. De Platt, GENEALOGICAL-HISTORICAL GUIDE TO LATIN AMERICA, Gale Research Co., Detroit, MI, 1978.

_(Sweden) N. E. Carlberg, BEGINNING SWEDISH RESEARCH, Carlberg Press, Anaheim, CA, 1989; C.-E. Johansson, CRADLED IN SWEDEN, Everton Publishers, Logan, UT, 1972; E. M. and G. P.

Korvallis, THE SCANDINAVIAN GENEALOGICAL HELPER, Everton Publishers, Logan, UT, 1969-72, 3 volumes; F. A. Thomsen, GENEALOGICAL GUIDEBOOK AND ATLAS OF SWEDEN, Thomsen's, Bountiful, UT, 1987.
_(Switzerland) J. H. Suess, HANDY GUIDE TO SWISS GENEALOGICAL RECORDS, Everton Publishers, Logan, UT, 1980; M. A. Wellauer, TRACING YOUR SWISS ROOTS, The Author, Milwaukee, WI, 1979; A. Nielsen, SWISS GENEALOGICAL RESEARCH, Donning Co., Virginia Beach, VA, 1979.
_(Uruguay) J. A. Apolant, GENESIS DE LA FAMILIA URUGUAYA, Imprenta Vinaak, Montevideo, Uruguay, 1975.
_(USSR) K. B. Mehr and D. M. Schlyter, SOURCES FOR GENEA-LOGICAL RESEARCH IN THE SOVIET UNION, Genun, Buffalo Grove, IL, 1983.
_(Wales) Family History Society of Wales, WELSH FAMILY HIS-TORY, The Society, Aberystwyth, Wales, 1993; G. K. S. Hamilton-Edwards, IN SEARCH OF WELSH ANCESTRY, Genealogical Publishing Co., Baltimore, MD, 1986; D. E. Gardner and F. Smith, GENEALOGICAL RESEARCH IN ENGLAND AND WALES, Bookcraft, Salt Lake City, UT, 1956-64, 3 volumes.

Once you have used all possible US records to locate the exact foreign place of origin of your ancestor, then have read the proper sections in Cerny-Elliott (3rd paragraph, this section), then have read the appropriate research guide or outline (3rd paragraph, this section), then have read a good guidebook (just above), you will be well versed in the sources available and the techniques. You should then proceed to your nearest Family History Center where you can use the International Gene-alogy Index, and the surname and locality sections of the Family History Library Catalog, to select records to order and examine. You may need to get help on the language from a local expert, such as a university professor or a person known to the staff of the Family History Center. If you need to continue your research after this, you can follow the instruc-tions and procedures recommended in the guide materials you have read.

64. Fraternal and occupational organizations

Fraternal organi-zations have a long history in the thirteen colonies and the US which was formed from them. The organizations are groups of people with some common benevolent, service, educational, religious, political, financial, commercial, ethnic, honorary, or social interest which unifies and motivates their activities. The records of these organizations sometimes contain genealogical information such as birth date, birth place, marital data, names of parents, biographical material, and death and burial information. Some of the major organizations of this sort are as follows. These have been selected because they all have sizable memberships and were organized before 1900. The date of establishment and the approximate number of members in thousands (K) are given in parentheses.

_American Federation of Labor (1881), now combined with Congress of Industrial Organizations, 815 16th St., NW, Washington, DC 20006. (15,000K)

_Athletic Union of the US, Amateur (1888), 3400 W. 86th St., Indianapolis, IN 46268. (235K)

_American Bible Society (1816), 1865 Broadway, New York, NY 10023. (500K)

_B'nai B'rith (1843), 1640 Rhode Island Ave., NW, Washington, DC 20036. (500K)

_Boy's Clubs of America (1860), 771 First Ave., New York, NY 10017. (1200K)

_Eagles, Fraternal Order of (1898), 12660 West Capitol Dr., Brookfield, WI 53055. (1100K)

_Eastern Star, Order of (1876), 1618 New Hampshire Ave., Washington, DC 20009. (3000K)

_Elks, Benevolent and Protective Order of (1868), 2750 N. Lakeview Ave., Chicago, IL 60614. (1500K)

_Elks, Improved Benevolent Protective Order (1898), 1522 N. 16th St., Philadelphia, PA 19121. (450K)

_Geographical Society, National (1888), 1145 17th St., NW, Washington, DC 20036. (10,000K)

_Gideons International (1899), 2900 Lebanon Rd., Nashville, TN 37214. (140K)

_Hebrew Immigrant Aid Society (1884), 200 Park Ave., S, New York, NY 10003. (15K)

_Jewish Women, National Council of (1893), 53 W. 23rd St., New York, NY 10010. (100K)

_Knights of Columbus (1882), One Columbus Plaza, New Haven, CT 06507. (1400K)

_Knights Templar, Grand Encampment of the USA (1816), 14 E. Jackson Blvd., Chicago, IL 60604. (300K) A Masonic organization.

_Masonic Relief Association of US and Canada (1885), 32613 Seidel Dr., Burlington, WI 53105. (15K)

_Masons, Ancient and Accepted Scottish Rite, Northern Jurisdiction Supreme Council 33° (1813), 33 Marrett Rd., Lexington, MA 02173. (436K)

_Masons, Ancient and Accepted Scottish Rite, Southern Jurisdiction, Supreme Council (1801), 1733 16th St., NW, Washington, DC 20009. (593K)

_Masons, Royal Arch, General Grant Chapter (1797), 1084 New Circle Rd., NE, Lexington, KY 40505. (299K)

_Moose, Loyal Order of (1888), Mooseheart, IL 60539. (1800K)

_Needlework Guild of America (1885), 1007 B St., Southampton, PA 18966. (400K)

_Norway, Sons of (1895), 1455 W. Lake St., Minneapolis, MN 55408. (84K)

_Odd Fellows, Independent Order of (1819), 422 N. Trade St., Winston-Salem, NC 27101. (1200K)

_Parents and Teachers, National Congress of (1897), 700 N. Rush St., Chicago, IL 60611. (7700K)

_PEO Sisterhood (1869), 3700 Grand Ave., Des Moines, IA 50312. (240K)

_Red Cross, American National (1881), 18th and D Sts., NW, Washington, DC 20006. (1200K)

_Rifle Association of America, National (1871), 1600 Rhode Island Ave., NW, Washington, DC 20036. (3000K)

_Rosicrucian Fraternity (1861), Beverly Hall, Quakertown, PA 18951.

_Salvation Army (1880), 120 W. 14th St., New York, NY 10011. (362K)

_Shrine, Imperial Council of the Ancient And Arabic Order of Nobles of the Mystic (1872), 323 N. Michigan Ave., Chicago, IL 60601. (799K) A Masonic organization.

_Sierra Club (1892), 730 Polk St., San Francisco, CA 94109. (440K)

_Turners, American (1848), 1550 Clinton Ave., N. Rochester, NY 14621. (17K)

_William Penn Association (1886), 709 Brighton Rd., Pittsburgh, PA 15233. (90K)

_Women's Christian Temperance Union, National (1874), 1730 Chicago Ave., Evanston, IL 60201. (200K)

_Women's Clubs, General Federation of (1890), 1734 N St., NW, Washington, DC 20036. (621K)

_Woodmen of America, Modern (1883), 1710 First Ave., Rock Island, IL 61201. (600K)

_Woodmen of the World (1890), 1450 Speer Blvd., Denver, CO 80204. (30K)

_Young Men's Christian Association of the USA (1851), 101 N. Wacker Dr., Chicago, IL 60606. (13,000K)

_Young Women's Christian Association of the USA (1858), 726 Broadway, New York, NY 10003. (2,400K)

_Zionist Organization of America (1897), 4 E. 34th St., New York, NY 10016. (140K)

Details on these and many other fraternal societies, along with addresses, will be found in:

_A. J. Schmidt, FRATERNAL ORGANIZATIONS, Greenwood Press, Westport, CT, 1980.

_THE WORLD ALMANAC, Newspaper Enterprise Association, New York, NY, latest annual edition.

_ENCYCLOPEDIA OF ASSOCIATIONS, Gale Research Co., Detroit, MI, latest edition.

Occupational and/or professional organizations are also good possibilities for ancestor information. Your progenitor may have had a profession or occupation which was represented by an association or society. Their records may contain valuable vital data and biographical information. Among the larger and earlier of these organizations are the following. The date of beginning of the group and the number of present members in thousands (K) are given in parentheses.

_Accountants, American Institute of Certified Public (1887), 1211 Ave. of the Americas, New York, NY 10036. (75K)

_Architects, American Institute of (1857), 1735 New York Ave., NW, Washington, DC 20006. (51K)

_Bar Association, American (1878), 750 N. Lake Shore Dr., Chicago, IL 60611. (360K)

_Chemical Society, American (1876), 1155 16th St., Washington, DC 20036. (135K)

_Civil Engineers, American Society of (1852), 345 E. 47th St., New York, NY 10017. (104K)

_Dental Association, American (1859), 211 E. Chicago Ave., Chicago, IL 60611. (136K)

_Economic Association, American (1885), 1313 21st Ave. S., Nashville, TN 37212. (20K)

_Education Association, National (1857), 1201 16th St., NW, Washington, DC 20036. (1900K)

_Electrical and Electronics Engineers, Institute of (1884), 345 E. 42nd St., New York, NY 10017. (300K)

_Forestry Association, American (1875), 1516 P St., NW, Washington, DC 20005. (30K)

_Geological Society of America (1888), 3300 Penrose Place, Boulder, CO 80301. (17K)

_Health, Physical Education, and Recreation, American Alliance for (1885), 1900 Association Dr., Reston, VA 22091. (50K)

_Historical Association, American (1884), 400 A St., SE, Washington, DC 20003. (14K)

_Library Association, American (1876), 50 E. Huron St., Chicago, IL 60611. (45K)

_Life Underwriters, National Association of (1890), 1922 F St., NW, Washington, DC 20006. (135K)

_Mathematical Society, American (1888), 201 Charles St., Providence, RI 02904. (23K)

_Mechanical Engineers, American Society of (1880), 345 E. 47th St., New York, NY 10017. (120K)

_Medical Association, American (1847), 535 N. Dearborn St., Chicago, IL 60610. (290K)

_Microbiology, American Society for (1899), 1913 Eye St., NW, Washington, DC 20006. (35K)

_Mining, Metallurgical, and Petroleum Engineers, American Institute of (1871), 345 E. 47th St., New York, NY 10017. (60K)

_Modern Language Association of America (1883), 10 Astor Pl., New York, NY 10003. (28K)

_Musicians, American Federation of (1896), 1500 Broadway, New York, NY 10036. (28K)

_Naval Architects and Marine Engineers, Society of (1893), 74 Trinity Pl., New York, NY 10006. (10K)

_Nurses Association, American (1896), 2420 Pershing Rd., Kansas City, MO 64108. (250K)

_Pharmaceutical Association, American (1852), 2215 Constitution Ave., NW, Washington, DC 20037. (50K)

_Photographers of America, Professional (1880), 1090 Executive Way, Des Plaines, IL 60018. (15K)

_Physical Society, American (1899), 335 E. 45th St., New York, NY 10017. (29K)

_Political and Social Science, American Academy of (1889), 3937 Chestnut St., Philadelphia, PA 19104. (10K)

_Psychological Association, American (1892), 1200 17th St., NW, Washington, DC 20036. (60K)

_School Administrators, American Association of (1865), 1801 N. Moore St., Arlington, VA 22209. (19K)

_Science, American Association for the Advancement of (1848), 1333 H St., NW, Washington, DC 20005. (132K)

_University Women, American Association of (1882), 2401 Virginia Ave., NW, Washington, DC 20037. (140K)

_Veterinary Medical Association, American (1863), 930 N. Meachan Rd., Schaumburg, IL 60172. (43K)

_Water Works Association, American (1881), 6666 W. Quincy Ave., Denver, CO 80235. (37K)

In addition to these national organizations, it is well to investigate your forebear's membership in regional, state, and local occupational and professional organizations. It is often the case that these groups will have richer records than their national counterparts. Many other occupational and professional organizations are listed in this volume:

_ENCYCLOPEDIA OF ASSOCIATIONS, Gale Research Co., Detroit, MI, latest edition.

If your ancestor was a member of a specialized occupation or a profession, it is possible that there was an organization to which he/she belonged. This book is the place to look in order to find such organizations.

---

65. Gazetteers

Gazetteers are of extraordinary assistance to genealogists because they list place names in alphabetical order and give their exact locations. Among the place names listed may be found hamlets, settlements, townships, towns, districts, counties, rivers, streams, creeks, ponds, lakes, canals, valleys, hills, and mountains. Sometimes population data, post offices, business directories, and maps are included. Place names are constantly occurring in all types of genealogical records, and it is important to know precisely where they are so that you can locate your ancestor. To find place names, use:

_F..R. Abate, editor, OMNI GAZETTEER OF THE USA, Omnigraphics, Detroit, MI, 1991.

_THE COLUMBIA LIPPINCOTT GAZETTEER OF THE WORLD, Columbia University Press, New York, NY, latest edition.

_BULLINGER'S POSTAL AND SHIPPERS GUIDE FOR THE US AND CANADA, Bullinger's Guides, Westwood, NJ, annual since 1871. Use the guide nearest to your ancestor's time.

_K. B. Harder, editor, ILLUSTRATED DICTIONARY OF PLACE NAMES, US AND CANADA, Van Nostrand Reinhold Co., New York, NY, 1976.

_GEOGRAPHIC NAMES ALPHABETICAL FINDING LIST, National Cartographic Information Center, US Geological Survey, Washington, DC, 1982-.

_G. R. Stewart, AMERICAN PLACE NAMES, Oxford University Press, New York, NY, 1970.

_H. Gannett, THE ORIGIN OF CERTAIN PLACE NAMES IN THE US, 1906, reprinted by Genealogical Publishing Co., Baltimore, MD, 1977.

_A. H. Holt, AMERICAN PLACE NAMES, 1938, reprinted by Gale Research Co., Detroit, MI, 1969.

There are a number of older gazetteers which are often of help with regard to places which no longer exist or whose names have been changed. In order of date, these are:

_J. Scott, THE US GAZETTEER, F. and R. Bailey, Philadelphia, PA, 1795.

_J. Morse, THE AMERICAN GAZETTEER, Hall, Thomas, and Andrews, Boston, MA, 1797.

_LIST OF POST OFFICES IN THE US, US Post Office, Washington, DC, 1803-81.

_J. and R. C. Morse, THE TRAVELLER'S GUIDE OR POCKET GAZETTEER OF THE US, Wadsworth, New Haven, CT, 1826.

_TABLE OF POST OFFICES IN THE US, 1846, US Post Office, Washington, DC, 1846.

_J. Hayward, A GAZETTEER OF THE USA, Case, Tiffany, and Co., Hartford, CT, 1853.

_FANNING'S ILLUSTRATED GAZETTEER OF THE US, Ensign, Bridgman, and Fanning, New York, NY, 1855.

_L. de Colange, THE NATIONAL GAZETTEER, A GEOGRAPHICAL DICTIONARY OF THE US, Hamilton, Adams, and Co., London, England, 1884.

In addition to national gazetteers, there are gazetteers of individual states. These are often quite useful since they tend to carry more detailed information. These state gazetteers, along with other national gazetteers are listed in:

_R. E. Grim, HISTORICAL GEOGRAPHY OF THE US, A GUIDE TO INFORMATION SOURCES, Gale Research Co., Detroit, MI, 1982.

_R. B. Sealock and others, BIBLIOGRAPHY OF PLACE-NAME LITERATURE, US AND CANADA, American Library Association, Chicago, IL, 1982.

_C. S. Brown, compiler, GAZETTEERS AND PLACE-NAME REFERENCES IN STATES AND TERRITORIES OF THE US, Genealogical Library, Salt Lake City, UT, 1985.

_P. W. Filby, AMERICAN AND BRITISH GENEALOGY AND
HERALDRY, New England Historical Genealogical Society, Boston,
MA, 1983, with periodic supplements,
Another way to identify and locate state gazetteers is to inquire at the
appropriate state libraries and to check the locality index at the nearest
Family History Center.

66. Genealogical book sources

There are numerous organizations which sell and/or publish genealogical books, pamphlets, microforms, record forms, maps, and supplies. Among the more prominent ones are those which follow. Send them an SASE, ask to be placed on their mailing lists, and request a catalog. Or if you are seeking a certain book, ask if they can supply it.

_A Press, PO Box 8796, Greenville, SC 29604.

_Accelerated Indexing Systems, 40 North Hwy. 89, North Salt Lake City,
UT 84054.

_Alice's Ancestral Nostalgia, 145 West, 200 North, #31, Salt Lake City,
UT 84103.

_Ancestors Unlimited, Intl., #226-1450 Johnston Rd., White Rock BC
V4B E59.

_Ancestral Genealogical Endexing Schedules, Inc., PO Box 2127, Salt
Lake City, UT 84110.

_American Genealogical Lending Library, and Precision Indexing, PO
Box 329, Bountiful, UT 84011.

_American Heritage Publishing, 1500 North Kansas Ave., Marceline,
MO 64658.

_Ancestree Genealogical Services, 204 Willowick Ave., Temple Terrace,
FL 33617.

_Ancestree House, PO Box 1121, Santa Maria, CA 93456.

_Ancestry Publishing, PO Box 476, Salt Lake City, UT 84110.

_Automated Archives, 1160 South State St., Orem, UT 84058.

_Banner Press, PO Box 20180, Birmingham, AL 35216.

_Barnett's Family Tree Bookstore, 1001 West Loop, North, Houston,
TX 77055.

_The Book House, Inc., 208 W. Chicago St., Jonesville, MI 49250.

_Boyd Publishing Co., PO Box 367, Milledgeville, GA 31061.

_Carl Boyer 3rd, PO Box 333, Newhall CA 91322.

_Clearfield Press, 200 E. Eager St., Baltimore, MD 21202.

_Closson Press, 1935 Sampson Dr., Apollo, PA 15613.

_Community Newscenter, Frandor Shopping Center, Lansing, MI 48912.

_The Corner Shelf, 102-B North Main St., Culpeper, VA 22701.

_Danbury House, PO Box 253, Oakland, ME 04963.

_Deseret Book Co., 2150 West 1500 South, Salt Lake City, UT 84101.

_E-D Book Co., 6510 Camino Venturosa, Goleta, CA 93117.

_Everton Publishers, PO Box 368, Logan, UT 84321.

_Family History World, PO Box 22045, Salt Lake City, UT 84122.

_Family Line Publications, Rear 63 E. Main St., Westminster, MD 21157.

_Fish's, 20 First St., Spreckels, CA 93962.

_Friends of the National Archives, 1557 St. Joseph Ave., East Point, GA 30344.

_The Friends' Shop, Public Library, 800 Vine St., Cincinnati, OH 45202.

_Frontier Press, 15 Quintana Dr., Galveston, TX 77554.

_Gale Research Co., 835 Penobscot Bldg., Detroit, MI 48226.

_Gateway Press, 1001 N. Calvert St., Baltimore, MD 21202.

_Genealogical Books In Print, 6818 Lois Dr., Springfield, VA 22150.

_Genealogical Publishing Co., 1001 N. Calvert St., Baltimore, MD 21202.

_Genealogical Sources, Unltd., 407 Ascot Ct., Knoxville, TN 37923.

_Genealogy Books & Consultation, 1217 Oakdale, Houston, TX 77004.

_Genealogy Center, 8213 Drew St., Englewood, FL 34224

_Genealogy Book Store, 1217 Oakdale, Houston, TX 77004.

_Genealogy Unlimited, 1367 West, 400 North, Orem, UT 84057..

_Gibbs Publishing Co., Q-359, Rd. 15, Napoleon, OH 43545.

_Goodspeed's Book Shop, 7 Beacon St., Boston, MA 02108.

_Heart of the Lakes Publishers, PO Box 299, Interlaken, NY 14847.

_Hearthstone Bookshop, 5735-A Telegraph Rd., Alexandria, VA 22303.

_Heritage Books, 1540-E Pointer Ridge Place, Suite 300, Bowie, MD 20716.

_Heritage Papers, PO Box 7776, Danielsville, GA 30604.

_Higginson Book Company, PO Box 778, Salem, MA 01970.

_History House, PO Box 30093, Raleigh, NC 27622.

_Holbrook Research Institute, Oxford, MA 01540.

_Brent H. Holcomb, PO Box 21766, Columbia, SC 29221.

_Hudson Heritage Books, 2807 Cedar Park Blvd., Ft. Worth, TX 76118.

_Hughes Ink, PO Box 1902, Irmo, SC 29063.

_Iberian Publishing Co., 548 Cedar Creek Dr., Athens, GA 30605.

_Ingmire Publications, 211 Downshire, San Antonio, TX 78216.

_Jensen Publications, PO Box 700, Pleasant Grove, UT 84062.

_Jonathan Sheppard Books, PO Box 2020, Empire State Plaza Station, Albany, NY 12220.

_The Learning Place, PO Box 3261, Beaumont, CA 92223.

_McDowell Publications, Route 4, Box 314, Utica, KY 42376.

_Diane Meilstrup Enterprises, 1711 Greenmeadow Ave., Tustin, CA 92680.

_The Memorabilia Corner, 1312 McKinley Ave., Norman, OK 73072.
_Mountain Press, PO Box 400, Signal Mountain, TN 37377.
_Museum of East TN History Bookshop, East TN Historical Society, 600 Market St., Knoxville, TN 37902.
_New Life Book Ministry, 384 Erbes Rd., Thousand Oaks, CA 91362.
_O'Brien's Book Store, 201 North Main, Sand Springs, OK 74063.
_Old Somersett House, PO Box 308, Prince George, VA 23875.
_Origins, 4327 Milton Ave., Janesville, WI 53546.
_Parker River Researchers, PO Box 86, Newburyport, MA 01950.
_Pathfinders, 1601 Bunker Hill Rd., Pueblo, CO 81001.
_Picton Press, PO Box 1111, Camden, ME 04843.
_Platte Valley Books, PO Box 271, Hastings, NE 68901.
_The Quest, 7484 Indian Rd., Temperance, MI 48182.
_Quintin Publications, 28 Felsmere Ave., Pawtucket, RI 02861.
_Reprint Company Publishers, PO Box 5401, Spartanburg, SC 29304.
_Researcher's Bookshelf, PO Box 40, Orting, WA 98360.
_Roots and Branches, 120 N. Salem St., Apex, NCC 27502.
_Root of It All, PO Box 404, Wildomar, CA 92395.
_Byron Sistler and Associates, 1712 Natchez Trace, Nashville, TN 37212.
_Sounds of Zion, 6973 South 300 West, Midvale, UT 84047.
_Southern Historical Press, PO Box 1267, Greenville, SC 29602.
_Southwest PA Genealogical Services, PO Box 253, Laughlintown, PA 15655.
_Stagecoach Library, 1840 S. Wolcott Ct., Denver, CO 80219.
_Stemmons Publishing, PO Box 612, West Jordan, UT 84084.
_Storbeck's Books, 16515 Dane Ct., Brookfield, WI 53005.
_Travel Genie, 620 West Lincolnway, Ames, IA 50010.
_Tuttle Antiquarian Books, PO Box 541, Rutland, VT 05702.
_Virginia Book Co., PO Box 431, Berryville, VA 22611.
_The Virginia Tree, 10600 Lilac Place, Silver Spring, MD 20903.
_Maralyn A. Wellauer, 3239 N. 58th St., Milwaukee, WI 53216.
_Ye Olde Genealogie Shoppe and Summit Publications, PO Box 39128, Indianapolis, IN 46239.

Two sets of books with unusually large listings of genealogical and local history books are the following. The second set gives places where the books may be purchased along with prices.
_P. W. Filby, AMERICAN AND BRITISH GENEALOGY AND HERALDRY, New England Historic Genealogy Society, Boston, MA, 1982, with supplements. Be sure to look at all supplements.

_N. Schreiner-Yantis, GENEALOGICAL AND LOCAL HISTORY BOOKS IN PRINT, The Compiler, Springfield, VA, 1975, with many later editions and supplements. Be sure to look at all of them.

67. Genealogical columns

In practically every city, county, and town in the US, there live genealogical searchers whose ancestors also lived there. Because of their presence in the location, they often have an excellent grasp of the records and the history of the area. If this is an area in which your ancestor lived, and if these resident genealogists could be contacted, they could probably be of help to you in your search. One of the best ways to make these contacts is to write a letter to the local newspaper and ask readers to respond. A number of newspapers carry a genealogical column, and many of these columns accept inquiries. These inquiries are generally free and readers of the column are invited to answer if they have pertinent information. A detailed listing of current newspapers in the US is provided in:

_GALE DIRECTORY OF PUBLICATIONS, Gale Research Co., Detroit, MI, latest annual issue.

And a compilation of newspapers which carry genealogical columns is available in:

_A. C. Milner, NEWSPAPER GENEALOGICAL COLUMN DIREC-TORY, Heritage Books, Bowie, MD, latest edition.

68. Genealogical compilations

Many individuals and groups have contributed greatly to genealogical research by gathering together or compiling genealogies. These compilations exist in many forms: manuscripts, card files, files of folders, typescripts, microfiche, and microfilm. Many have been copied by photocopying and microfilming. The major places in which these records or copies of them will be found are local libraries, state libraries, state archives, university libraries, large genealogical libraries, and the Family History Library. The holdings of the Family HIstory Library are obtainable through its numerous branch Family History Centers, as was detailed in a previous section. In all these repositories, the genealogical compilations may be found by looking in the manuscript and the publications catalogs under the pertinent localities (state, county, town), and especially under the heading GENEALOGY, both within the locality listings and as a separate independent major heading. These compilations are well worth locating because they can save you considerable time if they contain a genealogical sketch on one or more of your family lines.

However, you need to be warned, because the data cannot always be trusted. This means that all information should be verified in original records (or microfilm copies of the original records) before you add the material to your records.

The types of genealogical compilations that you should search for include the following. Materials of all these sorts are usually available for every state, and many of them may be located for counties and towns.

_Collections gathered by individuals (such as the Barbour Collection for CT, the Corbin Collection for MA, the Baldwin Collection for OH).

_Collections of particular record types (Bible, birth, cemetery, church, death, marriage, military, newspaper, probate, will).

_Collections from major genealogical journals (such as the New England Historical and Genealogical Journal, the William and Mary Quarterly, the SC Historical and Genealogical Magazine).

_Collections of members records of special organizations or records compiled by societies (such as the Daughters of the American Revolution, the Colonial Dames, the Holland Society).

_Collections for certain groups (such as Protestant immigrants to SC, Highland Scots of NC, MO Ozark families).

_Collections for given localities (such as Pioneers of Piscataqua Valley, Essex County Collection, Surnames of Anoka County, MN).

Please remember that these collections may be both published and non-published (manuscripts). You must be extremely careful not to overlook the latter. It is also well to recall that local histories (region, county, city, town) often have genealogical sections.

69. Genealogical periodicals　　A few national, and many state, county, regional, city, town and private genealogical associations and several individuals publish journals, pamphlets, reports, or newsletters on a regular schedule. These publications contain genealogies, local histories, county records, town records, cemetery records, Bible records, book reviews, research procedures, information on record repositories, church registers, and local information of many types. You can also publish queries in most of these journals. If your ancestor lived in one or more of these places, it is a good thing for you to subscribe to the local publications. To find these periodicals, take a look in:

__E. P. Bentley, THE GENEALOGIST'S ADDRESS BOOK, Genealogical Publishing Co., Baltimore, MD, latest edition.

_M. K. Meyer, DIRECTORY OF GENEALOGICAL SOCIETIES IN THE US, The Author, Mt. Airy, MD, latest edition.
_V. N. Chambers, editor, THE GENEALOGICAL HELPER, Everton Publishers, Logan, UT, latest May-June issue.
_J. Konrad, DIRECTORY OF GENEALOGICAL PERIODICALS, Summit Publications, Munroe Falls, OH, latest edition.
_A. Eichholz, ANCESTRY'S REDBOOK, Ancestry Publishing, Salt Lake City, UT, 1992.

Two widely-circulated general genealogical magazines are recommended to you. You should subscribe to or at least read one or both of them:
_HERITAGE QUEST, PO Box 329, Bountiful, UT 84011.
_THE GENEALOGICAL HELPER, Everton Publishers, PO Box 368, Logan, UT 84321.
These publications carry articles on research procedures, record repositories, news of meetings, activities of societies, ads of researchers, book reviews, queries, but seldom contain detailed genealogical data or records. Among the most important national periodicals are:
_THE AMERICAN GENEALOGIST, 128 Massasoit Dr., Warwick, RI 02888.
_GENEALOGICAL JOURNAL, PO Box 1144, Salt Lake City, UT 84110.
_NATIONAL GENEALOGICAL SOCIETY QUARTERLY, 4527 17th Street North, Arlington, VA 22207.
_THE AMERICAN GENEALOGIST, 1232 39th Street, Des Moines, IA 50311.
Practically every state has a good genealogical journal devoted to family history. Among the older (before 1960) and more notable ones are:
_NEW ENGLAND HISTORICAL AND GENEALOGICAL REGISTER, New England Historic Genealogical Society, 101 Newbury St., Boston, MA 02116.
_NY GENEALOGICAL AND BIOGRAPHICAL RECORD, NY Genealogical and Biographical Society, 122 E. 58th St., New York, NY 10022.
_PA GENEALOGICAL MAGAZINE, Genealogical Society of PA, 1300 Locust St., Philadelphia, PA 19107.
_GENEALOGICAL MAGAZINE OF NJ, Genealogical Society of NJ, New Brunswick, NJ 08903.
_DETROIT SOCIETY FOR GENEALOGICAL RESEARCH MAGAZINE, Detroit Society for Genealogical Research, 5201 Woodward Ave., Detroit, MI 48202.

_CO GENEALOGIST, CO Genealogical Society, PO Box 9671, Denver, CO 80209.

_ANSEARCHIN' NEWS, TN Genealogical Society, PO Box 12124, Memphis, TN 38112.

_LA GENEALOGICAL REGISTER, LA Genealogical and Historical Society, PO Box 3454, Baton Rouge, LA 70821.

_WI STATE GENEALOGICAL SOCIETY NEWSLETTER, WI State Genealogical Society, 5049 La Crosse Lane, Madison, WI 53705.

_NC GENEALOGY, W. P. Johnson, PO Box 1770, Raleigh, NC 27602.

_MS GENEALOGICAL EXCHANGE, PO Box 434, Forest, MS 39074.

_VA GENEALOGIST, J. F. Dorman, PO Box 4883, Washington, DC 20008.

_ID GENEALOGICAL SOCIETY QUARTERLY, Idaho Genealogical Society, 325 W. State St., Boise, ID 83702.

_KY GENEALOGIST, J. R. Bentley, 3621 Brownsboro Rd., Louisville, KY 40207.

_MD AND DE GENEALOGIST, R. B. Clark, Jr., PO Box 352, St. Michaels, MD 21663.

_THE TREESEARCHER, KS Genealogical Society, PO Box 103, Dodge City, KS 67801.

Many more journals for many more states, regions, counties, cities, and towns, as well as magazines dedicated to special groups (such as Huguenots or Germans from Russia) are being published. They can be identified by using the reference works listed in the first paragraph. The best places to find them are in pertinent state libraries, large genealogical libraries, appropriate local libraries, and the Family History Library (access through the Family History Centers). Many of them have extensive indexes which will simplify your use of them, so don't fail to seek out these indexes.

70. Genealogical periodical indexes

Numerous periodicals dealing with genealogical information are published in the US. In them thousands of names and data from many states, counties, cities, and towns are presented. Indexes are available for a large number of these publications. In some of these indexes, surnames are listed. In others, surnames are not listed, but you can look for the counties, cities, and towns in which your forebears lived, and then you can go to the referenced articles. In addition to these indexes for individual journals, there are collective indexes which list the contents of many genealogical magazines. An overall index is available for the period 1847-1985, and annual indexes are available from 1986 to the present.

_For periodicals 1847-1985, then annually 1986-present, consult Allen County Public Library Foundation, PERIODICAL SOURCE INDEX, The Foundation, Fort Wayne, IN, 1986-

The indexes should be consulted for your ancestors and for your ancestors' localities (states, counties, cities, towns) to see if data on them can be found. Please recognize that the dates refer to the years when the periodicals were published, not to years relating to the genealogical information.

71. Genealogical publications

For many years, organizations and individuals have been copying and publishing genealogical records of practically every type. This activity has been increasing in recent years such that a large number of volumes containing records is now available. Among the most widely published records are Bible, church, cemetery, census, colonial, immigration, military, newspaper, vital statistics (birth, death, marriage), and will. However, numerous others have been and are being printed. The four main forms in which records are published are books, CDROMs, journals, microfiche, and microfilms. Journals have been discussed in this Handbook in separate sections entitled Genealogical periodicals and Genealogical periodical indexes. CDROMs have also been treated in a separate section.

This section calls your attention to the thousands of books, microfiche, and microfilms which contain copies of genealogical records. A bit of caution is called for because errors are often made in copying records, so it is important that you use the convenient copied materials to lead you to the originals, which you must not fail to check. The many publications will be found listed in:

_THE FAMILY HISTORY LIBRARY CATALOG, LOCALITY SECTION AND SUBJECT SECTION, Family History Library, Salt Lake City, UT, and Family History Centers. Look under US, the state, the county, the city, and the town in the Locality Section, and under the subject in the Subject Section.

_P. W. Filby, AMERICAN AND BRITISH GENEALOGY AND HERALDRY, New England Historic Genealogical Society, Boston, MA, 1983, and supplements. Be sure and look at all supplements.

_N. Schreiner-Yantis, GENEALOGICAL AND LOCAL HISTORY BOOKS IN PRINT, The Compiler, Springfield, Va, 1975, with later editions and supplements. Be sure to look at them all.

_Library of Congress, MARVEL CATALOG, Washington, DC, accessible through Internet. Lists holdings of the Library of Congress.

In addition to searching the above reference works, you should look in the following journals. They review practically all new genealogical books, CDROMs, microfiche, and microfilms which are published. Since they come out several times per year, their listings tend to be up to date.

_THE GENEALOGICAL HELPER, Everton Publishers, PO Box 368, Logan, UT 84321.

_NATIONAL GENEALOGICAL SOCIETY QUARTERLY, 4527 17th Street North, Arlington, VA 22207.

The above reference books and the two journals will be found in state libraries, large genealogical libraries, numerous smaller genealogical libraries, and many city libraries. The publications to which they refer can be located in the Family History Library, other large genealogical libraries, state libraries, and pertinent local libraries (county, city, town).

72. Genealogical societies

There are hundreds of genealogical societies in the US and many in foreign countries. The US societies include ones for the entire country, almost all states, most regions, many counties, most large cities, and numerous towns. The members of many of these societies are residents who are interested in the genealogical history of the area and non-residents who had one or more ancestors in the area at some time in the past. Since they can therefore be of a great deal of help to other persons who have had ancestors in the locality, it is a good idea for you to consider joining the appropriate societies. They are listed in the following publications along with addresses:

_E. P. Bentley, THE GENEALOGIST'S ADDRESS BOOK, Genealogical Publishing Co., Baltimore, MD,. latest edition.

_M. K. Meyer, DIRECTORY OF GENEALOGICAL SOCIETIES IN THE USA AND CANADA, The Author, Mt. Airy, MD, latest edition.

_THE GENEALOGICAL HELPER, Everton Publishers, Logan, UT, latest July-Aug issue.

_A. Eichholz, ANCESTRY'S REDBOOK, Ancestry Publishing, Salt Lake City, UT, 1992.

These works can be located in large genealogical libraries, many smaller genealogical libraries, and state libraries.

73. German genealogy

When genealogists refer to Germany, they generally mean the area making up the German Empire in 1871-1918. This is in accordance with a standard set many years ago by the Family History Library. The area included the modern Federal Republic of Germany, small portions of east-central France, eastern Belgium, western Czechoslovakia, and southern Denmark; northern, west-central, and southwestern Poland; and an area now in western Russia. In 962, the several sizable duchies which made up Germany became a major portion of the Holy Roman Empire which loosely held them together and sporadically ruled over them. By about 1200, the duchies had broken up into numerous small and several large semi-independent states and some free cities. The emperor of the Holy Roman Empire was elected by the leaders of the larger states. The Empire persisted until 1806. During the many years 1200-1806, the German states formed various groupings, coalesced, divided, rearranged, and warred among themselves. Each state had its own government, laws, and its own archives, and kept and stored its own records. The records remain today in archives in or near the areas of these many states.

In 1517, Luther disrupted the major binding force of the Holy Roman Empire, namely its religion, by starting the Protestant Reformation. The result was well over a century of Catholic-Protestant warfare, which was further complicated by the coming into Germany of a second Protestant force, the Reformed Church (Calvin). In 1555, a temporary peace resulted with each state determining the religion of its people. Following this, the Catholic Counter-Reformation regained many areas during the period 1555-1600. The warfare exploded in the thirty Years War (1618-48) which left Germany devastated, with one third of its population dead, and the remainder destitute, starving, and homeless. Germany at the end of the war consisted of a loose confederation of a large number of states. During this time, Catholic parish registers were mandated (1545-63), and Lutheran parish records started in southwest Germany (1531), gradually spreading elsewhere. Over the next 140 years (1648-1788), the state of Prussia gathered strength and increasingly threatened Austria which had dominated the Empire. In 1805, Napoleon invaded Austria, defeated the Austrians, then in 1806 invaded and defeated Prussia. These events marked the end of the Holy Roman Empire, and under Napoleon the central German states came to be linked as the Confederation of the Rhine (1806). When Napoleon was defeated in 1815, the 39 German states organized as the German Confederation, with Austria and Prussia being the most powerful of the states. In 1848, the German Revolution shook the states, but the rebels, who fought for democratic changes, were defeated. Prussia slowly expanded its influence, and in the Austro-Prussian War (1866) expelled Austria and set itself up as the head of the North German Confederation. Following the defeat of France in 1870-1, the Confederation became the German Empire. Civil registration of births, marriages, and deaths was mandated in 1876, but some states had started it earlier, a few northern ones in 1809-11, and some areas west of the Rhine in the 1790s. The defeat of Germany in World War I (1918) dissolved the Empire, with lands being ceded to France, Poland, Denmark, Belgium, and Lithuania. Further, German territory was lost to the USSR and Poland following Germany's defeat in World War II, and the nation was divided into the Federal Republic of Germany (in the west) and the German Democratic Republic (in the east). In 1990, the two Germanies (West and East) were reunited. Through all this history, the records remained in archives in the leading cities of the various states, in the towns, and in the churches, which is where they are today.

Germans came to the American colonies and the US for many reasons, the chief ones being religious and political persecution, poverty, starvation, military devastation, oppressive taxation, and bitter winters. A few individual Germans probably settled in the 1660s in VA and MD, but the first German settlement was established as Germantown, PA in 1683 by 13 Mennonite families from Krefeld. In the year following, a group of German mystics came over and established themselves nearby. Then, in 1708, 61 emigrants from the Rheinland-Pfalz (Palatinate) came into NY and set up Newburgh, followed in 1709-10 by about 3000 more, who settled elsewhere in NY, with many soon moving to PA. The year 1710 also was marked by the founding of New Bern, NC by about 600 Palatinates. In 1714, miners from Westphalia came to VA to mine iron. Beginning about 1717, a steady stream of Germans came in PA, taking advantage of the colony's policies of religious toleration and cheap land. Baptist Dunkers came in 1719, Schwenkfelders in 1733, and Moravians in 1735. During these years, further small settlements of Germans were made in VA and NC. Eighty Salzburg families built the town of Ebenezer, GA in 1741. Numerous Germans coming into PA moved to other colonies. Many Germans who fought for Britain in the Revolutionary War deserted and remained in the US. All in all, over 200,000 Germans had come by 1780. After a lull, German immigration picked up after 1815, with the following numbers in thousands (K) coming in these periods: 1820s (8K), 1830s (152K), 1840s (435K), 1850s (952K), 1860s (787K), 1870s (718K), 1880s (1453K), 1890s (505K), 1900s (341K), 1910s

(144K). During the three centuries since the founding of Germantown (1683), over 7 million Germans have come. About half of the citizens of the US today have one or more German ancestors.

Every effort should be made here in the US to find the exact place of your German progenitor's origin. This is essential because of the decentralization of German records. The major German records for genealogical research are the church records and the civil registration records, the former providing birth, marriage, and death data before about 1876, and the latter after (sometimes earlier than 1876). These records are in archives in the pertinent states, cities, and towns, and in city and town offices. The Family History Library has microfilmed large numbers of them, so these should be thoroughly explored before any contacts with Germany are made. Further, there are large listings of Germans in the International Genealogical Index, which must not be overlooked. There are also many other valuable types of German records which are available: emigration, census, military, immigration, tax, guild, land. In addition, German genealogists have published several large genealogical compilations and some very sizable indexes to genealogies. These compilations and indexes are available in many large US genealogi-cal libraries. The vast holdings of the Family History Library are described in:
_J. Cerny and W. Elliott, THE LIBRARY, Ancestry Publishing, Salt Lake City, UT, 1988, pages 535-77.
You should study this material carefully before commencing your German research. In addition, you should read two or more of the following guidebooks:
__ Geo. K. Schweitzer, GERMAN GENEALOGICAL RESEARCH, Genealogical Sources,, Unltd., Knoxville, TN, 1995.
_A. Baxter, IN SEARCH OF YOUR GERMAN ROOTS, Genealogical Publishing Co., Baltimore, MD, 1994.
__ Germanic Genealogy Society, RESEARCH GUIDE TO GERMAN-AMERICAN GENEALOGY, The Society, St. Paul, MN, 1991.
_M. Lind, RESEARCHING AND FINDING YOUR GERMAN HERITAGE, The Linden Tree, Cloquet, MN, 1985.
_L. O. Jensen, GENEALOGICAL HANDBOOK OF GERMAN RESEARCH, The Author, Pleasant Grove, UT, 1980/3, 2 volumes.
A very useful journal for German genealogical researchers is:
_L. O. Jensen, editor, THE GERMAN GENEALOGICAL DIGEST, PO Box 700, Pleasant Grove, UT 84062.
There is also a society of German researchers which is well worth joining:

_GERMAN GENEALOGICAL SOCIETY OF AMERICA, PO Box
291818, Los Angeles, CA 90029. Publishes a very useful newsletter.

74. Group theory
It is often useful in genealogical research, especially on forebears with very common names, to remember that people in the early years of this country often travelled in groups for safety. People who were neighbors in one place banded together, then moved to another place together, where they settled together. This means that you can sometimes trace your elusive progenitors by tracing several of their neighbors. The easiest way to explain the technique is to give you an example.

Let us suppose you have an ancestor named William Smith who shows up in TN for the first time in the 1850 TN census. The 1850 census tells you also that he was born in VA. However, when you look back in the 1840 VA census index, you will find many, many persons named William Smith. So, which one is yours? What you do is go back to the original 1850 TN census (not the index) and copy the 10 families listed before your William Smith and the 10 families listed after him. Among the 20 families you will probably find some very uncommon surnames such as Latabton or Brekanatt or Prumduttle and some uncommon ones. Starting with the very uncommon names, you look them up in the 1840 VA census index, working your way down through the names in the order of increasing commonness. Following each name, list the names of the VA counties in which you find the name. For the rarer names, you may get only one or two counties. Now, glance down the lists, and see if there is a county in which most of the names appear. If there is such a county, and if your ancestor migrated and settled in a group, the William Smith in that county is probably your William Smith.

A similar procedure may be applied by using any sort of record which identifies neighbors and/or close friends of an ancestor with a common name. Possibilities are records of the following sorts: cemetery, church, deed (witnesses), land, maps of landowners, petitions, passenger list, society membership, tax, will and estate (witnesses, executors, administrators). The method is simply to locate the neighbors, friends, and associates of your forebear, then to trace the ones with less common names, and see if a person by your progenitor's name accompanies them. This approach does not always work because sometimes persons did not move in a group, but it often does. The technique is often appropriate for locating the place of origin of your immigrant ancestor by looking into the places or origin of his/her neighbors, friends, and associates.

---

75. Guardianships

When a person is unable to manage his/her property because of being too young, mentally deficient, or physically handicapped, the appropriate court in a county can appoint a guardian (or conservator). One common reason for guardianship appointments was the situation in which a minor child inherited property upon the death of a parent. These appointments gave rise to records which are filed in the court which had jurisdiction. The records may include appointments, bonds, petitions, inventories, accounts, settlements, and releases. They often kept a listing of guardianship cases called a guardianship docket. In many states, it is the Probate Court which handles guardianships, but in some states, other courts are the proper ones. The states which use other courts for this function and the courts are: AL (Superior), AZ (Superior), CA (Superior), CO (District), DE (Orphans' and Chancery), FL (County Judge), GA (Chancery), HI (Circuit), ID (District), IL (Circuit), IN (Probate or Superior or Circuit), KY (County), LA (District), MD (Equity or Orphans'), MS (Chancery), MT (District), NE (County), NV (District), NJ (Surrogate's or County or Superior), NM (County or Superior), NY (Surrogate's), NC (Superior), ND (County), OK (County), OR (Circuit or District or County), PA (Register of Wills), SD (County), TN (County or Probate or Chancery), TX (County), UT (District), VT (District), VA (Circuit or Chancery), WA (Superior), WV (County), WI (County), WY (District).

Guardianship records often contain name and age of the person, name(s) of parents, name of guardian, lists of property and other items belonging to the person, disbursal of funds, date and circumstances of termination of the guardianship. Some of these records have been microfilmed and are available at the Family History Library (and from its branch Family History Centers). However, most of them remain in the courts where they were filed. You may write the counties (or independent cities in VA), being sure to enclose an SASE, or you may hire a searcher to investigate for you. County courthouse addresses are available in:

__E. P. Bentley, COUNTY COURTHOUSE BOOK, Genealogical Publishing Co., Baltimore, MD, latest edition.
__A. Eichholz, ANCESTRY'S REDBOOK, Ancestry Publishing, Salt Lake City, UT, 1992.
These volumes may be found in practically every genealogy library.

76. Hired researchers

There are many persons practicing today as professional genealogists, most of them part-time. They can be of considerable help to you in examining records which are available only in places far distant from you, in cases in which you have been unsuccessful in getting replies from local officials, in difficult situations for which you need expert advice and searching, and in the event that you simply wish a certain portion of the research to be carried out by someone you pay to do it. It is well to exercise caution of several types in employing a researcher. First, you need to remember that some researchers are good, and some are not. Therefore, give every researcher you hire a trial run in which you do not commit too much money. Second, be careful to send a hired researcher everything you know on the line being worked on, so as to avoid duplication of effort. Third, have a firm, written agreement with the researcher as to what is to be done and what it will cost. Under no circumstances should you give a researcher open book, that is, the right to charge you an unlimited amount of money. Set a precise maximum. Fourth, you pay a researcher for her/his time in searching, not for finding certain data. Whether the researcher finds the desired information or not, the time has been spent, and you owe for it.

Several routes are available for locating a professional researcher. Two organizations test and certify or accredit such professionals. You may write them, enclosing an SASE, and ask for their listings.

_Board for Certification of Genealogists, PO Box 19165, Washington, DC 20036.

_Accreditation Committee, Family History Library, 35 North West Temple Street, Salt Lake City, UT 84150.

These organizations assume no responsibility for the genealogical researchers on their lists. They only present them to you with the information that those listed have passed certain tests. Other places where listings of genealogical searchers may be found are:

_Association of Professional Genealogists, PO Box 11601, Salt Lake City, UT 84147. Write for list.

_P. W. Filby and M. K. Meyer, WHO'S WHO IN GENEALOGY AND HERALDRY, Genealogical Publishing Co., Baltimore, MD, latest edition.

_THE GENEALOGICAL HELPER, Everton Publishers, Logan, UT, listing in the latest September-October issue. Also see the ads in other issues, but be careful.

Again, these offer no guarantees and take no responsibility for searchers who appear in their pages. For locating researchers in specific localities, write the local libraries and local genealogical societies for names.

77. Historical societies

As is the case for genealogical societies, there are numerous historical societies in the US. They represent regions, states, counties, cities, and towns, and also special groups. Some of them are concerned with genealogy; others are not. If you find a historical society in your ancestor's area or a historical society for a group with which your forebear was associated, dispatch them an SASE and a letter. Ask them about their activities, membership dues, genealogical interests, and publications. If their answer indicates they could be of assistance to you in your searches, join. Historical societies are listed in:

_DIRECTORY, HISTORICAL SOCIETIES AND AGENCIES IN THE US AND CANADA, American Association for State and Local History, Nashville, TN, latest edition.

78. Homestead records

In 1862 the US Congress passed a law that a settler could gain title to 160 acres or more of public land for a small filing fee and/or a 5-year residency on the land cultivating and improving it. There were also requirements that the age of the settler be 21 and that the settler be a US citizen or have declared in court an intention to become one. Homestead records are filed in the National Archives in Washington, DC, and in the Washington National Records Center in Suitland, MD. A file of homestead records may contain an application, a publication of the claim, proofs of the homestead, naturalization papers, and military discharge records. The application gives much data on the land and the applicant: description, location, and improvements of the land, description of the house, nature of crops, number of acres under cultivation; name, address, and age of the applicant, number and relationship of members of the family. About 1,970,000 entries for homestead land were made, but only about 780,000 were completed and had patents (the first deeds) issued. However, the most valuable genealogical materials, the applications, are available for all entries.

In order to obtain copies of homestead records for before 1908, it is necessary to send a legal description of the land to:

_General Branch, Civil Archives Division, National Archives, Washington, DC 20408.

The easiest way to obtain the legal description is to obtain it from the county deed records, plat maps, or tax records. If this search is unsuccessful, you can then search the tract books which were kept by the land offices. You need to know the general location. Microfilm copies of the tract books are available at the Family History Library and may be borrowed through Family History Centers. A third possibility is to use a county atlas which shows your ancestor's land. And a fourth way is to use township plats (maps) which are in the National Archives, Regional Branches of the National Archives, the Bureau of Land Management in Alexandria, VA, and Bureau of Land Management Offices in the western states. There are further homestead records, but they rarely carry extra genealogical information. For details, consult:

_GUIDE TO GENEALOGICAL RESEARCH IN THE NATIONAL ARCHIVES, National Archives and Records Service, Washington, DC, 1985, Chapter 15.

---

79. Immigrant ancestor origins

Sooner or later every genealogical researcher traces back to one or more ancestors who were the first to arrive here. These immigrant ancestors came from foreign countries, and if your research is to continue they must be traced there. It is usually fairly easy to discover the country of an immigrant ancestor, but that is not ordinarily enough information. What is needed is the exact town, city, or locality. There are exceptions, of course, but you will find that this information greatly simplifies your research because long and sometimes expensive procedures are often called for if you don't know it. Therefore, when you arrive at an immigrant ancestor, you must make every possible effort to find the exact place of origin from records here in the US.

In addition to making a thorough investigation of family records (Bibles, diaries, notes, photographs, letters, birth certificates and announcements, marriage certificates and invitations, death certificates, funeral programs, newspaper clippings), the following categories will probably be the most likely for finding the exact place of origin: Bible, biographies, birth records of children, cemetery, church, city and county histories, death, the International Genealogical Index, marriage, military, mortuary, naturalization, newspapers carrying obituaries, passports, passenger lists, published genealogies, societies, wills and probate. If these all fail, then you might try looking into these same records of neighbors, friends, and associates of your forebear in the hope that they came with her/him from the same place. Sections in this Handbook are devoted to these record types.

80. Immigration records

Since 1607 about 50 million people have immigrated to the area that is now the US from other countries. The immigrations can be divided into four periods. (1) Before 1820, approximately 1.1 million came, including about 350 thousand slaves. The majority were English, Scots-Irish, and Scottish from the British Isles. Sizable numbers came from Germanic-speaking countries and Africa, and there were smaller numbers of Irish, Dutch, Swedes, French, Welsh, and others. (2) From 1820-70, approximately 10 million entered the US. The major groups were from the German states, Ireland, and Great Britain (England, Scotland, Wales). (3) In the era 1870-1920, about 24 million came. The main groups were from Germany, Ireland, Italy, Austria-Hungary (including Czechs and Slovaks), Russia, Scandinavia (Denmark, Norway, Sweden), Poland, and England. (4) After a lull, a 4th era of immigration began about 1965, with Mexicans, Cubans, West Indians, and Asians in notable numbers coming.

Early immigration records are generally poor. As time went on, some improvements were made, but good records do not begin until the early 1800s, in most places not until 1820. There are both direct and indirect records of the arrival of immigrants. The direct records consist of actual lists of passengers arriving at a port. Such passenger lists give the names of persons on the ship, the date and place of arrival, the date and place of origin, and sometimes the country from which the persons are coming. These very important lists will be discussed in detail in a later section entitled Passenger lists. The indirect immigration records consist of ones which list persons who had to be recent immigrants to qualify for inclusion in the list. For example, certain colonies offered land to new immigrants. Records of those who took up the land imply that they had recently entered the colony. These indirect records will be the subject matter of this section.

The major period of time for which indirect immigration records are important is the period up to 1820. This represents the years during which passenger lists are usually very poor. The types of indirect records that may be sought are illustrated by the following:
_PA oaths of allegiance, 1727-1808
_VA headrights listed in land patents, 1623-1732

_Church records of transfers of memberships, especially Church of
  England (Episcopal), Congregational, Quaker, Huguenot, Reformed
_Early naturalizations, military lists, colonial government records
_Newspaper ads of indentured servants for sale
_Land granted to early MD settlers, 1633-80
_Land granted to Protestant refugees by SC, 1763-73
_Censuses, vital records, tax lists, probate records, court records, military
  records, church records during a colony's first 20-30 years

        In addition to these indirect indications of immigration, there are
also emigration records, that is, departure records in the countries from
which your ancestors came. In British Archives, there are:
_Colonial emigration licenses, oaths, and lists
_Colonial censuses and land title lists
_Colonial transportations to the colonies of felons, political prisoners,
  military prisoners, paupers, vagrants
_Colonial naturalization records
_Servants and apprentices sent to the colonies
_Foreigners who came through Britain, then went to colonies [Palatine
  Germans, French Huguenots]
_Probate records of colonists
In German and Swiss Archives, the following are often found:
_Emigration permission certificates and passports
_Emigration information in parish registers
_Civil emigration and colonization records
Some similar records are in archives in other European countries such as
The Netherlands and Sweden. A number of the records described in this
and the previous paragraph have been published. Both the published and
the unpublished records are described in detail in:
_M. Tepper, AMERICAN PASSENGER ARRIVAL RECORDS,
  Genealogical Published Co., Baltimore, MD, 1994.
Many of the published works are listed in:
_P. W. Filby, AMERICAN AND BRITISH GENEALOGY AND
  HERALDRY, New England Historic Genealogical Society, Boston,
  MA, 1983, and supplements.

81. Indian genealogy   This section deals with tracing family lines
among Native Americans or American
Indians. Prior to interaction with westward-
moving white people, lineage tracing among
Indians is almost impossible because of the lack of records, Indian naming
practices, and Indian family and kinship patterns. As Indian lands were

taken over, most Native Americans were forced westward and/or put on reservations. Some were integrated into white society. The colonies, the eastern states, and finally the US government set up officials and agencies to administer Indian affairs. In 1824 the US established the Bureau of Indian Affairs to manage matters for Indians on reservations and those remaining in tribal groups. A local field agency was put in place to serve each tribe. The colony, state, and US Indian agencies and officials kept many records. These are available in the pertinent state archives, state historical societies, state offices of Indian affairs, Regional Branches of the National Archives, and the National Archives. Many of these records are also on microfilm at the Family History Library.

Once you have found an Indian ancestor in your lineage, you need to locate the place of residence and the tribe. A useful volume for identifying the tribe is:
_C. Waldman, ATLAS OF THE NORTH AMERICAN INDIAN, Facts on File, New York, NY, 1985.
Then it is important for you to read about the history of the tribe so that you know the places it was located, the moves it made, and how it was related at various times to governmental agencies. Appropriate books for this include:
_F. W. Hodge, HANDBOOK OF AMERICAN INDIANS NORTH OF MEXICO, Pageant Books, New York, NY, 2 volumes.
_US Department of the Interior, BIOGRAPHICAL AND HISTORICAL INDEX OF AMERICAN INDIANS, G. K. Hall, Boston, MA, 1966, 8 volumes.
_J. R. Swanton, THE INDIAN TRIBES OF NORTH AMERICA, Smithsonian Institution Press, Washington, DC, 1952.
_REFERENCE ENCYCLOPEDIA OF THE AMERICAN INDIAN, Todd Publishers, Rye, NY, 1973, 2 volumes.
Following this, if the tribal history so indicates, you can seek the records in the pertinent state agencies. Or, as is more likely, you can look into the records of the Bureau of Indian Affairs. Your first step in this latter case is to discover which Bureau agency managed your ancestor's tribe and where the records are. These data will be found in the following volumes:
_GUIDE TO GENEALOGICAL RESEARCH IN THE NATIONAL ARCHIVES, The National Archives and Records Service, Washington, DC, 1985. See chapter 11.
_L. D. Szucs and S. H. Luebking, THE ARCHIVES, A GUIDE TO THE NATIONAL ARCHIVES FIELD BRANCHES, Ancestry

Publishing, Salt Lake City, UT, 1988. See section on Bureau of Indian Affairs, Record Group 75, pages 176-211.

The types of records that will be found in the various repositories are removal records; tribal censuses, registers, rolls, and lists; annuity rolls of payment to Indians; school reports and censuses; land allotment records including applications which trace forebear's ancestral lines to establish his tribal membership; claims records for those seeking compensation for confiscated land; health and welfare records; vital statistics (birth, marriage, death). The most valuable of these records are those in which an Indian was required to document his/her descent from an ancestor who was a tribal member several generations back. In order to do effective Indian family history research, you should be thoroughly acquainted with the following materials:

_A. Eichholz, ANCESTRY'S REDBOOK, Ancestry Publishing, Salt Lake City, UT, 1992. See sections on Native Americans under each state.

_C. S. Carpenter, HOW TO RESEARCH AMERICAN INDIAN BLOOD LINES, Heritage Quest, Orting, WA, 1987.

_E. E. Hill, GUIDE TO RECORDS IN THE NATIONAL ARCHIVES OF THE US RELATING TO AMERICAN INDIANS, The Archives, Washington, DC, 1984.

_M. V. Gormley, CHEROKEE CONNECTIONS, Family Historian Books, Tacoma, WA, 1995.

_National Archives, AMERICAN INDIANS, A SELECT CATALOG OF NATIONAL ARCHIVES MICROFILMS, The Archives, Washington, DC, 1984.

_A. Eakle and J. Cerny, THE SOURCE, A GUIDEBOOK OF AMERICAN GENEALOGY, Ancestry Publishing, Salt Lake City, UT, 1984, pages 109-112, 535-557.

_J. McEvers, INDIAN GENEALOGY, A GUIDEBOOK TO NATIVE AMERICAN ANCESTRY, Polyanthos, New Orleans, LA, 1981.

_E. K. Kirkham, OUR NATIVE AMERICANS, THEIR RECORDS OF GENEALOGICAL VALUE, Everton Publishers, Logan, UT, 1980-4.

Remember that many Indian genealogical records on microfilm at the Family History Library are available through the numerous branch Family History Centers.

---

82. International Genealogical Index

One of the most valuable genealogical indexes is the International Genealogical Index. It can be found on microfiche in the Family History Library in Salt Lake City and in each of its numerous branch Family History Centers. The index is also available in computer data-base form (CDROM), which allows entries to be directly called up. The index contains an exceedingly large number of names, well over 200 million in its most recent edition. The International Genealogical Index contains chiefly christening, birth, and marriage information. These data have been obtained from birth records, marriage records, church records, censuses, probate records, will records, and personal records of genealogists. Each individual entry gives the name, sex, names of parents (for births) or name of spouse (for marriages), date, and a reference to the source. The index is divided into sections. Entries for the US are subdivided by state, for Canada by province, Ireland and Germany are not subdivided, and most other countries are by county. The areas having the greatest numbers of entries are England, Mexico, Germany, US, MA, OH, MO, TN, NY, PA, VA, CT, and KY.

All you need to do to use this index is go to the nearest Family History Center (see separate section in this Handbook). Ask for the proper portion of the index, then search it for your ancestor, being careful to keep spelling variations in mind. When you find an entry in which you are interested, copy down the full entry, including all the reference numbers. Show the entry to the attendant and ask that the referenced material be ordered from Salt Lake City. Please remember that the International Genealogical Index is just an index. Everything that you obtain from it and from the materials to which it refers must be checked (in the original sources, if at all possible) and verified. At the end of the microfiche edition of the International Genealogical Index is a microfiche which gives detailed instructions for its use. Pamphlets are also available for guiding you in the use of both the microfiche and the CDROM versions.

83. Irish genealogy

The island which is Ireland today was invaded in the 5th century BC by Celtic tribal peoples, who developed a high culture which flourished into the 8th century AD: literature, music, sculpture, monasteries, scholars, far-ranging missionaries. During the 5th century AD, St. Patrick had completed the Christianization of the land. In 795, Viking invaders began raids, then established coastal cities, and exercised control over large areas. These Vikings were defeated in 1014, and Ireland returned to self-rule until 1169. In that year, at the invitation of one of the Irish contestants for the kingship, the English began the conquest of the island. This was the start of an Irish-English struggle which would last over 800 years. Early on, the English took large tracts of land, and many Irish became tenant farmers, subject to English landlords. English control over the next 365 years rose and fell until 1534, when all Ireland was finally brought under English domination. Over the next 70 years, English rulers outlawed Catholicism, tried to impose Protestantism on Ireland, seized land and gave it to English landlords and settlers, and put down several Irish revolts. In 1603, the British monarch confiscated land in Ulster (northeast Ireland) and gave it to English and Scottish Protestants, creating the Protestant majority in what is today the country of Northern Ireland. Catholic Irish revolt defeats in 1649 and 1690 were followed by further land seizures, so that by 1700, Catholics held only 15% of the country's land. Catholics were forbidden to buy, inherit, or rent land, to hold political office, their worship was restricted, and they were exploited in the English landlord-Irish tenant system. English trade policy in the early 1700s depressed the Protestant Irish economy, and many Scots-Irish left for America. Rebellions continued into the 1800s, with a resulting unification of Ireland with Great Britain, followed by changes which relieved Catholic discontent, including restoration of freedom for Catholic worship. However, continuing absentee landowner oppression and a rising population produced an acute economic situation. This was compounded by a potato blight in 1845-9 which led to about one million deaths and about 1.6 million emigrants, mostly to the US. The numbers of Irish coming to the US remained high for several decades. After several decades of agitation for self rule, including several unsuccessful rebellions, the dominion of the Irish Free State was established in 1921, with six northeastern counties splitting off as the dominion of Northern Ireland. The six counties of Northern Ireland were those with the largest Protestant populations. In 1937, the Irish Free State became the sovereign country of Eire, and in 1949, an independent nation, the Republic of Ireland.

Even though some Irish (Catholics) came to America in colonial times and to the US after the Revolution, a rapid increase started in 1820. There were over 54 thousand 1821-30, more than 207 thousand 1831-40, and in the two decades 1861-90, the influx continued at about 500 thousand per decade. After 1890, Irish immigration declined as conditions in Ireland improved. There are numerous published compilations of Irish immigrants which you should seek in large and medium-sized genealogical libraries.

Research in Ireland is made difficult because many Irish were not landholders, church records were adversely affected by the religious conflict, Ireland is divided and sub-divided into many sorts and sizes of regions which sometimes overlap, the majority of early deeds were not registered, and a fire in 1922 at the Public Record Office destroyed many of the records most useful for genealogical purposes. It is, therefore, of great import that you exhaust every possible source in the US in an effort to locate the precise place in Ireland from which your ancestor came. Without this information, your task will become doubly difficult. The major records for doing Irish research are censuses and census substitutes [lists of inhabitants, taxpayers, freeholders, tax valuations, leaseholders], civil registration records from 1864- (birth, marriage, death), the extensive compilations and indexes in the Public Record Office, church records [Church of Ireland or Episcopalian mostly 1720-, Catholic mostly 1820-, Presbyterian mostly 1819-], directories [commercial, professional, city inhabitants], published family histories, gravestone inscriptions, newspapers, wills and administrations, and genealogical periodicals. The major places in Ireland where these will be found are in the county libraries and record offices, and several places in Dublin [National Library of Ireland, Public Record Office of Ireland, Genealogical Office, Registrar-General's Office, Registry of Deeds, State Paper Office, Representative Church Body Library (Church of Ireland), Society of Friends Library, Trinity College Library]. These Dublin record repositories are for all of Ireland, but the nine northern counties, particularly the six in Northern Ireland, are more fully covered by repositories in Belfast. See the section on Scots-Irish genealogy in this Handbook for more detail. Many Irish records are on microfilm at the Family History Library in Salt Lake City, UT, and are available on loan through its many Family History Centers. Please make thorough use of these before you even think about investigating in Ireland.

Because of the above-mentioned research difficulties, you should make yourself extensively acquainted with Irish research before you delve very deeply into it. The following articles and volumes are recommended:
_J. Cerny and W. Elliott, THE LIBRARY, Ancestry Publishing, Salt Lake City, UT, 1988, section on Ireland, pages 475-487.
__J. Grenham, TRACING YOUR IRISH ANCESTORS, Gill and MacMillan, Dublin, Ireland, 1992.
_T. McCarthy, THE IRISH ROOTS GUIDE, Lilliput Press, Dublin, Ireland, 1991.
_A. Baxter, IN SEARCH OF YOUR BRITISH AND IRISH ROOTS, Genealogical Publishing Co., Baltimore, MD, 1994.
__K. J. Betit and D. A. Radford, IRELAND, A GENEALOGICAL GUIDE FOR NORTH AMERICANS, The Irish at Home and Abroad, Salt Lake City, UT, 1993.

_J. G. Ryan, IRISH RECORDS, Ancestry Publishing, Salt Lake City, UT, 1988.

__S. E. Quinn, TRACE YOUR IRISH ANCESTORS, Magh Itha Teoranta, Bray, Ireland, 1989.

_M. D. Falley, IRISH AND SCOTCH-IRISH ANCESTRAL RE-SEARCH, Genealogical Publishing Co., Baltimore, MD, 1981.

_D. F. Begley, HANDBOOK ON IRISH GENEALOGY, Ancestry Publishing, Salt Lake City, UT, 1993.

_M. C. O'Laughlin, THE COMPLETE BOOK FOR TRACING YOUR IRISH ANCESTORS, Irish Genealogical Foundation, Kansas City, MO, 1984.

84. Jewish genealogy

A few Jewish people came to the colonies and the US before 1850. The first known came into New York in 1654, and Jewish communities were established in Newport, Savannah, Charleston, Philadelphia, and Richmond before the 1800s. Many Jews came to the US from Germany during 1850-80, but the great majority of Jewish immigrants came after 1880. They were largely of German and Eastern European origin, and they tended to settle in large cities.

For the most part, tracing your Jewish ancestors in the US is done by the use of the ordinary sources as outlined in other sections of this Handbook. The residential concentration, the institutional separation, and the religious conventions of Jewish forebears often provide special advantages. This makes certain records especially helpful: synagogue records (minutes, accounts, school registers, circumcision lists, bar and bat mitzvah records, marriage records, death records, burial records, congregational histories), cemetery records, tombstone inscriptions, mortuary records, newspaper (especially Jewish) obituaries, city directories, city business directories. Particularly useful for tracking your ancestors overseas are family records, censuses, naturalization records, and passenger lists. The records kept by Jewish immigrant aid societies in major port cities often contain information on places of origin. The main Jewish archives in the US are the American Jewish Archives in Cincinnati, the American Jewish Historical Society in Waltham, MA, and the Leo Baeck Institute, and the Yivo Institute in New York City. The Family History Library in Salt Lake City has microfilmed many Jewish records.

Initially, you should read some good articles and books concerning the specifics of Jewish genealogical research. Recommended works include:

_A. Eakle and J. Cerny, THE SOURCE, Ancestry Publishing, Salt Lake City, UT, 1984, article on Jewish-American Research, pages 603-649.

_K. Stryker-Rodda, GENEALOGICAL RESEARCH, METHODS AND SOURCES, American Society of Genealogists, Washington, DC, 1983, section on Jewish migration, pages 341-359.

_A. Kurzweil, FROM GENERATION TO GENERATION, Schocken Books, New York, NY, 1981.

_D. Kranzler, MY JEWISH ROOTS, Sephen-Harmon Press, New York, NY, 1979.

_D. Rottenberg, FINDING OUR FATHERS, Random House, New York, NY, 1977.

If your ancestor was in this country by 1840, you need to check the following important volume. It is a compilation of genealogies of American Jewish families who were here by 1840. It traces many to the date of the book.

_M. H. Stern, AMERICANS OF JEWISH DESCENT, A COMPENDIUM OF GENEALOGY, KTAV Publishing, New York, NY, 1971.

Two other works which will be useful to many searchers are ones that index numerous Jewish genealogies:

_D. S. Zubatsky, JEWISH GENEALOGY, A SOURCEBOOK, Garland Publishing Co., New York, NY, 1984.

_D. S. Zubatsky, SOURCES FOR JEWISH GENEALOGIES, The Author, Champaign, IL, 1982.

85. Land grants The foreign countries which settled what is now the US, the American colonies, the US states, and the US federal government made land grants to the first private owners of land. These first private owners were both individuals and groups. In general, the process included filing an application with the government, receiving a warrant exchangeable for the land, presentation of the warrant to a local land office, survey of the land if it had not been done, recording of the location in a tract book and on a plat map, issuance of a patent that was a certificate of title, and often the filing of a copy with the county, city, or town. The grants of land included those bought for cash or credit, donated to promote settlement and development, and given for military service. The federal government also awarded land to states and to railroads, both of which then sold or leased part or all of it to private owners. And the federal government granted (or re-affirmed) titles to land previously granted to residents of areas taken over by the US (from France, Mexico, Britain, and Spain).

In colonial times, the 13 American colonies (CT, DE, GA, MA, MD, NJ, NH, NY, NC, PA, RI, SC, VA) made land grants on behalf of their parent countries, and France, Spain, Mexico, and Britain made grants of land in areas adjacent to the US (which the US would later take over). The records of the colonial grants should be sought in the state land offices, state archives, and state libraries of the states indicated above. Many of the American colony land grants have been transcribed, abstracted, indexed, microfilmed, and/or published, and they can be located in the same places. Records of the land grants made by France, Spain, Mexico, and Britain should be sought in the states now occupying the areas, in the archives of the countries, and in the National Archives. The re-affirmation of these grants when the US took over will be discussed below. A sizable number of copies of all the above records and published materials derived from them are available at the Family History Library. Details on the colonial records, along with descriptions of what is available for each colony, will be found in:
_A. Eakle and J. Cerny, THE SOURCE, Ancestry Publishing Co., Salt Lake City, UT, 1984, pages 216-253.
And brief descriptions of what is available for each colony will also be found in:
_A. Eichholz, ANCESTRY'S REDBOOK, Ancestry Publishing, Salt Lake City, UT, 1992.

In the many years following the Revolutionary War, the following states, called state-land states, retained the right to grant their own land: the states derived from the thirteen colonies (CT, DE, GA, MA, NH, NY, MD, NJ, NC, PA, RI, SC, VA), plus HI, KY, ME, TN, TX, VT, and WV. Therefore, it is in these state land offices, archives, and state libraries where the original land grant records, indexes, published transcripts, and microfilmed copies may be found. Some are also available at the Family History Library and obtainable through its numerous branch Family History Centers.

The other 30 states of the US (AL, AK, AZ, AR, CA, CO, FL, ID, IL, IN, IA, KS, LA, MI, MN, MS, MO, MT, NE, NV, NM, ND, OH, OK, OR, SC, UT, WA, WI, WY) are known as public domain land states. The land making up these states was the property of the federal US government, and they made the land grants. More than one billion acres were granted to private individuals, private groups, and to the states.

About 300 million acres were sold or donated (1800-1908), about 285 million were in homestead grants (1862-), about 225 million were given to some of the above states (who sold or leased part or all), about 126 million for railroads and timber culture and other developmental purposes, about 73 million for military bounty grants (see separate section), and 22 million in private land claims. Each of these transactions generated records which are gathered together in a case file. The case files for all grants except to states, railroads, and for timber culture are stored in the Washington National Records Center, 4205 Suitland Road, Suitland, MD 20409. To order photocopies of the case files, you should give the legal description of the land to the following agency:

_General Branch, Civil Archives Division, National Archives, Washington, DC 20408.

The legal description of your forebear's land consists of state, county, township, and range. These data can often be located in a deed or patent saved in family records, county land records (deeds, mortgages, plat maps, surveys, tax records), or by searching tract books at the state archives or the Family History Library.

Case files of private land claims (1789-1837) are stored in the Washington National Records Center. They apply to these states: AL, AZ, AR, CA, CO, FL, IL, IN, IA, LA, MI, MS, MO, NM, WI. Many applications submitted 1789-1837 have been published and indexed in:

_AMERICAN STATE PAPERS, CLASSES VIII AND IX, Gales and Seaton, Washington, DC, 1832-61.

An overall index to these materials is available:

_O. W. McMullin, GRASSROOTS OF AMERICA, Gendex Corp., Salt Lake City, UT, 1972.

Many of these case files are available at the Family History Library and at state archives. Further details on land grant records will be found in the two volumes named at the end of the second paragraph of this section and in:

_GUIDE TO GENEALOGICAL RECORDS IN THE NATIONAL ARCHIVES, The National Archives and Records Service, Washington, DC, 1985, Chapters 8 and 15.

86. Land records As indicated in the section above, the colonies, states, and the US government issued land to groups (land companies, land speculators, town proprietors or selectmen, railroads), and to individuals. The groups usually subdivided the large areas they had obtained into smaller units which they sold or gave away or leased to promote settlement. The records of the town proprietors and selectmen (who operated in New England) are generally to be found in the town records, with microfilm copies often in the state archives and the Family History Library. The records of the land companies, land speculators, railroads, and other such groups are widely dispersed. To locate them, inquiries to the appropriate state archives and state libraries are often effective. You may also search for them in the index to the following volumes:

_THE NATIONAL UNION CATALOG OF MANUSCRIPT COLLEC-
TIONS, Edwards, Ann Arbor, MI, 1959-present, annual volumes, index in each volume, cumulative indexes also, and also overall name and subject indexes.

These indexes will lead you to the repositories where the records are stored. However, you may experience some difficulty in locating certain ones, since they may be in private hands. Some of these group records are available in microfilm form at the Family History Library.

Once an individual received title to land from the government, most subsequent transfers of the land were by deed. A previous section entitled Deed records will give you detail. The ownership of land also usually gave rise to tax records, which will be discussed in a later section. In addition, in the places where deed records are kept, there are generally mortgage and lease records, and in conjunction with tax records, you will often find plat maps. These are detailed maps which show the names of the land owners on their pieces of land. In most states, these records (deed, tax, mortgage, lease, plat maps) will be found in the counties, but in CT, RI, and VT, the deeds, mortgages, and leases are in the towns, and in CT, ME, MA, NH, RI, and VT, land tax and plat records must also be sought in the towns. The Family History Library holds microfilm copies of a number of these records.

---

87. Large genealogical libraries

Spread around the US there are a number of large genealogical libraries. Fifteen of them which are among those with the largest genealogical collections of US materials are as follows. Guidebooks and/or large indexes to all or part of the holdings are given in parentheses.

_Family History Library of the Genealogical Society of UT, 35 North West Temple St., Salt Lake City, UT 84150. (J. Cerny and W. Elliott, THE LIBRARY, Ancestry Publishing, Salt Lake City, UT, 1988.)

_Public Library of Fort Wayne and Allen County, 900 Webster St., Fort Wayne, IN 46802. (K. B. Cavanaugh, A GENEALOGIST'S GUIDE TO THE FT. WAYNE, INDIANA, PUBLIC LIBRARY, The Author, Ft. Wayne, IN, 1980.)

_New England Historic Genealogical Society Library, 101 Newbury St., Boston, MA 02116. (W. P. Greenlaw, THE GREENLAW INDEX OF THE NEW ENGLAND HISTORIC GENEALOGICAL SOCIETY, Hall, Boston, MA, 1979.)

_NY Public Library, Research Libraries, 5th Avenue and 42nd St., New York, NY 10022-1939. (NY Public Library, DICTIONARY CATALOG OF THE LOCAL HISTORY AND GENEALOGY DIVISION, Hall, Boston, MA, 1974.)

_Library of Congress, 10 First St., SE, Washington, DC 20540. (M. J. Kaminkow, GENEALOGIES IN THE LIBRARY OF CONGRESS, with SUPPLEMENTS, Magna Carta, Baltimore, MD, 1976-86; M. J. Kaminkow, US LOCAL HISTORIES IN THE LIBRARY OF CONGRESS, Magna Carta, Baltimore, MD, 1975-6; J. C. and M. C. Neagles, THE LIBRARY OF CONGRESS: A GUIDE TO GENEALOGICAL AND HISTORICAL RESEARCH, Ancestry, Salt Lake City, UT, 1990.)

_NY Genealogical and Biographical Society Library, 122-126 East 58th St., New York, NY 10022.

_Library of the National Society, Daughters of the American Revolution, 1776 D St., NW, Washington, DC 20006-5392. (National Society, DAR, LIBRARY CATALOG, The Society, Washington, DC, 1982/6.)

_Western Reserve Historical Society Library, 10825 East Blvd., Cleveland, OH 44106.

_Detroit Public Library, 5201 Woodward Avenue, Detroit, MI 48202. (J. Oldenburg, A GENEALOGICAL GUIDE TO THE BURTON HISTORICAL COLLECTION, DETROIT PUBLIC LIBRARY, Ancestry Publishing, Salt Lake City, UT, 1988.)

_Newberry Library, 60 West Walton St., Chicago, IL 60610. (P. T. Sinko, GUIDE TO LOCAL AND FAMILY HISTORY AT THE NEWBERRY LIBRARY, Ancestry Publishing, Salt Lake City, UT, 1987).

_State Historical Society of WI Library, 816 State St., Madison, WI 53703. (J. P. Danky, GENEALOGICAL RESEARCH, AN INTRODUCTION TO THE RESOURCES OF THE STATE HISTORICAL SOCIETY OF WI, The Society, Madison, WI, 1986.)

_Dallas Public Library, 1515 Young St., Dallas, TX 75201.

_Sutro Library, 480 Winston Drive, San Francisco, CA 94132. (G. E. Strong and G. F. Kurutz, LOCAL HISTORY AND GENEALOGI-

CAL RESOURCES OF THE CA STATE LIBRARY AND ITS SUTRO BRANCH, CA State Library Foundation, Sacramento, CA, 1983.)
_Clayton Library, 5300 Caroline, Houston, TX 77004.
_Public Library of Cincinnati and Hamilton County, 800 Vine St., Cincinnati, OH 45202-2071.

Among other large libraries which have good genealogical collections are the following:
_In AL: Birmingham Public Library, Davis Library at Samford University, in AZ: AZ State Genealogical Library in Phoenix, in AR: AR History Commission in Little Rock, in CA: see above, Los Angeles Public Library, San Diego Public Library, San Francisco Public Library, in CO: Denver Public Library,
_In CT: CT Historical Society in Hartford, CT State Library in Hartford, in DE: Historical Society of DE in Wilmington, in DC: see above, in FL: Miami-Dade Public Library, Orange County Library in Orlando, FL State Library in Tallahassee, Tampa-Hillsborough County Public Library, in GA: Atlanta-Fulton County Public Library, GA Department of Archives in Atlanta, Washington Memorial Library in Macon, in HI: Hawaii State Library in Honolulu,
_In ID: ID Historical Society in Boise, in IL: see above, IL State Historical Society in Springfield, in IN: see above, IN State Library in Indianapolis, in IA: IA State Historical Society in Des Moines, in KS: KS State Historical Society in Topeka, Wichita Public Library, in KY: KY Historical Library in Frankfort, Filson Club Library in Louisville,
_In LA: LA State Library in Baton Rouge, New Orleans Public Library, in ME: ME State Library in Augusta, ME Historical Society in Portland, in MD: MD Historical Society in Baltimore, in MA: see above, Boston Public Library, in MI: see above, Library of MI in Lansing, in MN: MN Historical Society in St. Paul, Minneapolis Public Library, in MS: MS Department of Archives and History in Jackson,
_In MO: Mid-Continent Public Library in Independence, Kansas City Public Library, St. Louis Public Library, in MT: MT Historical Society in Helena, in NE: NE State Historical Society in Lincoln, in NV: NV State Library in Carson City, NV Historical Society in Reno, Las Vegas Family History Center, in NH: NH Historical Society in Concord, NH State Library in Concord, in NJ: Joint Free Public Library of Morristown, NJ Historical Society in Newark, NJ State Library in Trenton, Newark Public Library,

_In **NM**: Albuquerque Public Library, in **NY**: see above, NY State Library in Albany, Buffalo and Erie County Public Library, Rochester Public Library, Onondaga County Public Library in Syracuse, in **NC**: Public Library of Charlotte, NC State Library in Raleigh, in **ND**: Red River Valley Genealogy Society in West Fargo, in **OH**: see above, OH Genealogical Society in Mansfield, OH Historical Society in Columbus, in **OK**: OK City Public Library, OK State Historical Society in Oklahoma City,

_In **OR**: OR Historical Society in Portland, Genealogical Forum of Portland, Multnomah County Library in Portland, in **PA**: State Library of PA in Harrisburg, Historical and Genealogical Societies of PA in Philadelphia, Carnegie Library of Pittsburgh, in **RI**: RI Historical Society in Providence, in **SC**: South Caroliniana Library in Columbia, Greenville County Library in Greenville, in **SD**: SD Historical Society in Pierre,

_In **TN**: Knox County Library in Knoxville, Memphis Public Library, TN State Library in Nashville, in **TX**: see above, TX State Library in Austin, Fort Worth Public Library, Clayton Library in Houston, in **UT**: see above, Brigham Young University Library in Provo, in **VT**: VT Historical Society in Montpelier, in **VA**: National Genealogical Society Library in Arlington, VA State Library in Richmond, in **WA**: Seattle Public Library, Spokane Public Library, Tacoma Public Library, in **WV**: see above, Milwaukee Public Library, in **WY**: Laramie County Library in Cheyenne.

Details on the holdings of many of the above libraries and numerous others are given in:

_P. W. Filby, DIRECTORY OF AMERICAN LIBRARIES WITH GENEALOGY OR LOCAL HISTORY COLLECTIONS, Scholarly Resources, Wilmington, DE, 1988.

__A. Eichholz, REDBOOK, Ancestry Publishing, Salt Lake City, UT, 1992.

Many genealogy libraries are also listed in:

_V. N. Chambers, editor, THE GENEALOGICAL HELPER, Everton Publishers, Logan, UT, latest Jul-Aug issue.

Practically all libraries in the US, with descriptive data, are listed in:

_American Library Association, AMERICAN LIBRARY DIRECTORY, Bowker, New York, NY, latest issue.

88. Legal appeals

If your ancestor was involved in a case which was appealed from a trial court to a higher court, there is a very good possibility that you can locate the records easily. There is a very large set of volumes available in most sizable law libraries (such as those at law schools) with an index which includes many appeal cases from 1658 through 1906. The indexes are:

_AMERICAN DIGEST, 1906 DECENNIAL EDITION, TABLE OF CASES, 1658-1906, West Publishing Co., St. Paul, MN, 1911, Volumes 21-25. Over 550,000 cases. With supplemental indexes (Tables of Cases) for 1907-16, 1917-26, etc.

Unfortunately, the cases are listed by the plaintiff (the one bringing the case) only. You should look up your ancestors' surnames in these volumes noting carefully that the listings are arranged under each surname according to state. The listings refer you both to summaries of the cases in the AMERICAN DIGEST, and also to STATE REPORTS (published records) for each state. Details of the cases along with complete names of the parties are given in these state records which a law librarian can help you locate. The state records will then direct you back to the trial court records which will usually be even more detailed. This approach is quite appropriate if the surnames you are seeking are uncommon, but if a surname is common, there will be a vast number of listings to sort through.

If you have the usual good fortune of knowing your progenitor's state, you should request the individual state record indexes (Tables of Cases) for that state. These records are indexed by both the plaintiff and the defendant, and thus give you much fuller coverage.

89. Libraries A library is a place where published records are collected, preserved, organized, and made available. Published records include books, serials, journals, magazines, pamphlets, newspapers, newsletters, microfilm, microfiche, and computer disks and diskettes. Many libraries also act in an archival capacity, that is, they collect original records, usually ones relating to their immediate locales. There are many libraries in the US, both governmental and private, which have materials of value for genealogical research. These include:

_The Library of Congress in Washington, DC. This is the US national library, established in 1800. It is the largest library in the world. Since 1870, copies of all books copyrighted in the US must be deposited.

_The State Libraries, one in each state at the state capital. See later section for a listing.

_State University and College Libraries, at least one large important one in each state.

_County, City, and Town Libraries, in county seats, cities, and towns.

_Private Libraries: libraries sponsored by state and local historical societies, genealogical societies, hereditary societies, private colleges and universities, religious denominations, ethnic societies, fraternal societies, patriotic societies, professional societies, corporations, and specialized-purpose libraries.

The largest genealogical libraries among those mentioned above have been treated in a previous section. Practically all libraries in the US, along with some indications of their genealogical holdings, are listed in:

_American Library Association, AMERICAN LIBRARY DIRECTORY, Bowker, New York, NY, latest issue.

Specialized listings of genealogical libraries will be found in:

_P. W. Filby, DIRECTORY OF AMERICAN LIBRARIES WITH GENEALOGY OR LOCAL HISTORY COLLECTIONS, Scholarly Resources, Wilmington, DE, 1988.

__A. Eichholz, REDBOOK, Ancestry Publishing, Salt Lake City, UT, 1992.

__E. P. Bentley, THE GENEALOGIST'S ADDRESS BOOK, Genealogical Publishing Co., Baltimore, MD, latest edition.

_V. N. Chambers, editor, THE GENEALOGICAL HELPER, Everton Publishers, Logan, UT, latest Jul-Aug issue.

When you go into a library, register, then ask for and read the regulations. Next, request the main catalog, which may be a card catalog, a computer catalog, or a microfiche catalog. These are generally arranged alphabetically according to one or more of the categories suggested by the five letters in the word SLANT: by Subject, by Locality (state, county, city, town), by Author (or compiler or editor), by Name (surnames), and by Title. Now, search this main catalog for the Names of your ancestors, for the Localities in which they lived, and the Subjects which relate to their activities, and then, search out appropriate Titles and Authors of materials you need. When you find references which you believe could contain ancestor information, copy the name of the source and its code or call numbers (and/or letters). Use these call numbers to locate the materials on the shelves or to request them at the appropriate desk. Following these extensive investigations, ask about the other catalogs, indexes, and finding aids which will lead you to items not included in the main catalog. Examine all these under all the above categories (SLANT) that apply, copy the call numbers, and obtain the items. When you obtain materials, treat them with extreme care so that no damage is done to them, and return them to the designated places (carts, boxes, shelves). Many libraries prefer that you not try to return items to the shelf positions where you found them, so pay careful attention to any return instructions that are posted. Never fail to consult a librarian in your particular search. Briefly describe what you are seeking so she or he can indicate sources that may not be obvious from the finding aids.

In smaller libraries, such as many county and town institutions, the finding and accessing procedures may be simpler and more informal than those mentioned above. Consultation with the librarian is a must since this can save you much time. Do not fail to ask the librarian about other repositories in the area, especially other libraries, but also museums, newspaper offices, mortuaries, cemetery offices, and collections in private hands.

90. Locating an ancestor   One of the more common problems in genealogical research is to know the colony or state of an ancestor but not the county and/or town. Discovery of the county and/or town is usually essential because the most valuable and the larger numbers of genealogical records are usually locally (county and/or town) based. Fortunately, there are generally a number of colony or state records which reveal the county and/or town and which are indexed.

Especially valuable for the period up to 1790 are the following indexed records:
_The International Genealogical Index and Ancestral File.
_Colonial and early state land records (bounty, deed, grant, headright, patent, rent, survey, warrant).
_Colonial governor, council, court, and legislative records.
_Special record type indexes in state archives and/or state libraries (Bible, claims, marriage, biography, manuscript, obituary, cemetery, genealogical compilations, newspaper).
_Colonial, French and Indian, and Revolutionary War military service, bounty land, and pension records.
_Surname indexes in state libraries.
_Series of published volumes of materials in state archives.
_Name indexes to genealogical periodical articles relating to pre-1790 ancestors.

_Early colonial censuses.

_Volumes listing early settlers or inhabitants.

_Volumes listing early immigrants (especially those by Filby and Meyer, see section on Immigration Records).

_Volumes of early special record types (marriage, newspaper abstracts, oaths of allegiance, probate, tax, vital, will).

Many of the above are discussed in detail in other sections of this volume. They can be found in the appropriate state archives and state libraries, in large genealogical libraries, and many of them are available through Family History Centers from the Family History Library.

For the period of time after 1790, the materials listed below are among the most important indexed records which can lead you to the county and/or town of your forebear:

_Indexes to the federal census records.

_The International Genealogical Index and Ancestral File.

_State-wide vital record indexes.

_Revolutionary War, War of 1812, Mexican War, Civil War, Spanish-American War military service, bounty land, and pension records (both federal and state records).

_State land grant records, especially for states entering the Union after 1800.

_Special indexes in the state archives and state libraries (Bible, biography, cemetery, genealogical compilations, names in county histories, marriage, newspaper abstracts, obituary).

_State census record indexes.

_Volumes of special record types for the early years of the territory and state (marriage, petitions, probate, tax, vital, will,territorial).

You recognize, of course, that not all of these will be available for all states, but all should be looked for. The best sources are the state archives, state libraries, large genealogical libraries, and the Family History Library (records accessible through Family History Centers).

91. Manufactures censuses

In several of the regular population census years, there also were taken censuses of establishments (organizations, companies, businesses) which manufactured articles, items, or products. In some years the records are called censuses of manufactures, and in other years they are titled industrial schedules. A few of the 1810 records still exist, but most of them for 1820, 1850, 1860, 1870, and 1880 are available. In 1850 and after, the coverage was broadened as an attempt was made to list all manufacturing, mining, fishing, commercial, mercantile, and trading businesses with an annual production of $500 or more. The records give the name of the owner and/or the company plus considerable detail on the investment, materials, labor, machinery, and product. If you know your ancestor owned a business, it is often worthwhile to try to find his company in these records which are grouped by county within each state. Most of the original manufactures censuses are now in state libraries, state archives, or university libraries. Many of them have been microfilmed by the National Archives and other agencies. The best places to start your search for them are the state libraries and state archives. They usually have the records or copies of them, and if they do not, they can tell you who does. Microfilm copies of some of them can also be found at the National Archives, the Regional Branches of the National Archives, and at the Family History Library. The microfilm copies at the latter repository can be borrowed through the numerous Family History Centers.

92. Manuscripts There are thousands of collections of manuscripts (unpublished hand-written materials) in hundreds of repositories (archives, libraries, societies, churches, businesses, organizations, museums, private) all over the US. Manuscript collections consist of all sorts of records of religious, educational, patriotic, business, social, civil, professional, governmental, and political organizations; documents, letters, memoirs, notes and papers of early settlers, ministers, politicians, business men, educators, physicians, dentists, lawyers, judges, land speculators, storekeepers, and farmers; records of churches, cemeteries, mortuaries, schools, corporations, and industries; works of artists, musicians, writers, sculptors, photographers, architects, and historians; and records, papers, letters, and reminiscences of participants in various wars, as well as records of military organizations and campaigns. It is quite possible that some of these materials may relate to your progenitors.

The holdings of many manuscript repositories in the US are briefly described in the following volumes:
_P. M. Hamer, A GUIDE TO ARCHIVES AND MANUSCRIPTS IN THE US, Yale University Press, New Haven, CT, 1961.
_US National Historical Publications and Records Commission, DIRECTORY OF ARCHIVES AND MANUSCRIPT REPOSITORIES IN THE US, The Commission, Oryx Press, New York, NY, 1988.

_H. Cripe and D. Campbell, AMERICAN MANUSCRIPTS, 1763-1815,
Scholarly Resources, Wilmington, DE, 1977.
The major finding aid for locating manuscripts is a series of indexed
annual volumes which have been published since 1959.
_US Library of Congress, THE NATIONAL UNION CATALOG OF
MANUSCRIPT COLLECTIONS, The Library, Washington, DC,
issued annually 1959-. Volumes indexed individually.
There is also an overall name index covering the volumes for 1959-84 and
an overall subject index for the same years:
_E. Altham and others, INDEX TO PERSONAL NAMES IN THE
NATIONAL UNION CATALOG OF MANUSCRIPT COLLEC-
TIONS, 1959-84, Chadwyck-Healey, Arlington, VA, 1988, 2 volumes.
_E. Altham and others, INDEX TO SUBJECTS IN THE NATIONAL
UNION CATALOG OF MANUSCRIPT COLLECTIONS, 1959-84,
Chadwyck-Healey, Arlington, VA, 1994, 3 volumes.
Examine all the above indexes for your family surnames, then look under
pertinent states, counties, cities, and towns to see what records are
available. Don't overlook the many listings in the NATIONAL UNION
CATALOG indexes under the heading genealogy. You will find all the
above volumes in large libraries, including large genealogical libraries. If
you discover materials which you suspect relate to your forebears, write
the appropriate repository asking for details. Be sure to send a long
SASE and to request names of searchers if you cannot go in person.

93. Maps Maps are very important instruments for locating your
progenitors and for understanding their geographical
surroundings. They can lead to an identification of
exactly where your ancestors lived, the hills, valleys, and
water courses in their areas, the sites of nearby churches and cemeteries,
how far it was to the county seat and/or nearby towns, what roads they
travelled, how county boundaries changed while they were there, and what
other cities, towns, and counties were close by.

One of the most frequent uses of maps is to locate a county within
a state. For counties as they now exist, state road maps are often useful
for this. They may be obtained from state tourist agencies, state highway
departments, book stores, and gasoline stations. The following book
contains state outline maps of county (or town) boundaries as they now
exist:
_A. Eichholz, ANCESTRY'S REDBOOK, Ancestry Publishing, Salt Lake
City, UT, 1989.

It is important in many cases to trace the parent counties of your fore-bear's counties, especially when county jurisdictions and boundary changes occurred during their residence. The book just mentioned lists the parent county or counties of each county along with the dates of the changes. This permits you to track back to previous counties in which you should seek data on your forebears. A very useful volume in this regard is:

_W. Thorndale and W. Dollarhide, MAP GUIDE TO FEDERAL CENSUSES, Genealogical Publishing Co., Baltimore, MD, 1987.

This volume shows you county boundaries as they were in each census year from 1790-1920. State archives and state libraries can often refer you to maps showing county boundaries during many past years. And you must not forget that older state atlases also contain them.

Once you locate the county or town, then it will help you to obtain detailed maps of the county or town, since they will give you much more information. Such maps can be found in county or town atlases, and obtained from county and town tourist bureaus, highway departments, book stores, and often from state highway departments. County and town land and tax offices frequently have plat books which show property boundaries. These offices and other agencies have from time to time issued landowner maps which show property lines with the names of the land owners shown within the lines. There is a sizable collection of such maps in the Library of Congress, from which copies can be ordered. A listing of many of these is:

_R. W. Stephenson, LAND OWNERSHIP MAPS, Library of Congress, Washington, DC, 1967.

The US Geological Survey has issued a series of inexpensive highly-detailed maps. Each map usually shows only part of a county or only a few towns. The maps may be purchased from the US Geological Survey (169 Federal Building, 1961 Stout St., Denver CO 80294 or 503 National Center, 12201 Sunrise Valley, Reston, VA 22092). Write them or call 1-800-USA-MAPS and request a price list for maps in the state(s) with which you are concerned. The maps are also available in many university libraries. Do not fail to obtain or look at these exceedingly valuable maps for your progenitor's areas.

Older detailed maps of cities can be located in city atlases and city directories, and recent ones can be obtained from book stores, city tourist agencies, and travel clubs. Contemporary city directories often contain ward maps which can assist you in locating an ancestor in an unindexed census (city censuses were usually taken by wards). The ward information will narrow your search to only the pertinent ward. There is also a large

collection of ward maps in the Library of Congress. Copies can be ordered from the listing in:
_M. H. Shelley, WARD MAPS OF US CITIES, Library of Congress, Washington, DC, 1975.

Many of the above maps and numerous other specialized ones are available in map collections which are to be found in state archives, state libraries, large genealogical libraries, and state university libraries. The map holdings of over 3000 repositories in the US are inventoried in:
_D. A. Cobb, GUIDE TO US MAP RESOURCES, American Library Association, Chicago, IL, 1986.

94. Marriage records
Many sorts of official governmental records of marriage have come to be made beginning early in colonial times. These records include marriage intentions (announcements of coming marriage), marriage bonds (money posted to guarantee the legality of a marriage), marriage applications, marriage licenses, and more rarely marriage consents (by parents for underaged). Copies of some of these may be in the governmental records in the place of the marriage. In addition, the officials usually entered the marriage in a register when the license or application was returned or a certificate was presented, authenticating that the marriage had been performed. Marriage records at their best will reveal the couple's full names, the marriage date and place, their places and dates of birth (or ages), their residences, their marital statuses, their parents' names, the groom's occupation, names of witnesses, and the minister or presiding official. In early times, not many of these data are likely to be found, but as time went on, more and more information appeared in the documents.

In most places, a county or town office was the place for the recording of marriage information. Some time later, many (but not all) states required that copies or originals of marriage records be sent to a central state registry. You may obtain records by addressing inquiries to these county, town, city, and/or state offices. In some cases, the State Archives or State Historical Society has been made the repository for earlier records. Because of their value, numerous marriage records have also been microfilmed, and many have been published, especially the earlier ones, in both book and CDROM form. The microfilmed records should be sought in the appropriate State Archives, State Library, State Historical Society, and the Family History Library (with its branch Family History Centers). Published marriage records can be sought in the relevant state, county, and/or town libraries, and in large genealogical libraries.

The following listing presents the places where original marriage records for each of the states may be found. You may write to the appropriate offices. County and town addresses will be found in:

_A. Eichholz, ANCESTRY'S REDBOOK, Ancestry Publishing, Salt Lake City, UT, 1992.

_NAMES AND PLACES, Wiley and Sons, New York, NY, latest edition.

_L. K. Meitzler, THE US COUNTY COURTHOUSE ADDRESS BOOK, Heritage Quest, Orting, WA, 1988.

It could be that you would first rather check your nearest Family History Center for microfilms and/or your nearest large genealogical library for published marriages.

_AL: Since 1936, Bureau of Vital Statistics, State Department of Public Health, Montgomery, AL 36130. Before 1936, Probate Judge in county. Records usually available from county origin.

_AZ: Clerk of Superior Courts in county. Some records as far back as 1860s.

_AR: Since 1917, Division of Vital Records, 1815 West Markham Street, Little Rock, AR. Before 1917, County Clerk. Records usually available from county origin.

_CA: Since 1905, Vital Records Branch, 410 N Street, Sacramento, CA 95814. Before 1905, County Recorder. Records usually available from county origin.

_CO: County Clerk. Statewide index at Vital Records Section, 4210 East 11th Avenue, Denver, CO 80220. Records usually available from county origin.

_CT: Since 1897, Vital Records Section, 79 Elm Street, Hartford, CT 06115. Before 1897, Registrar of Vital Statistics in town. Records date back to origins of towns. Large marriage record collection 1640-1900 at CT State Library, 231 Capitol Avenue, Hartford, CT 06106.

_DE: Since 1930, Bureau of Vital Statistics, State Health Building, Dover, DE 19901. For 1744-1928 and some earlier, DE State Archives, Hall of Records, Dover, DE 19901.

_DC: Since 1811, Marriage License Bureau, 515 5th Street, NW, Washington, DC 20001.

_FL: Since 1927, Office of Vital Statistics, PO Box 210, Jacksonville, FL 32231. Before 1927, Clerk of Circuit Court in county. In most counties records go back to or almost back to the origin.

_GA: Probate Judge in county. In general records go back to county origin, except in many cases of record loss.

_HI: Since 1853, Research and Statistics Office, PO Box 3378, Honolulu, HI 96801. Earlier records from 1826 at HI State Archives, 478 South King Street, Honolulu, HI 96813.

_ID: Since 1947, Bureau of Vital Statistics, Statehouse, Boise, ID 83720. Before 1947, County Recorder. Records often date back to origin of county.

_IL: Since 1962, Office of Vital Records, 535 West Jefferson Street, Springfield, IL 62761. Before 1962, County Clerk. Many records date from origin of county.

_IN: Clerk of Circuit Court or Clerk of Superior Court in county. State-wide index since 1958 at Division of Vital Records, PO Box 1964, Indianapolis, IN 46206. Records date back to origin of county.

_IA: Since 1880, Vital Records Section, Lucas State Office Building, Des Moines, IA 50319. Before 1880, Clerk of District Court in county. Many records date back to origin of county.

_KS: Since 1913, Bureau of Registration, 6700 South Topeka Avenue, Topeka, KS 66620. Before 1913, Probate Judge in county. Records usually date from county origin or shortly after.

_KY: Since 1958, Office of Vital Statistics, 275 East Main Street, Frankfort, KY 40621. Before 1958, Clerk of Circuit Court in county. Records usually date back to origin of county.

_LA: Clerk of Court in parish, except for Orleans Parish, from Division of Vital Records, PO Box 60630, New Orleans, LA 70160. Some parish records date back to origin of parish, some later, a few earlier (incomplete).

_ME: Since 1892, State Board of Vital Statistics, State House, Augusta, ME 04330. Before 1892, check both County Clerk and ME State Archives, State House, Station 84, Augusta, ME 04333.

_MD: Since 1951, Division of Vital Records, PO Box 13146, Baltimore, MD 21203. For 1914-50, MD State Archives, 350 Rowe Boulevard, Annapolis, MD 21401. Before 1914, Clerk of Circuit Court in county, except for Baltimore City, from Clerk of Court of Common Pleas of city. Also check MD State Archives.

_MA: Since 1841, Registry of Vital Records, 150 Tremont Street, Boston, MA 02111. Before 1841, Town Clerk.

_MI: Since 1867, Office of Vital and Health Statistics, 3500 North Logan Street, Lancing, MI 48914. Before 1867, County Clerk. Records in some counties date back to or almost to the origin.

_MN: Clerk of District Court in county and MN Historical Society, 690 Cedar Street, St. Paul, MN 55101. State-wide index since 1958 at Section of Vital Statistics, 717 Delaware Street, SE, Minneapolis, MN 55440.

_MS: Circuit Clerk in county. Records usually date to origin of county.

_MO: Recorder of Deeds in county. Statewide index since 1948 at Bureau of Vital Records, State Department of Health, Jefferson City, MO 65101. Records usually date back to or near the origin of the county.

_MT: Clerk of District Court in county. Records usually date back to county origin.

_NE: Since 1909, Bureau of Vital Statistics, PO Box 95007, Lincoln, NE 68509. Before 1909, County Court Clerk. Records usually date back to county origin.

_NV: County Recorder in county. Statewide index since 1968 at Division of Health-Vital Statistics, Capitol Complex, Carson City, NV 89710. Records date from county origin.

_NH: Since 1640, Bureau of Vital Records, Hazen Drive, Concord, NH 03301. Or Town Clerk. Records date to town origin.

_NJ: Since 1848, Archives and History Bureau, State Department of Education, Trenton, NJ 08625. Before 1848, County Clerk and Archives and History Bureau.

_NM: County Clerk. Statewide index at Vital Statistics Office, PO Box 968, Santa Fe, NM 87504. Records often go back to 1880s, a few to 1869-70.

_NY: For 1880-1907 and since 1915, Vital Records Section, Empire State Plaza, Tower Building, Albany, NY 12237. For 1908-15, County Clerk, or City Clerk in Albany or Buffalo, or Registrar of Vital Statistics in Yonkers. Some records before 1880 in NY State Archives, especially 1847-52, some published. For New York City 1847-1937, from Municipal Archives, for after 1937, City Clerk in borough.

_NC: Since 1962, Vital Records Branch, PO Box 2091, Raleigh, NC 27602. For 1868-1962, Registrar of Deeds in county. Before 1868, NC Division of Archives, 109 East Jones Street, Raleigh, NC 27611.

_ND: Since 1925, Division of Vital Records, State Department of Health, Bismarck, ND 58505. Before 1925, County Judge. Most records date from county of origin.

_OH: Probate Judge in county. Most records date from county origin.

_OK: Clerk of Court in county. Most records date from county origin, in some cases, back into territorial times.

_OR: Since 1906, Vital Statistics Section, PO Box 116, Portland, OR 97207. Before 1906, County Clerk. Most records date from county origin.

_PA: Marriage License Clerk in county for records back to 1885. Some of these also at PA Bureau of Archives, PO Box 1026, Harrisburg, PA

17108. Also there are records 1860-93 for Lancaster, Philadelphia, Pittsburgh.

_RI: Since 1853, Division of Vital Statistics, 75 Davis Street, Providence, RI 02908. For 1850-53, City or Town Clerk. For 1636-1850 use published records or City or Town Clerk.

_SC: Since 1950, Office of Vital Records, 2600 Bull Street, Columbia, SC 29201. For 1911-50, Probate Judge in county.

_SD: Since 1905, Health Statistics Program, Joe Foss Office Building, Pierre, SD 57501. Before 1905, Register of Deeds or Clerk of County Court. Some records date back to 1882.

_TN: Since 1945, Division of Vital Records, Cordell Hull Building, Nashville, TN 37219. Before 1945, Clerk of Court in county. Records sometimes go back to county origin.

_TX: County Clerk. Records usually go back to date of county origin.

_UT: County Clerk. Many records go back to 1887/88, a few earlier.

_VT: Town or City Clerk. Records before 1857 incomplete. Statewide index at Public Records Division, 6 Baldwin Place, Montpelier, VT 05602.

_VA: Since 1853, Division of Vital Records, PO Box 1000, Richmond, VA 23208. Before 1853, Clerk of Court in county or City Clerk in city. Often date back into 1700s, sometimes much earlier.

_WA: Since 1968, Vital Records, PO Box 9709, LB11, Olympia, WA 98504. Before 1968, County Auditor. Many date back to county origin, some not quite that far.

_WV: Since 1964, Division of Vital Statistics, State Office Building No. 3, Charleston, WV 25305. Before 1964, County Clerk. Many records go back to or near the county origin.

_WI: Since 1836, Bureau of Health Statistics, PO Box 309, Madison, WI 53701. Records often date back to early 1820s or to county origin.

_WY: Since 1941, Vital Records Services, Hathaway Building, Cheyenne, WY 82002. Before 1941, County Clerk. For 1869-1970, also at WY State Archives, Barrett State Office Building, Cheyenne, WY 82002.

As can be seen from the above listings, in many instances official (state, county, city) marriage records cease to be available when you go back far enough. You will also often find that early records are incomplete, especially in frontier areas and times, and that they contain nothing on your forebears. In such situations, you will need to seek marriage information or indications from other sorts of records. The most likely sources include records of the following types: Bible, biography, cemetery, census, church, city directory, county and city history, directories, family records, fraternal organizations, gravestones, hereditary societies, military, mortuary, <u>newspaper</u>, <u>pension</u>, <u>probate</u>, published genealogy, tax, <u>will</u>. All of these are discussed in detail in other sections of this Handbook. Those that are usually the most helpful have been underlined.

---

95. Migration patterns

A knowledge of the general westward migration which resulted in the settlement of the US can be exceptionally valuable to you. Such knowledge will often assist you to predict where your forebears went when they left a place. In many cases, it will also help you to make a good guess as to the route they followed.

The settlement of the US largely began on the east coast with the coming of five major groups. These large groups followed fairly quickly upon the heels of smaller groups of earlier settlers who came as early as 1607. (1) the Congregationalist Puritans, mostly from Eastern England during 1629-41 to MA, (2) the Episcopalian Cavaliers and their servants and laborers mostly from south and southwest England during 1642-74 to the Chesapeake Bay area [VA, MD], (3) the Quakers mostly from the north midlands of England during 1675-1715 to the DE Valley [PA, DE, western NJ], (4) the Presbyterian and Anglican peoples from northeastern Ireland and the counties on both sides of the English-Scottish border during 1717-75 to the backcountry, that is, the country immediately behind the coastal settlements of the above three groups, and (5) German Pietists and German Lutherans during 1708-75 into the DE Valley and the backcountry. These five migrations represent the major ones, but you must remember that smaller groups and groups with other ethnic origins settled in between and among them.

Now, let us look at the basic periods of settlement: (1) the early colonial era, 1607-1700, chiefly English settlers, (2) up to the Appalachian mountains, 1700-63, continuing English, with many Germans and Scots-Irish, (3) through the Appalachian mountains, 1763-83, (4) into the trans-Appalachian region, 1783-1812, (5) up to the MS River, 1812-50, (6) across the MS River 1821-63, (7) the jump to the far West, 1825-46, and (8) the filling in between, 1861-90, that is, the settlement of what was jumped over in 1825-46. The most important factors in setting this pattern were (a) four passages through or around the Appalachian mountains and (b) the region along the IL-MO border where the OH River enters the MS River from the east and the MO River enters it from the west. The four passages through the Appalachian Mountains are the Cumberland Gap into KY, the passage from southeastern PA and northeastern MD into southwestern PA (Pittsburgh), the southern coastal route around the Appalachian Mountains (MD-VA-NC-SC-GA-AL), and the large gap in NY defined by the Mohawk Valley and the Lake Erie Plain which leads to western NY.

The early colonial era (1607-1700) involved the settlement of the eastern coast, the coastal river valleys, and the lowlands. The English settled VA (1607), MA (1620), and MD (1634), with the Dutch coming to NY (1624). The English moved into ME (1630s), CT (1636), RI (1636), and NH (1638). Swedes settled in DE and NJ (1638), but the Dutch took over in 1655, with the English taking all Dutch territory (NY, DE, NJ) in 1664. The English went from VA to NC (1670s), and other English settled SC (1670) and PA (1682). GA was not to be settled until 1733.

In the period 1700-63, the land between the coastal lowlands and the Appalachian mountains was settled. The Appalachians run all the way from northeastern NY down to northwestern GA. When you move just over the eastern-most range of these mountains, you will find a rich fertile valley (the Great Valley) also running from northeastern NY to northwestern GA, and enclosed on both sides by Appalachian Mountains. In the western Appalachians and beyond were Indians and the French. Immigrants in sizable numbers began entering at Philadelphia (Germans 1709- and Scots-Irish 1717-), filled southeastern PA, then turned south down the Great Valley (1727-), moved from it into central VA and NC and western SC, and filled the Valley almost to TN. Meanwhile, Scots-Irish also came to New England and joined in the movement into the uplands of MA, CT, NH, ME, and VT.

In 1763, the British won the French and Indian War, expelling the French and driving the Indians back. This included the takeover of Fort Duquesne (Pittsburgh) which stood at the westward-flowing OH River. This war effectively opened up two gaps in the Appalachian Mountains, the Cumberland Gap into KY, and the gap to Pittsburgh. So settlers moved (1) from PA-MD-VA-NC through the Valley through the Cumberland Gap into KY, (2) from PA-VA-NC-MD through the Valley into TN, and (3) from PA-NJ-MD-VA to Pittsburgh and its surrounding area. Then came the American Revolution which left the US with all land E of the MS River, gave Spain FL and the land west of the MS River, and left hostile Indians in northern OH and AL-MS.

The trans-Appalachian region was occupied during 1783-1812. This was because Indians were driven out of western NY during the

Revolution, thus opening the Mohawk Valley-Erie Plain gap through the Appalachians. In addition, the OH Indians were defeated in 1795, and the US acquired the LA Territory (west of MS River) in 1803. These were the major movements which occurred: (1) New Englanders into western NY, (2) NJ-DE-PA-MD-VA to Pittsburgh then down the OH River [northern KY, southern OH, IN, and IL], (3) NJ-PA-MD down the Valley to TN-KY and across KY into southern OH, (4) NC-SC to TN-KY, and (5) SC into GA and northern AL. Note carefully the dates at which the next four states entered the Union: VT(1791), KY(1792), TN(1796), OH(1803).

Settlement during 1812-40 moved up to the MS River. As of 1812, the OH Valley from Pittsburgh down to the MS River represented the center line of settlement. North of this in northern IN and IL, and south of this in AL and MS, there were strong hostile Indians. They were defeated and pushed west in the War of 1812, and the westerly movement resumed. During 1815-30 southerners (KY-TN-VA-NC-SC) crossed KY, western VA, and southern OH to southern IN and IL, then to mines in northwestern IL and southwestern WI. In 1830-50, people from NY-OH-PA-Germany settled northern IN and IL, and southern MI and WI. The importance of the NY gap (Mohawk Valley-Erie Plain), the Erie Canal along this gap, the heavy immigration into NY City, and the Erie Canal's connection with the Great Lakes should be recognized in this 1830-50 movement. During the entire period 1815-50, western GA, AL, MS, and western TN were filled by people from NC-SC-GA and east TN.

Settlement across the MS River had begun quite early in LA (French, Spanish, Acadians), the US acquired the area in 1803, and people from MS-AL-GA-Ireland-Germany came in, with LA becoming a state in 1812. However, the main thrust westward occurred as MO was settled by people from KY-TN-VA-OH-Germany-Ireland, and became a state in 1821. It became the trade center of the west, and became the center for movement further west. AR became a state in 1836 following settlement from TN-AL-MS-NC-KY-GA. The areas of the states of KS and OK were set aside for relocation of displaced eastern Indians 1825-40, and this reserve acted as a migration barrier. People from LA-MS-AR-MO-KY chose to go south to TX or to go to northwestern MO and then jump to CA-OR. The upper MS River was crossed by people from OH-IN-IL-PA-NY-KY, who brought IA to statehood in 1846. Then MN was settled by persons from NY-WI-Germany-Ireland, with statehood coming in 1858. During this time, Americans had started moving into TX in 1821, TX became independent of Mexico in 1836, and was annexed to the US in 1845. The state was largely settled from TN-AL-GA-MS and by Germans. People from OH-IL-MO-IN-IA-Germany-Ireland began entering KS in 1854 and it became a state in 1861. NE statehood was acquired in 1867 as a result of migrations from IL-IA-OH-NY-PA-Germany-Sweden.

The next movement is often a surprise to people when they first hear of it. What occurred was that many people jumped from the MO-IA-KS-NE area to OR-CA during 1825-50. The generally accepted reasons are that it was believed the intervening land was unproductive (not true, but thought to be) and that sizable portions of it were inhabited by hostile Indians (true). The western valleys of the British OR area began to fill in the 1830s, with sizable migrations by the OR Trail occurring after 1842. The British gave up the area in 1846, and it became the OR Territory in 1848, most of its settlers having come from MO-IL-IA-OH. In 1847-8, persecuted Mormons settled in the UT desert, and in 1850 the settlement became the Territory of UT. As early as 1841, US settlers were moving overland into Mexican CA, in 1848 the US took CA from Mexico along with NM and AZ, the gold rush occurred in 1849, and CA became a state in 1850.

Following the Civil War during 1861-90, the remainder of the US was settled. The mining frontier moved eastward from the west coast (CA to NV-CO, OR to WA-ID-MT-WY-SD), farmers following the miners into these areas. NV received statehood in 1864 (settled from CA-NY-OH), CO in 1876 (settled from IL-NY-MO-OH-IA), WA in 1889 (settled from IL-NY-IA-OR-OH-MO-Canada-Germany-Sweden), MT in 1889 (settled from MO-IL-IA-NY), SD in 1889 (settled from IA-WI-IL-NY-Norway-Germany), ID in 1890 (settled from UT-MO-IL-IA-WA), and WY in 1890 (settled from IA-NE-IL-MO-UT). All these invasions of Indian lands precipitated bloody wars, ending with the Indians on reservations, and the opening up of the Great Plains. During 1865-85 the Great Plains filled with ranchers and their cattle, spreading north from TX (west TX-western OK-KS-NE-CO-WY-MT-SD-ND, then moving into NM-AZ-eastern OR). The ranchers were followed in some places by sheepherders, then by farmers 1875-90 who came from the MS Valley and overseas (Ireland, Germany, Scandinavia). Settlement was successfully encouraged by the states and the new railroads, both of which recruited in Europe. In 1889, the US opened a portion of central OK country to white settlers, the eastern portion being occupied by Indians. Shortly after, more tracts in western OK were made available to white settlers, and in 1907 the two areas (Indians in east, whites in center and west) became the state of OK.

If you care to read in detail about all the above settlements or about one or more of them in particular, the best volume is:
_R. A. Billington and M. Ridge, WESTWARD EXPANSION, Macmillan, New York, NY, 1982.
And if you wish to examine maps showing detailed migration routes, you will find an extensive listing in:
_R. S. Ladd, MAPS SHOWING EXPLORERS' ROUTES, TRAILS, AND EARLY ROADS IN THE US, Library of Congress, Washington, DC, 1962.

96. Military records

The 13 colonies which became the US and the US have engaged in a sizable number of wars. The records kept on the participants in these wars began essentially as only lists of names, but as time went on, more and more data were kept. The major wars, that is, those with the largest numbers of fighting men, were the French and Indian War (1754-63), the Revolutionary War (1775-83), the War of 1812 (1812-5), the Civil War (1861-5), and the two World Wars. Others included many colonial wars, Indian wars (1817-98), the Mexican War (1846-8), and the Spanish-American War (1898-1902). The first four mentioned are of the greatest importance because of the numbers of men and the need for genealogical information during those years.

In general, five main types of records were generated by the wars. First, there were service records (enlistment, muster, pay, rosters, account, discharge, hospital, wounded, prisoner, deserter, death, capture, prison, parole). These can give dates and places and events during service, and sometimes descriptions, birthdates or ages, birthplaces, and places of residence. Second, there were pension records, mostly US, but after the Civil War, Confederate pensions were given by some states. These records are often quite rich: applications, supporting documents (birth, age, marriage, children, residences after the war, description, health, occupation), actions, payments (including moves from one place to another, death date, death place), then another application by the widow followed by similar events and information. Third, there were bounty land awards by both states and the US, none being given by the US for service after 1855. These records involved applications and supporting documents, actions, and warrants. Some of the warrants were redeemed for land by the veteran, but many were sold. Fourth, there were claims filed by both military men and civilians who were owed money for service and/or supplies. Finally, there were histories and reports of military units (such as regiments) written as both official and non-official accounts, many of them being published.

The original records on colonial wars are in the pertinent state archives. Most of the more important ones have been published, as was indicated in the previous section entitled Colonial war records. The original records on those who fought for the united colonies in the Revolutionary War and on those who fought in federal US forces in the following wars are in the National Archives. So are the original service records for men who fought for the Confederacy (1861-5). Many of these records (service, bounty land, pension, claim) and indexes to them have been microfilmed. These microfilmed copies are available at the National Archives, its branches, the Family History Library, other large genealogical libraries, and at appropriate state libraries and archives. In addition to the above federal records, the state archives usually have more data on their own men who fought in federal forces, but they also often have data on men who fought only in state units and whose records never made it to the federal level. This was especially the case in the earlier wars. In other words, the state archives and/or adjutant general's offices often know of many war participants for which there are no federal records.

The first step in a search for your ancestor who may have fought in the wars is to look in major indexes to service, pension, and bounty land records in order to locate his exact state and regiment (or unit or ship). These major indexes are:
_(Revolutionary War) Daughters of the American Revolution, DAR PATRIOT INDEX, DAR, Washington, DC, 1966/79, 2 volumes; National Genealogical Society, INDEX OF REVOLUTIONARY WAR PENSION APPLICATIONS IN THE NATIONAL ARCHIVES, The Society, Washington, DC, 1976; F. Rider, AMERICAN GENEALOGICAL-BIOGRAPHICAL INDEX, Godfrey Memorial Library, Middletown, CT, 1942-, two series; National Archives, GENERAL INDEX TO COMPILED MILITARY SERVICE RECORDS OF REVOLUTIONARY WAR SOLDIERS, Microfilm M860, Washington, DC, 58 rolls. The service and pension records are all available on microfilm.
_(War of 1812) National Archives, INDEX TO COMPILED SERVICE RECORDS OF VOLUNTEER SOLDIERS WHO SERVED DURING THE WAR OF 1812, MICROFILM M602, Washington, DC, 234 rolls; National Archives, WAR OF 1812 MILITARY

BOUNTY LAND WARRANTS, 1815-58, Microfilm M848, Washington, DC, 14 rolls; National Archives, INDEX TO WAR OF 1812 PENSION APPLICATION FILES, Microfilm M313, Washington, DC, 102 rolls; National Archives, OLD WAR INDEX TO PENSION FILES, 1815-1926, Microfilm T316, Washington, DC, 7 rolls.

_(Indian wars) National Archives, INDEX TO COMPILED SERVICE RECORDS OF VOLUNTEER SOLDIERS WHO SERVED DURING INDIAN WARS AND DISTURBANCES, 1815-58, Microfilm M629, Washington, DC, 42 rolls; National Archives, OLD WAR INDEX TO PENSION FILES, 1815-1926, Microfilm T316, Washington, DC, 7 rolls; National Archives, INDEX TO INDIAN WARS PENSION FILES, 1892-1926, Microfilm T318, 12 rolls; National Archives, POST-REVOLUTIONARY BOUNTY LAND WARRANT APPLICATIONS, arranged alphabetically.

_(Mexican War) National Archives, INDEX TO COMPILED SERVICE RECORDS OF VOLUNTEER SOLDIERS WHO SERVED DURING THE MEXICAN WAR, Microfilm M616, 41 rolls; National Archives, INDEX TO MEXICAN WAR PENSION FILES, 1887-1926, Microfilm T317, 14 rolls; National Archives, OLD WAR INDEX TO PENSION FILES, 1815-1926, Microfilm T316, 7 rolls; National Archives, POST-REVOLUTIONARY BOUNTY LAND WARRANT APPLICATIONS, arranged alphabetically.

_(Civil War-Confederate) National Archives, CONSOLIDATED INDEX TO COMPILED SERVICE RECORDS OF CONFEDERATE SOLDIERS, Microfilm M253, 535 rolls. The service records are all available on microfilm.

_(Civil War-Union) National Archives, INDEXES TO COMPILED SERVICE RECORDS OF VOLUNTEER UNION SOLDIERS WHO SERVED IN ORGANIZATIONS FROM THE STATE OF AL* (Microfilm M263), AZTerritory (M532), AR* (M383), CA (M533), CO Territory (M534), CT (M535), Dakota Territory (M536), DE (M537), DC (M538), FL* (M264), GA* (M385), IL (M539), IN (M540), IA (M541), KS (M542), KY* (M386), LA* (M387), ME (M543), MD* (M388), MA (M544), MI (M545), MN (M546), MS* (M389), MO* (M390), NE Territory (M547), NV (M548), NH (M549), NJ (M550), NM Territory* (M242), NY (M551), NC* (M391), OH (M552), OR (M553), PA (M554), RI (M555), TN* (M392), TX* (M393), UT Territory* (M556), VT (M557), VA* (M394), WA Territory (M558), WV* (M507), WI (M559), separate index for each state. No overall consolidated index. The service records for all states marked * are available on microfilm. National

Archives, GENERAL INDEX TO PENSION FILES, 1861-1934, Microfilm T288, 544 rolls.

_(Spanish-American War) National Archives, GENERAL INDEX TO COMPILED SERVICE RECORDS OF VOLUNTEER SOLDIERS WHO SERVED DURING THE WAR WITH SPAIN, Microfilm M871, 126 rolls; National Archives, GENERAL INDEX TO PENSION FILES, 1861-1934, Microfilm T288, 544 rolls.

If you do not locate your progenitor in the above indexes, inquire by mail at the appropriate state archives, library, and office of the adjutant general.

When you have located a forebear who was a war participant, the state and the regiment (unit) are what are important. This will let you proceed to get the records (service, bounty land, pension). The service records for the Revolutionary War, Confederates in the Civil War, Union troops in states marked * in the previous paragraph, and a few others are on microfilm.

_National Archives, COMPILED SERVICE RECORDS OF SOLDIERS WHO SERVED IN THE AMERICAN ARMY DURING THE REVOLUTIONARY WAR, Microfilm M881, 1097 rolls: National Archives, COMPILED SERVICE RECORDS OF AMERICAN NAVAL PERSONNEL AND MEMBERS OF THE DEPARTMENTS OF THE QUARTERMASTER GENERAL AND THE COMMISSARY GENERAL OF MILITARY STORES WHO SERVED DURING THE REVOLUTIONARY WAR, Microfilm M880, 4 rolls.

_National Archives, COMPILED SERVICE RECORDS OF VOLUNTEER SOLDIERS WHO SERVED DURING THE WAR OF 1812 FROM THE TERRITORY OF MS, Microfilm M678, 22 rolls.

_National Archives, COMPILED SERVICE RECORDS OF VOLUNTEER SOLDIERS WHO SERVED DURING THE MEXICAN WAR FROM MS (Microfilm M863), PA (M1028), TN (M638), TX (M278), in Mormon organizations (M351).

_National Archives, COMPILED SERVICE RECORDS FOR UNION ARMY VOLUNTEERS FROM AL (Microfilm M276), AR (M399), FL (M400), GA (M403), KY (M397), LA (M396), MD (M384), MS (M404), MO (M405), NM Territory (M427), NC (M401), TN (M395), TX (M402), UT Territory (M692), VA (M398), WV (M508).

_National Archives, COMPILED SERVICE RECORDS FOR CONFEDERATE VOLUNTEER ARMY VOLUNTEERS FROM AL (Microfilm M311), AZ Territory (M318), AR (M317), FL (251), GA (M266), KY (M319), LA (M320), MD (M321), MS (M269), MO

(M322), NC (M270), SC (M267), TN (M268), TX (M323), VA (M324), Confederate Government Organizations (M258), General and Staff Officers (M331).

Revolutionary War pension and bounty land records are also available on microfilm.

_National Archives, REVOLUTIONARY WAR PENSION AND BOUNTY LAND WARRANT APPLICATIONS, Microfilm M804, 2670 rolls.

The above microfilms are available as indicated in the third paragraph of this section. Almost all records not on microfilm are available only at the National Archives, Washington, DC 20408. They (service, pension, bounty land, claim records) may be obtained by your personal visit, your hired researcher, or they may be ordered using NATF Form 80. These forms may be received by requesting them from the National Archives. Many other military records in the National Archives are described in

_National Archives, MILITARY SERVICE RECORDS, A SELECT CATALOG OF NATIONAL ARCHIVES MICROFILM PUBLICA-TIONS, The Archives, Washington, DC, 1985.

_National Archives, GUIDE TO GENEALOGICAL RESEARCH IN THE NATIONAL ARCHIVES, The Archives, Washington, DC, 1985.

After obtaining copies of the National Archives records, your next step is to write to three agencies in the appropriate state(s): the state archives, the state library, and the office of the state adjutant general. Addresses for the state archives and libraries are given in separate sections of this Handbook, and the state libraries can give you the addresses of the offices of the adjutants general. Ask these agencies about service, pay, bounty land, pension, claims and manuscript records. Inquire also about histories of the military unit (regiment) in which your progenitor served. These contacts with state agencies are absolutely essential for colonial military records, French and Indian War records, and Confederate records. Remember that Confederate pensions were granted by Confederate states and border states which had sizable Confederate participants (KY, MO).

Many other sources of military records are discussed in several guidebooks. If you care to pursue your searches further, consult:

_Geo. K. Schweitzer, REVOLUTIONARY WAR GENEALOGY, The Author, Knoxville, TN, 1991.

_J. C. and L. L. Neagles, LOCATING YOUR REVOLUTIONARY WAR ANCESTORS, Everton Publishers, Logan, UT, 1983.

_Geo. K. Schweitzer, WAR OF 1812 GENEALOGY, The Author, Knoxville, TN, 1994.
_B. H. Groene, TRACING YOUR CIVIL WAR ANCESTOR, Blair, Winston-Salem, NC, 1987.
_Geo. K. Schweitzer, CIVIL WAR GENEALOGY, The Author, Knoxville, TN, 1988.
_J. C. Neagles, CONFEDERATE RESEARCH SOURCES, Ancestry Publishing, Salt Lake City, 1987.
__J. C. Neagles, US MILITARY RECORDS, Ancestry, Salt Lake City, UT, 1994.

97. Mortality censuses When the federal censuses of 1850, 1860, 1870, and 1880 were taken, extra records were accumulated by inquiring about persons who had died during the year preceding 01 June of each of the census years. The information in the records includes name, age, sex, state or county of birth, month of death, and cause of death. It is estimated that only about 60% of the deaths were recorded in the three earlier mortality censuses. There were also 1885 mortality censuses for CO, FL, NE, NM, NC, ND, OH, and SD.

Many of the mortality records are on microfilm, including the following, which were done by the National Archives:
_National Archives, FEDERAL MORTALITY CENSUS SCHEDULES, 1850-80, for AZ (Microfilm T655), CO (T655), CT (A1165), DE (A1155), DC (T655), FL (T1168), GA (T655, T1137), IL (T1133), IA (T1156), KS (T1130), KY (T655), LA (T655, T1136), MA (T1204), MI (T1163), MT (GR6), NE (T1128), NJ (GR21), NC (GR1), OH (T1159, T1163), PA (T956), SC (GR22), SD (GR27), TN (T655, T1135), TX (T1134), UT (GR7), VT (GR7), VA (T1132), WA (T1154).
Those listed and those not listed are available as originals or as microfilm ycopies in the Family History Library, and/or the Daughters of the American Revolution Library (Washington, DC), and/or in pertinent state libraries, state archives, state historical societies, and from the American Genealogical Lending Library. Sometimes you will need to make an inquiry or two in order to find them. Almost all the mortality records have also been published and indexed, an indexed publication being available for each state. These are available at large genealogical libraries and state libraries.

98. Mortuary records

Mortuary establishments often have records dating quite far back (a few before the Civil War). In addition, these businesses are usually very well acquainted with the cemeteries in the area. In many instances they can therefore be of considerable help to you in locating records of death and burial sites. To locate mortuaries in or near any given place, consult:

_AMERICAN BLUE BOOK OF FUNERAL DIRECTORS, National Funeral Directors Association, New York, NY, latest issue.
_THE NATIONAL YELLOW BOOK OF FUNERAL DIRECTORS, Nomis Publications, Youngstown, OH, latest issue.

99. National Archives

The US National Archives, located at Pennsylvania Avenue between 7th and 9th Streets, Washington, DC 20408 is a giant storehouse of federal records. Many of these contain genealogical information of importance. It is well to remember that only _federal_ records (not state nor local) are to be found there, very few records for the period before the Revolutionary War (before the federal government) are to be found there, and many of the records do not have name indexes (because they were organized for nongenealogical purposes). Among the most useful records are the census records (population, mortality, agricultural, manufactures, slave, pensioner), passenger arrival lists (customs lists, immigration lists), naturalization records, military records (service, pension, bounty land records for the regular and volunteer army, and for the navy, marines, and coast guard), civilians during war periods, American Indian records, black American records, merchant seaman, civilian government employee records, public land records, private land claims, claims, federal court records, DC records, and cartographic records (maps, plats, surveys).

Many of these records have been discussed more thoroughly in other sections of this Handbook. Even more detailed descriptions of the numerous records in the National Archives are provided in:
_National Archives Staff, GUIDE TO GENEALOGICAL RESEARCH IN THE NATIONAL ARCHIVES, National Archives and Records Service, Washington, DC, 1985.
Quite a sizable number of the genealogically-useful records in the National Archives have been microfilmed. The following catalog lists them:
_NATIONAL ARCHIVES MICROFILM PUBLICATIONS, The Archives, Washington, DC, latest edition.
And these catalogs describe them:

_MILITARY SERVICE RECORDS, IMMIGRANT AND PASSEN-
GER ARRIVALS, GENEALOGICAL AND BIOGRAPHICAL
RESEARCH, BLACK STUDIES, AMERICAN INDIANS,
DIPLOMATIC RECORDS, National Archives, Washington, DC, 6
volumes, various dates.
_A GUIDE TO PRE-FEDERAL RECORDS IN THE NATIONAL
ARCHIVES, National Archives, Washington, DC, 1989.
These films are available in the National Archives, the eleven National
Archives Field Branches, and the Family History Library. Many of the
microfilms are available in large genealogical libraries, state libraries, and
state archives. Many may also be borrowed from the American Genea-
logical Lending Library, PO Box 329, Bountiful, UT 84011 and the National Archives Microfilm Rental Program, PO Box 30, Annapolis
Junction, MD 20701.

100. National Archives Branches

The National Archives, which
was discussed in the previous
section, has eleven National
Archives Regional Centers
(Branches) located near or in major cities in the US. Each of the eleven
Branches serves certain states. Each Branch has many of the microfilms
produced by the National Archives, and, in addition, each has many
original records pertaining to its own region. These special original
records include those of the federal courts, Indians, naturalizations, taxes,
ships, seamen, land offices, mining, customs, marine inspection, naviga-
tion, and army engineers. For details concerning the holdings of the
Branches, look into:
_L. D. Szucs and S. H. Luebking, THE ARCHIVES, A GUIDE TO
THE NATIONAL ARCHIVES FIELD BRANCHES, Ancestry
Publishing, Salt Lake City, UT, 1988.
There are also separate guides to each of the Branches which are avail-
able from the National Archives and the Branches:
_GUIDE TO NATIONAL ARCHIVES ATLANTA (or BOSTON or
CHICAGO or DENVER or FORT WORTH or KANSAS CITY or
LOS ANGELES or NEW YORK or PHILADELPHIA or SAN
FRANCISCO or SEATTLE) BRANCH, The Archives, 1987.

The eleven National Archives Field Branches, their addresses, and
the states they serve are:
_National Archives, New England Region, 380 Trapelo Road, Waltham,
MA 02154. CT, ME, MA, NH, RI, VT.

_National Archives, Northeast Region, 201 Varick St., New York, NY 10014. NY, NJ, Puerto Rico, US Virgin Islands.

_National Archives, Mid-Atlantic Region, Room 1350, 9th and Market Streets, Philadelphia, PA 19107. PA, DE, MD, VA, WV.

_National Archives, Southeast Region, 1557 St. Joseph Avenue, East Point, GA 30344. AL, FL, GA, KY, MS, NC, SC, TN.

_National Archives, Great Lakes Region, 7358 South Pulaski Road, Chicago, IL 60629. IL, IN, MI, MN, OH, WI.

_National Archives, Central Plains Region, 2312 East Bannister Road, Kansas City, MO 64131. IA, KS, MO, NE.

_National Archives, Southwest Region, 501 West Felix Street, Fort Worth, TX 76115. AR, LA, OK, TX, NM.

_National Archives, Rocky Mountain Region, Building 48, Denver Federal Center, Denver, CO 80225. CO, MT, ND, SC, UT, WY.

_National Archives, Northwest Region, 6125 Sand Point Way, NE, Seattle, WA 98115. AK, ID, OR, WA.

_National Archives, Pacific Sierra Region, 1000 Comodore Drive, San Bruno, CA 94066. Northern CA, HI, NV (all except Clark County), Samoa, Pacific Ocean Islands.

_National Archives, Pacific Southwest Region, 24000 Avilla Road, Laguna Niguel, CA 92677. Southern CA, AZ, NV (Clark County).

Every one of the above Branches has a research room staffed by trained archivists. Researchers are welcome and the microfilms and original records are available for use.

101. Naturalization records

In the colonial period, most of the immigrants to what later would be the US were British citizens, so no naturalization processes were required. When other nationalities began to arrive, they were supposed to take oaths of allegiance to the colony and the Crown as they got off the ship, in the presence of an official, or in a court. In 1740, the English Parliament passed a law setting forth naturalization requirements: 7 years residence in one colony plus an oath of allegiance to the Crown. The oath records usually carry a minimum of information, ordinarily the name and date, and the country of origin.

In 1776-7, all those who supported the Revolution were automatically considered citizens. In many of the colonies oaths of allegiance were required to establish patriotism. During the period 1777-91, immigrants were required by the new states to take an oath of allegiance. In 1778, the articles of Confederation of the newly-established US made all citizens of the states citizens of the new nation. The US Congress in 1790 enacted a national naturalization act which required one year's state residence, two year's US residence, and a loyalty oath taken in court. In 1795, a five year's residence came to be required along with a declaration of intent three years before the oath. Then in 1798, these times became 14 and 5 years respectively. Revised statutes of 1802 reverted to the 5 and 3 years. The declaration and oath could be carried out in any court of record (US, state, county, city). Wives and children of naturalized males became citizens automatically (until 1922). Foreigners who served in the US military could apply directly for citizenship without a prior declaration. The declarations and final papers (at the oath) contain many of the following: name, original country, port of arrival, date of arrival, description, birth date, birthplace, present address, and name of spouse.

In 1906, the Bureau of Immigration and Naturalization was set up and this agency has kept records on all naturalizations since then. Thus, if your progenitor was naturalized after September 1906, write to the following address for an application form which you can use to request records:
_Immigration and Naturalization Service, 425 Eye Street, NW, Washington, DC 20536.
For naturalization records before October 1906, you need to realize that the process could have taken place in any of many courts. As was stated above, any court of record could have been used. These courts must be searched. Often, they will have indexes, but sometimes you will find them unindexed and/or mixed in with other types of records. Don't forget the federal court records (in the National Archives Field Branches). Quite a number of naturalization records are available on microfilm at the Family History Library.

102. Newspapers

Thousands of old newspapers are in libraries, archives, and historical society repositories. Many have also been microfilmed. And a fair number have been indexed. The first newspaper in the American colonies was started in Boston in 1690. By 1765, over 30 were being published, and by 1830 there were about 1000. Early on, newspapers contained very little information of genealogical value, but as time went on useful items increased. Among them were births, engagements, marriages, anniversaries, deaths (obituaries), divorces, family reunions, land sales, legal notices, local news, social events, court cases, accidents, military news, unclaimed letters, organization meetings, public announcements, and advertisements by businesses, physicians, dentists, morticians, and attorneys.

If you know or can approximate the dates of significant events in your progenitor's life, it will probably be rewarding to examine newspapers of the area during these dates. To discover what newspapers are available and where they are located, consult the following sources:
_C. S. Brigham, HISTORY AND BIBLIOGRAPHY OF AMERICAN NEWSPAPERS, 1690-1820, American Antiquarian Society, Worcester, MA, 1947, 2 volumes.
_W. Gregory, AMERICAN NEWSPAPERS, 1821-1936, H. W. Wilson Co., New York, NY, 1937.
_NEWSPAPERS IN MICROFORM, US, Library of Congress, Washington, DC, latest edition. Many of these can be borrowed.
_US NEWSPAPER PROGRAM, NATIONAL UNION LIST, Online Computer Library Center, Dublin, OH, latest edition.

Should the above sources not lead you to papers which you need, write the local library, the state library, the state historical society, and the state university library (see sections on Libraries and State libraries for addresses). Enclose an SASE, and be sure to ask about both newspapers and newspaper indexes, as well as published and typescript abstracted newspaper records. Don't overlook the possibilities of ethnic, foreign language, and religious newspapers. A couple of good reference books, one listing newspaper indexes, the other guiding you to obituaries are:
_A. C. Milner, NEWSPAPER INDEXES, A LOCATION AND SUBJECT GUIDE, Scarecrow Press, Metuchen, NJ, latest edition.
_B. M. Jarboe, OBITUARIES, A GUIDE TO SOURCES, G. K. Hall, Boston, MA, 1989.
The Family History Library does not actively collect newspapers, but you should examine the catalog at your nearest Family History Center for newspaper abstracts and indexes, which they do collect.

Another valuable use of newspapers is to place a notice in a current newspaper in the community where your forebear lived. Ask if anyone can give you information. To find the name and address of the appropriate newspaper, look in:
_GALE DIRECTORY OF PUBLICATIONS, AN ANNUAL GUIDE TO NEWSPAPERS, MAGAZINES, JOURNALS, AND RELATED PUBLICATIONS, Gale Research Co., Detroit, MI, latest annual edition.

| **103. Orphans** | In the colonial and early US years, county and/or town officials (usually called overseers of the poor) dealt with orphaned children. If orphaned children had inherited property, the courts appointed guard- |

ians. Orphan children were placed with relatives or friends or in homes or orphanages. Often when they became old enough, they were bound out to learn a trade or to be servants. Records of these actions may be found in overseers' minutes, probate court records, or county court records. Orphanages could be maintained by the local government, the state government, churches, other benevolent organizations, or private parties. The records should be sought at the county and town level in the various courts, and the local library should be consulted. Some of the orphanages may still exist, and the local library may know where records of defunct ones are.

| **104. Other local repositories** | In doing research in counties, cities, and towns, it is easy to overlook several very important possibilities for finding records. Chief among |

these are: (1) abstract and title insurance companies, (2) older businesses, (3) cemetery offices, (4) church offices, (5) mortuaries, (6) newspaper offices, (7) organizations, associations, lodges, fraternities, societies, (8) insurance agencies, and (9) schools. (1) Abstract and title insurance companies function to authenticate and insure titles to land. They maintain detailed records on land grants, sales, purchases, mortgages, and liens. (2) Older businesses in communities may still have employment, sales, and credit records. (3) Cemetery offices are often overlooked. Don't forget that in addition to tombstone inscriptions, further data may be available in a cemetery office. (4) Local churches frequently have kept their records, and they often go back quite far. See the separate section on Church records in this Handbook.

(5) Mortuary records should not be by-passed. The older funeral establishments are the most likely to have records which may be of use to you. (6) Newspapers often maintain extensive files of their own issues dating back many years. Often they are the only source of such collections. (7) Organizations, associations, societies, lodges, and fraternities sometimes have kept the older records on their members. Applications are especially to sought, since they may give vital record data and parents' names. (8) Insurance agency records, particularly those at the local level, might have been saved. Again, the applications can carry useful information. (9) School records can provide birth and parentage data, but they

usually do not go very far back, they have often been lost or destroyed, and they are generally hard to locate.

105. Passport applications

Even though not required before 1916, many US citizens applied for and obtained passports. The National Archives has many of the applications for 1795-1925. These passport applications contain differing amounts of information, the data being more sparse for the earlier ones. Among the items often found are name, signature, residence, age, personal description, and sometimes birthdate and place, date and port of arrival in US, name of ship, and date and place of naturalization. If other family members accompanied the passport holder, they too were listed, and data on them were given. The passport records are in Record Groups 59 and 84 at the National Archives. They are variously indexed for different periods of time. The Family History Library has microfilm copies of the applications and most of the indexes. You may borrow them through a Family History Center, or inquiries concerning these records and requests for the records may be addressed to:

_Record Groups 59 and 84, National Archives, Washington, DC 20408. Give them as much information as you can, but try to include the residence and the approximate date. For passport applications in 1925 and after, write:

_Passport Office, US Department of State, 1425 K Street, NW, Washington, DC 20520.

A good survey of the history of US passports is provided in:

_US Passport Office, THE US PASSPORT, PAST, PRESENT, FUTURE, The Office, Washington, DC, 1976.

106. Passenger lists

The year 1820 is a very important one with regard to the keeping of lists of passengers of ships arriving in the US from overseas. Before 1820, there are only a few records resulting from a federal mandate for the filing of such lists of passengers. The lists before 1820 (with a few exceptions) are widely scattered, quite incomplete, have largely been published, and the majority have been indexed. After 1820, the records are a result of federal law which was followed carefully in most major ports. The post-1820 records document the arrival of millions of immigrants. With some variances according to the port, the records from 1820 into the 1882/93 time are called customs passenger lists and those afterwards are the immigration passenger lists. Ship passenger arrival lists ordinarily give only a minimum of genealogical data. Family relationships are the major items which are often found, along with the ship, date, port of arrival, and the country or area of departure. Sometimes you will find the exact city, town, district, parish, or local area, but not usually.

If your ancestor arrived before 1820, the largest and most comprehensive set of indexes should be used. This multi-volumed publication indexes almost 2 million names which have been gathered from over 1300 sources of passenger lists from 1607 onward:
_P. W. Filby and M. K. Meyer, PASSENGER AND IMMIGRANT LISTS INDEX, Gale Research Co., Detroit, MI, 1981, with annual SUPPLEMENTS, 1982ff.

If your ancestor arrived after 1820 (or 1800-19 at Philadelphia), use the following indexes:
_National Archives, BALTIMORE PASSENGER ARRIVAL LIST INDEXES, 1820-1952, Microfilms M326, M327, M334, T520, Washington, DC. Lead to microfilm lists M255, M596, T844, and original records.
_National Archives, BOSTON PASSENGER ARRIVAL LIST INDEXES, 1820-1940, Microfilms M265, M334, T521, T617, T790, Washington DC. Lead to microfilm lists M277, T843.
_National Archives, NEW YORK PASSENGER ARRIVAL LIST INDEXES, 1820-46, 1897-1943, Microfilms M261, T519, T612, T621, Washington, DC. Lead to microfilm lists M237, T715.
_National Archives, PHILADELPHIA PASSENGER ARRIVAL LIST INDEXES, 1800-1948, Microfilms M334, M360, T526, T791, Washington, DC. Lead to microfilm lists M425, T840.
_National Archives, NEW ORLEANS PASSENGER ARRIVAL LIST INDEXES, 1820-1952, microfilms M334, T527, T618, Washington, DC. Lead to microfilm lists M259, M272, T905.
_National Archives, A SUPPLEMENTAL INDEX TO PASSENGER LISTS OF VESSELS ARRIVING AT ATLANTIC AND GULF COAST POSTS, EXCLUDING NEW YORK, 1820-74, Microfilm M334, Washington, DC. Leads to microfilm list M575, which gives passengers to many ports. The records have many years missing for most ports.
These microfilms are available at the National Archives, its Field Branches, at the Family History Library, and in pertinent large genealogical libraries, state libraries, and state archives. There are also numerous published lists and indexes, most dealing with special ethnic groups, special dates, or special ports. These may be found listed in:

_M. Tepper, AMERICAN PASSENGER ARRIVAL RECORDS, Genealogical Publishing Co., Baltimore, MD, 1994.
_P. W. Filby, AMERICAN AND BRITISH GENEALOGY AND HERALDRY, New England Historic Genealogical Society, Boston, MA, 1983, and periodic SUPPLEMENTS, 1987, etc.
The numbers of immigrants coming into the major ports during the period 1820-1952 are approximately as follows (figures given in thousands, K): New York City (23,960K), Boston (2050K), Baltimore (1460K), Philadephia (1240K), New Orleans (710K), and San Francisco (500K).

For further information on passenger records and for a detailed list of ports and dates covered in A SUPPLEMENTAL INDEX (M334), look into:
_National Archives, GUIDE TO GENEALOGICAL RESEARCH IN THE NATIONAL ARCHIVES, The Archives, Washington, DC, 1985, Chapter 2.
In addition to passenger arrival lists, there are also passenger departure lists from European ports. A good listing of many of those available is found in:
_A. Eakle and J. Cerny, THE SOURCE, A GUIDEBOOK TO AMERICAN GENEALOGY, Ancestry Publishing, Salt Lake City, UT, 1984, Chapter 15.
Such departure lists may also be located in the Family History Library. The locality section of the catalog available in every Family History Center will lead you to them. Look under the country of departure.

Please notice that the very important New York immigration records for most of the latter half of the 19th century (1847-96) are not as yet indexed. This indexing is now in process, but until it is completed, the records must be gone through page-by-page. Any information you might have on date of immigration, port of origin, and name of ship could shorten your work considerably. If your immigrant ancestor was German, you may be fortunate, because many Germans coming during this time period have been indexed in:
__I. A. Glazier and P. W. Filby, GERMANS TO AMERICA, Scholarly Resources, Wilmington, DE, 1988ff., numerous volumes.
Other ethnic group passenger compilations include:
__I. A. Glazier and P. William Filby, ITALIANS TO AMERICA, 1880-1899, Scholarly Resources, Wilmington, DE, 1992ff., numerous volumes.

__R. P. Swierenga, DUTCH IMMIGRANTS IN US SHIP PASSENGER
MANIFESTS, 1820-1880, Scholarly Resources, Wilmington, DE, 1983,
2 volumes.

107. Patriotic and hereditary societies

Patriotic, hereditary, and lineage societies are made up of people with ancestors from some historical event, organization, group, place, or time. Examples are societies whose membership is composed of individuals with a forebear who served in a war, belonged to a particular military group, came from a certain country, was an early settler of a state or area, had a royal heritage, lived during a certain period (colonial, pre-1700, etc.), had a particular occupation, came on a certain ship, or was of a particular religious persuasion. Many of these societies publish a periodical or a newsletter, and many of them have issued volumes listing the ancestors they have traced, the lines of descent, and present and past members. These societies can be of assistance to genealogists in two ways: (1) their publications can be looked at to see if any member has traced back to an ancestor of yours, and (2) you can write them for information and for details concerning membership, if you care to join.

Detailed listings of these societies along with their addresses will be found in:
_THE HEREDITARY REGISTER OF THE US OF AMERICA,
Hereditary Register, Publications, Yoncalla, OR, latest edition.
__R. R. Davenport, HEREDITARY SOCIETY BLUEBOOK, Clearfield
Press, Baltimore, MD, latest edition.
_E. P. Bentley, GENEALOGIST'S ADDRESS BOOK, Genealogical
Publishing Co., Baltimore, MD, latest edition.
_ENCYCLOPEDIA OF ASSOCIATIONS, Gale Research Co., Detroit,
MI, latest edition.
Among the larger societies of the patriotic, hereditary, and lineage type are the following. Each of those listed publishes membership lists, lineages, and lists of ancestors. The volumes containing these data may be located by looking in library card or computer catalogs under the name of the society. Such volumes will be found in large genealogical libraries.
_The Colonial Dames of America, 421 East 61st Street, New York, NY
10021.
__Daughters of Union Veterans of the Civil War, 503 South Walnut St.,
Springfield, IL 62704.

_The General Society of Colonial Wars, 840 Woodbine Avenue, Glendale, OH 45246.

_General Society of Mayflower Descendants, 4 Winslow Street, Plymouth, MA 02361.

_General Society of the War of 1812, PO Box 106, Mendenhall, PA 19357.

__Ladies of the Grand Army of the Republic, 46 Chassin Avenue, Eggertsville, NY 14226.

__Military Order of the Stars and Bars, Sons of Confederate Veterans, PO 59, Columbia, TN 38402.

_National Society Daughters of Colonial Wars, 1307 New Hampshire Avenue, NW, Washington, DC 20009.

_National Society Daughters of the American Revolution, 1776 D Street, NW, Washington, DC 20006.

_The National Society of the Colonial Dames of the 17th Century, 1300 New Hampshire Avenue, NW, Washington, DC 20036.

_National Society of the Colonial Dames of America, Dumbarton House, 2715 Q Street, NW, Washington, DC 20007.

_The National Society of the Daughters of the Founders and Patriots of America, 2025 I Street, NW, Washington, DC 20006.

__National Society of the Sons and Daughters of the Pilgrims, 3917 Heritage Hills Dr., 104, Bloomington, MN 55437.

_National Society Sons of the American Revolution, 1000 South Fourth Street, Louisville, KY 40203.

_National Society US Daughters of 1812, 1461 Rhode Island Avenue, NW, Washington, DC 20005.

_The Order of Founders and Patriots of America, 15 Pine St., New York, NY 10005.

__United Daughters of the Confederacy, 328 North Boulevard, Richmond, VA 23220.

You should seek the publications of the above societies, but also look for the lineage books of the National Society of Colonial Daughters of the Seventeenth Century.

108. Pension records   The US government, some states, and some colonies gave pensions to many of the citizens who served in the military, and to widows and orphans of veterans. Not all veterans, widows, and orphans were awarded pensions because there were varying requirements which had to be met and proved. These usually related to need and the period of service. The government agency which granted a pension would keep a pension file on each applicant, with the application itself and the payment records being the documents of greatest genealogical value. An application might include the following: name, wife's name, rank, military unit, dates of service, age, residence, dates and places of birth and marriage, names and ages of minor children, and documents proving the service. A widow's or descendant's application had also to prove the relationship to the veteran (marriage records, birth records).

There are several indexes to federal pension records. Among those carrying the largest number of names are:
_National Genealogical Society, INDEX OF REVOLUTIONARY WAR PENSION APPLICATIONS IN THE NATIONAL ARCHIVES, The Society, Washington, DC, 1976. Leads to microfilmed records, National Archives, REVOLUTIONARY WAR PENSION AND BOUNTY LAND WARRANT APPLICATION FILES, Microfilm M804, The Archives, Washington, DC.
_National Archives, OLD WAR INDEX TO PENSION FILES, 1815-1926, Microfilm T316, Washington, DC. Leads to original records, copies available from National Archives.
_National Archives, INDEX TO WAR OF 1812 PENSION APPLICA-TION FILES, Microfilm M313, Washington, DC. Leads to original records, copies available from National Archives.
_National Archives, INDEX TO INDIAN WAR PENSION FILES, FOR SERVICE 1817-98, Microfilm T318, Washington, DC. Leads to original records, copies available from National Archives.
_National Archives, INDEX TO MEXICAN WAR PENSION FILES, FOR SERVICE 1846-8, Microfilm T317, Washington, DC. Leads to original records, copies available from National Archives.
_National Archives, GENERAL INDEX TO PENSION FILES, FOR SERVICE 1861-1916, Microfilm T288, Washington, DC. Includes Union Civil War pensions, and those given later. Leads to original records, copies available from the National Archives.

The microfilm indexes and the microfilm Revolutionary War pension and bounty land warrant applications are available at the National Archives, its Field Branches, the Family History Library, and some large genealogical libraries. They may also be borrowed from the American Genealogical Lending Library (PO Box 329, Bountiful, UT 84011). The index book to Revolutionary War pension applications is available in large genealogical libraries and most state libraries. When you locate an ancestor in the 2nd, 3rd, 4th, 5th, or 6th index above, you

will need to request copies of the records from the National Archives. This must be done on a special request form which is available from:
_National Archives, Washington, DC 20408.
For more detail on pensions, and for other similar records, including pension payment records, consult:
_National Archives, GUIDE TO GENEALOGICAL RESEARCH IN THE NATIONAL ARCHIVES, The Archives, Washington, DC, 1982, Chapter 7.

For colonial pension records and for pension records of Confederates which were given by Confederate states and two border states (AL, AR, FL, GA, KY, LA, MS, MO, NC, OK, SC, TN, TX, VA), dispatch inquiries with SASEs to the appropriate state library and state archives.

109. Published genealogies

Many people have written up and published their family histories in book form. One of the first things every genealogist should do is to find out if someone has published all or a part of his/her family history. However, care is called for because the quality of family histories varies widely. Some are essentially nothing but family legend and unfounded hearsay; others are tightly crafted from original documents and cautiously drawn interpretive conclusions with every source referenced in detail. No material in any family history should be accepted uncritically. All data should be personally checked by reference to original documents or photocopies (prints, microfilms, microfiche, microcards) of them.

Fortunately, there are a number of alphabetically-arranged listings or indexes of family histories according to the principal surname. A few also list other surnames. These should all be looked into to ascertain if there are books which might contain data of value to you.
_M. J. Kaminkow, GENEALOGIES IN THE LIBRARY OF CONGRESS, with SUPPLEMENTS, Magna Carta Book Co., Baltimore, MD, 1976-86.
_ GENEALOGIES CATALOGED BY THE LIBRARY OF CONGRESS SINCE 1986 (UP TO JULY 31, 1991), Library of Congress, Washington, DC, 1991.
_M. J. Kaminkow, COMPLEMENT TO GENEALOGIES IN THE LIBRARY OF CONGRESS, Magna Carta Book Co., Baltimore, MD, 1981. Lists family histories in 45 other large genealogical libraries.

_SURNAME SECTION, FAMILY HISTORY LIBRARY CATALOG, Family History Library, Salt Lake City, UT, latest issue. On microfiche and CDROM; also available at every Family History Center.
_New York Public Library, DICTIONARY CATALOG OF THE LOCAL HISTORY AND GENEALOGY DIVISION, Hall, Boston, MA, 1974.
_J. Munsell, INDEX TO AMERICAN GENEALOGIES, Genealogical Publishing Co., Baltimore, MD, 1967 (originally published in 1900/8). Refers to family histories published before 1908.
_F. Rider, AMERICAN GENEALOGICAL INDEX, Godfrey Memorial Library, Middletown, CT, 1942-51. And F. Rider, AMERICAN-GENEALOGICAL-BIOGRAPHICAL INDEX, Godfrey Memorial Library, Middletown, CT, 1952-.
_CARD CATALOGS in large genealogical libraries and state libraries. Check those in or near your ancestor's state.

110. Revolutionary War records

The Revolutionary War was fought 1775-83 between rebels in the 13 colonies aided by the French and the British, their Loyalist supporters in the colonies, Indian supporters, and mercenaries hired by the British. Approximately 250,000 fought on the Patriot side, which means that 1 out of every 5 men participated in the rebellion against the British government. There are three main types of records that the war generated which are of use to genealogists: (1) service records, (2) pension records, and (3) bounty land records. Service records include rolls and rosters (enlistment, muster in, muster out, monthly, pay) and lists (description, wounded, death, deserter, casualty, missing, hospital, prisoner, burial, oath of allegiance, exchange, court martial, promotion). Among the items which may be found in service records are dates and places and events of service, and sometimes description, birthdate, birthplace, and places of residence. Pension records consist of an application with supporting documents, action taken on the application, and payment records, sometimes for a veteran, sometimes for his widow, sometimes for both. Data may include birth, age, marriage, children, residences after the war, description, health, occupation, migrations, and death. Bounty land records could consist of an application with supporting documents, action taken on the application, a warrant for the land, and records of warrant redemption or sale.

It is important to recognize that there were two major types of service in the American Revolution. The first was service in the Continental (united colony) forces. The resulting service, pension, and bounty land records are chiefly in the National Archives, which has microfilmed many of them. These microfilms are available in large genealogical libraries, state libraries, and/or state archives, or they may be borrowed from the American Genealogical Lending Library, PO Box 329, Bountiful, UT 84011. The second type of service was in the state militia or other state-based forces. The originals of these records are in the pertinent state archives, a few got into the National Archives, and there are some published state lists. These records may be sought in the state archives and libraries. In short, your search must involve both the Continental and the state records or else you may miss your ancestor.

The first step you should take in your Revolutionary War progenitor search is to examine five major reference indexes (2 books, 2 multi-volumed sets of books, one microfilm set). These works list most of the Continental Army and many of the state forces, plus some civilian patriots:

_Daughters of the American Revolution, DAR PATRIOT INDEX, The Daughters, Washington, DC, 1966/79, 2 volumes. Lead to lineage information in Daughters of the American Revolution, LINEAGE BOOKS, The Daughters, Washington, DC, 1890-1921, 166 volumes, with INDEX to the first 160 volumes.

_National Genealogical Society, INDEX OF REVOLUTIONARY WAR PENSION APPLICATIONS IN THE NATIONAL ARCHIVES, The Society, Washington, DC, 1976. Leads to National Archives, REVOLUTIONARY WAR PENSION AND BOUNTY LAND WARRANT APPLICATIONS, Microfilm M804, Washington, DC.

_J. Pierce, REGISTER OF CONTINENTAL PAY CERTIFICATES, Genealogical Publishing Co., Baltimore, MD, 1973. Leads to service records as indicated below.

_F. Rider, AMERICAN GENEALOGICAL-BIOGRAPHICAL IN-DEX, Godfrey Memorial Library, Middletown, CT, 1952-, over 170 volumes. Leads to published state records and records in state archives.

_National Archives, GENERAL INDEX TO COMPILED MILITARY SERVICE RECORDS OF REVOLUTIONARY WAR SOLDIERS, Microfilm M860, Washington, DC. Leads to National Archives, COMPILED SERVICE RECORDS OF SOLDIERS WHO SERVED IN THE AMERICAN ARMY DURING THE REVOLU-TIONARY WAR, Microfilm M881, Washington, DC; and National

Archives, COMPILED SERVICE RECORDS OF AMERICAN NAVAL PERSONNEL AND OTHERS WHO SERVED DURING THE REVOLUTIONARY WAR, Microfilm 880, Washington, DC.

Your second step is to obtain the materials to which the indexes above have led you. As mentioned before, you will find them in large genealogical libraries, the National Archives and its Branches, the Family History Library and its branch Centers, and you can borrow the microfilms from the American Genealogical Lending Library. Your third step is to visit or write the appropriate state library and state archives. Seek both Continental and state information: service records, pay rolls, bounty land, pension records, claims, military unit histories. Don't fail to do this because the states of GA, MD, MA, NY, NC, PA, SC, and VA gave bounty land and some of the states gave a few pensions. If you care to go further, it is often rewarding to search in the counties and/or towns where your veteran enlisted, lived after the war, and died. Seek Bible, cemetery, church, court, militia, tax, and newspaper records in local libraries, court houses, and town halls.

It has been estimated that as many as one-third of the people in the 13 colonies were British sympathizers (Tories). Of these, quite a number fought for the British (Loyalists). Numerous Tories and Loyalists went to Canada, Florida, England, and the West Indies. If you suspect that your forebear was pro-British, there are published volumes which list some of them. See the following for the names and coverage of many of these volumes:
_V. D. Greenwood, THE RESEARCHER'S GUIDE TO AMERICAN GENEALOGY, Genealogical Publishing Co., Baltimore, MD, 1990, pages 512-7.
Detailed bibliographies which direct you to Loyalist and Tory source materials in archives and libraries are:
_G. Palmer, A BIBLIOGRAPHY OF LOYALIST SOURCE MATERIAL IN THE US, CANADA, AND GREAT BRITAIN, Meckler Publishing Co., Westport, Ct, 1982.
_P. J. Bunnell, RESEARCH GUIDE TO LOYALIST ANCESTORS, Heritage Books, Bowie, MD, 1990.
Contact with pertinent state libraries and archives is also recommended, since records of confiscation of property of Loyalists are available for most of the states. Both the Archives of Canada (395 Wellington St., Ottawa, ON, Canada K1A 0N3) and the Archives of Ontario (77 Grenville St., Toronto, ON, Canada M7A 2R9), as well as the Public Record

Office in London have Loyalist records (Series AO12 and AO13). The Family History Library has microfilm copies of some of them.

If you care to go more deeply into Revolutionary War research, look into the following volumes:
_J. C. and L. L. Neagles, LOCATING YOUR REVOLUTIONARY WAR ANCESTOR, Everton Publishers, Logan, UT, 1983.
_Geo. K. Schweitzer, REVOLUTIONARY WAR GENEALOGY, The Author, Knoxville, TN, 1991.
The latter volume refers you to works which give data on Germans and French who participated in the War.

111. Scots-Irish genealogy The Scotch-Irish, or better the Scots-Irish, or even better the Ulster Scots, were a group of people who descended from Scottish Protestants (mostly Presbyterians) who were transplanted to northeastern Ireland in the 1600s. This transplantation was begun by James I of England who moved people from Scotland to Ulster (northeastern Ireland) during 1607-9, displacing many of the Catholic Irish. During the remainder of the century there were further migrations of Scots into Ulster. However, during these same years, conditions slowly began to turn unfavorable for the Ulster Scots. By about 1700, there were adverse economic, political, and religious factors making life increasingly uncomfortable for them. Most of their farms were owned by absentee English landlords who raised their rents. English laws were enacted which debilitated the previously-profitable cattle and sheep raising industries. In 1704, Parliament passed an act which excluded Presbyterians from holding political offices, and taxed them for the support of the Anglican church. As a consequence, the Ulster Scots began to leave, many going to the colonies. Only a few came before 1717, but after that, several thousands per year came, the number getting as high as 10 thousand in a few years.

The Ulster Scots came into every one of the thirteen colonies, most of them arriving at Philadelphia during 1717-75, with Baltimore receiving the next largest number. Their tendency was to go into the frontier areas where they settled along rivers and in valleys where there was good land. Many went south into the Shenandoah Valley, then turned southeastward to occupy the back country of MD, VA, NC, and SC. Others went westward to southwestern PA and northwestward to central PA. After the French and Indian War (1763), they began to move into KY and TN and down the OH River to southern OH. In succeeding years, particularly after the Revolution (1783), their migrations took them to southern IN and IL, and then into MO.

Research in the Ulster area of Ireland, now Northern Ireland, is complicated by many factors: many people were not landholders but leased or rented from landlords (often absentee), church records were adversely affected by the continuing Catholic-Presbyterian-Anglican conflicts, the area is divided and sub-divided into many sorts and sizes of regions which sometimes overlap (counties, baronies, provinces, dioceses, parishes, townlands), records were generated by all of these regions at various times and with varying degrees of efficiency, and a fire at the Public Record Office in Dublin in 1922 burnt many of the records most useful for genealogical research. It is therefore of great import that you exhaust every possible source here in the US in an effort to locate the precise place in Northern Ireland from which your Scots-Irish ancestor came. Without this information your task will be doubly difficult. The major records for doing Scots-Irish research are censuses and census substitutes [lists of inhabitants, taxpayers, freeholders, tax valuations, householders], the extensive indexes in the Public Record Offices in Belfast and Dublin, church records [Church of Ireland or Episcopalian 1720-, Catholic mostly 1820-, Presbyterian mostly 1819-], directories, published family histories, gravestone inscriptions, newspapers, wills and administrations, and genealogical periodicals. The major places where these will be found are in the county libraries and record offices, several repositories in Belfast [Public Record Office of Northern Ireland, Northern Ireland Registrar-General's Office, Presbyterian Historical Society, Linen Hall Library, Irish and Local Studies Department of the Central Library], and several repositories in Dublin [National Library of Ireland, Public Record Office of Ireland, Genealogical Office, Registrar-General's Office, Registry of Deeds, State Paper Office, Representative Church Body Library of the Church of Ireland, Society of Friends Library, Trinity College Library]. Many Scots-Irish records are on microfilm at the Family History Library in Salt Lake City, UT, and are available on loan through its numerous branch Family History Centers. Please make use of these before you even think about making contacts in Northern Ireland.

Because of the above-mentioned research difficulties, you should make yourself extensively acquainted with Scots-Irish research before you delve very deeply into it. The following volumes are recommended:

_K. Neill, HOW TO TRACE FAMILY HISTORY IN NORTHERN IRELAND, Irish Genealogical Association, Belfast, Northern Ireland, 1986.

_M. Rubincam, GENEALOGICAL RESEARCH METHODS AND SOURCES, American Society of Genealogists, Washington, DC, 1980, section on Ireland, pages 446-474.

_A. Baxter, IN SEARCH OF YOUR BRITISH AND IRISH ROOTS, Genealogical Publishing Co., Baltimore, MD, 1987.

_J. G. Ryan, IRISH RECORDS, Ancestry Publishing, Salt Lake City, UT, 1988.

_M. D. Falley, IRISH AND SCOTCH-IRISH ANCESTRAL RESEARCH, Genealogical Publishing Co., Baltimore, MD, 1981.

112. Scottish genealogy

When the Romans invaded what is now Scotland in 80 AD, they called the inhabitants, who had been there a long time, Picts. The Romans defeated the Picts, built roads, forts, and towns in Scotland, but were unable to control the area, and finally left in the early 400s. Christianity was introduced in the 5th century, and about 500 a Celtic tribe, the Scots, came from Ireland. In 563, Christian missions began to convert large numbers of Picts. In 844, the Scottish king came to rule over the Picts also. This was followed by two centuries of violent struggles for the throne with numerous murders of kings. After the Norman conquest of England in 1066, many anti-Norman English settled in Scotland, and feudalism was established. Over 150 years of warfare followed as the English tried to take control of the entire island of Great Britain. Scotland maintained her independence, frequently allying herself with France against England. The English invaded Scotland in 1296 and won the Battle of Dunbar, but the Scots revolted several times, and in 1314 defeated the English and reestablished Scottish independence at the Battle of Bannockburn. The Stuart family took the throne of Scotland in 1371, renewed close ties with France, survived much internal dissension, and fought constantly with England. In 1513, the Scots invaded England, and were defeated.

In the 1560s, the Protestant Reformation surged through Scotland rapidly changing the official church of Scotland from Roman Catholic to Presbyterian. When the queen of England died in 1603, her cousin, the king of Scotland, inherited the English throne. He moved to London, ruled over the two countries, promoted Scottish colonies in America and northeastern Ireland, and began to reorganize the Presbyterian Church with the aim of establishing the Episcopal Church. In 1642, civil war between Puritans and Royalists broke out in England, the Puritans won, Scotland first sided with them, then defied them, were defeated by them in 1650, and were forced to unite with Puritan England in 1654. Many prisoners taken by the Puritans were sent to the colonies, and many others also emigrated. When the English monarchy was restored in 1660, the king dissolved the unity, and ruled the countries separately. The English monarchs attempted to establish the Episcopal Church of England in Scotland, but opposition reestablished the Presbyterian Church as of 1691. In 1707, the two countries negotiated unification along with Wales to form the Kingdom of Great Britain. The laws of Scotland and its established Presbyterian Church were maintained, but the Scottish parliament was abolished and the country sent representatives to the British Parliament. The House of Hanover took the British throne in 1714, but many Highland Scots (Jacobites) who supported the Stuarts revolted unsuccessfully in 1715 and again in 1745-6. The feudal land system slowly began giving way to leasing. During the late 1700s and early 1800s much of the grazing land of the Highlands was fenced off, depriving many people of their livelihood, and resulting in emigration to the US and other places.

It is of great importance for you to make every possible attempt here in US records to locate the precise place of origin of your Scottish ancestor. It is usually very difficult to locate your progenitor in the records of Scotland without this information. The major records for doing Scottish research are censuses (1841/51/61/71/81/91), civil vital records (birth, marriage, death, all 1855-), council and session records (miscellaneous court records, 1554-), gravestone inscriptions, parish registers (Presbyterian in the General Record Office, some as early as 1560, most 1750-; most others in individual churches or in Episcopal or Catholic archives in Edinburgh), published family histories, retours and services of heirs (land inheritance, 1850-), sasines (land transfers, some before 1599, many after), tax, testaments (wills, some as early as 1529, many more later). The major places in Scotland where these and other records will be found are in the county, town, and city libraries and record offices, regional and district record archives, and several national repositories in Edinburgh. Included in the latter are the General Record Office (New Register House), the Scottish Record Office (General and West Register Houses), and the National Library of Scotland. Many of the above Scottish records and others are on microfilm at the Family History Library in Salt Lake City, UT, and are available on loan through its numerous Family History Centers. Thorough use of all these records at the Family History Library should be made before making contacts in Scotland or going there.

You should acquaint yourself in detail with Scottish records and research before you do any detailed searching. The following volumes are recommended:
_D. Moody, SCOTTISH FAMILY HISTORY, Genealogical Publishing Co., Baltimore, MD, 1994.
_D. B. Goldie, IN SEARCH OF HAMISH McBAGPIPES, A CONCISE GUIDE TO SCOTTISH ANCESTRY, xxxx, 1992.
_C. Sinclair, TRACING YOUR SCOTTISH ANCESTORS, HMSO, Edinburgh, Scotland, 1991.
_K. B. Cory, TRACING YOUR SCOTTISH ANCESTRY, Polygon, Edinburg, Scotland, 1990.
_G. Hamilton-Edwards, IN SEARCH OF SCOTTISH ANCESTRY, Genealogical Publishing Co., Baltimore, MD, 1984.
_A. James, SCOTTISH ROOTS, Macdonald Publishers, Loanhead, 1981.
_D. Whyte, INTRODUCING SCOTTISH GENEALOGICAL RESEARCH, Scottish Genealogical Society, Edinburgh, latest edition.
_B. S. Mitchell, POCKET GUIDE TO IRISH GENEALOGY, Closson Press, Apollo, PA, 1988.

113. Slave-holder censuses

If your ancestor lived in AL, AR, DE, DC, FL, GA, KY, LA, MD, MS, MO, NJ, NC, SC, TN, TX, or VA in 1850 and/or 1860, and owned slaves, you may be able to locate the family in the slave-holder census records. These records show the name of each slave-owner along with the number of slaves. A line for each slave gives age, color, sex, and some other data, but names of slaves are not shown. These records have been microfilmed by the National Archives, and are available as follows:
_National Archives, SEVENTH CENSUS OF THE US, 1850, Microfilm M432, AL(rolls 17-24), AR(roll 32), DE(roll 55), DC(roll 57), FL(roll 60), GA(88-96), KY(223-228), LA(242-247), MD(300-302), MS (383-390), MO(422-424), NJ(466), NC(650-656), SC(861-868), TN(902-907), TX(917-918), VA(983-993).
_National Archives, EIGHTH CENSUS OF THE US, 1860, Microfilm M653, AL(rolls 27-36), AR(rolls 53-54), DE(roll 100), DC(105), FL(110), GA(142-153), KY(401-406), LA(427-431), MD(484-485), MS(595-604), MO(661-664), NC)920-927), SC(1229-1238), TN (1281-1286), TX(1309-1312), VA(1386-1397).

These census records have also been published in both book and micro-fiche form:

_1850 SLAVE SCHEDULES, AL-VA, Accelerated Indexing Systems, North Salt Lake City, UT, 1988, both book and microfiche.

_1860 SLAVE SCHEDULES, AL-VA, Accelerated Indexing Systems, North Salt Lake City, UT, 1988, both book and microfiche.

The microfilms are available in the National Archives, the National Archives Field Branches, the Family History Library, state libraries, and large genealogical libraries. The published indexes to the regular census records (see sections Census 1850 and Census 1860) will let you locate your family in the regular census records, where you can take note of the county and the district or region in the county. This will then let you turn to the approximate place in the slave-holder censuses where your forebear may be found. The books and microfiche slave schedules are indexed, and will be found in the Family History Library, large genealogical libraries, and in some of the pertinent state libraries.

114. Soundex system

Soundex is an indexing system which has been used for partially indexing the 1880 census (only families with children age 10 or under), for indexing the 1900 census, for indexing some of the states of the 1910 census (AL, AR, CA, FL, GA, IL, KS, KY, LA, MI, MS, MO, NC, OH, OK, PA, SC, TN, TX, VA, WV), and for indexing the 1920 census. Some of the states for 1910 are actually indexed by Miracode, but the same principles are used for the indexes. In Soundex and Miracode, surnames are indexed by a code which involves a capital letter followed by three numerals, for example, S326 or P630 or B653. The aim of this system is to gather together all surnames which sound alike, so as to facilitate your handling of spelling variations of the surnames you are looking for.

In order to obtain the code for a given surname, you need to apply the following steps:

First, write down the name using a capital for the first letter and lower case for the rest.

Second, look at the first letter of the name. Find it in the list below. Then find the second letter of the name in the list. If they occur on the same line of the list, mark out the second letter.

1 b, p, f, v
2 c, s, k, g, j, q, x, z
3 d, t
4 l
5 m, n
6 r
   a, e, i, o, u, y, w, h

Third, starting at the second letter of the name, mark out all occurrences of a, e, i, o, u, y, w, and h. Don't mark out the first letter of the name.

Fourth, look for double letters and mark the second one out.

Fifth, look to see if any letter is followed by a letter on the same line in the list above. If so, mark the second one out.

Sixth, write down the first letter of the name, then the numbers (from the above list) corresponding to the small letters you have left.

Seventh, if you don't have three numerals, add enough zeroes to make three numerals.

Now, let's illustrate with the surname Schuller. The first step was to write the name. The second step is to find the first letter of the name (an S) in the chart. It is on line 2. Now find the second letter of the name (c) on the chart. It is also on line 2, so mark it out: S¢huller. The third step is to mark out all small letters a, e, i, o, u, y, w, and h: S¢h∥ll¢r. The fourth step is to locate double letters and mark the second one out (the double l): S¢h∥ll¢r. The fifth step is to look for two letters from the same line in the chart which occur together, and to mark out the second. There are none. The sixth step is to write the first letter of the name (S), then the numbers from the chart corresponding to the letters which remain (l=4 and r=6) to get S46. The seventh step is to add zeroes, if necessary, to make three numerals: S460. This is the code you look up in the Soundex or Miracode index. Here are some other examples: Keen (K500), Heinold (H543), Schissler (S246), Dhow (D000), Pfinmat (P530). Remember only three numerals are used, so Cabotsen would be C132, not C1325.

All surnames which have the same code number will be gathered together in the indexes. All of them are arranged alphabetically by the person's first name. The references in the indexes also give you much of the information carried by the original census records, but it is always well to check. A very useful book giving the proper Soundex(Miracode) codes for over 125 thousand names is:

_B. W. Steuart, THE SOUNDEX REFERENCE GUIDE, Precision
    Indexing, Bountiful, UT, 1990.

115. Special censuses and lists

In addition to the numerous censuses taken under federal and state authority, there are many censuses taken for counties, districts, cities, townships, and towns. Further, there are many compilations (lists of inhabitants) similar to censuses which can yield valuable information on your ancestor. These lists include tax lists, assessment lists, petitions, poll lists, resident lists, land lottery lists, rent rolls, debt books, school censuses, and church-wardens' enumerations. These may be located in the catalog of the Family History Library (available at every Family History Center), by writing to the appropriate state archives and state libraries, and by contacting the pertinent county, district, city, township, or town library. Many of them, particularly the earlier ones, are listed in:

_J. D. Stemmons, THE US CENSUS COMPENDIUM, Everton
    Publishers, Logan, UT, 1973.

Be sure and examine the Family History Library Catalog because it shows many lists which are not included in the book by Stemmons. And even more lists are usually held by the state libraries and archives.

116. Spelling variations

All genealogists face a problem which sometimes produces enough difficulty that you miss an ancestor. This problem is that there are many ways names can be spelled. In fact, every name has at least one, usually numerous, possible spellings. The problem becomes greater as you go further back. This is because few people were literate back then, those who did read and write often did not do it well, spelling was not standardized to the degree it now is, and writers spelled names the way they heard them. This latter was complicated by differences in linguistic (ethnic) background between the writer of records and the person who gave the writer his/her name. A German-speaking county clerk and a Scots-Irish farmer, or vice versa, just might both speak and spell names differently. In actuality, you will once in a while discover that a name will be spelled several ways in the same document.

When seeking records for your ancestor, it is absolutely necessary to take into account spelling variations. What you must do is attempt to predict what variations are likely and then to look for them in the indexes and records. The rest of this section will tell you how to predict many of the major spelling variations. It will certainly not predict all, since you will often encounter some incredibly distorted ones. The key to this method is that it is the <u>first</u> <u>three</u> <u>sounds</u> in a name that are important. The first three sounds of a name are usually carried in the first three to seven letters. And if you set out similarly sounding combinations of these first three to seven letters, you will have before you most possible spelling variations. In other words, what you do is: (1) identify the first three sounds of the name, (2) write down all combinations of letters which produce each of these three sounds, then (3) look for these combinations of letters (plus further letters, if the name is longer) in indexes and records.

The first sound in a name is generally produced by the initial (capitalized) letter sometimes plus one or two other letters. The most likely similar sounds for various initial letters are as follows:

For	Try
A	A/Ai/Ay/Au/E/Ha
Ai	Ai/A/Ay
Au	Au/O/A/Aw
Ay	Ay/A/Ai
Aw	Aw/O/A/Au
B	B/P/Bh
C	C/K/Ch/S/Kh
Ch	Ch/C/K
D	D/T
E	E/Ea/I/Ei
Ea	Ea/E/A/Ee
Ee	Ee/E/Ea
Ei	Ei/E/I/A/Ea
Eu	Eu/U/Ew/Ue
Ey	Ey/I/Y
F	F/Ph/V
G	G/C/J/Gh
H	H/omit H (to give A/E/I/O/U)
I	I/E/U
Ie	Ie/I/Y/A/E
J	J/G/Gh/Y
K	K/C/Ch/Kh
L	L
M	M/N
N	N/Kn/Gn/M

O	O/Oa/U
Oa	Oa/O/Ow/Ou
Oi	Oi/Oy
Oo	Oo/U/Ou/O
Ou	Ou/O/A/I/E/Oo
Oy	Oy/Oi
Ow	Ow/O/A/I/E/U
P	P/B/Bh
Qu	Qu/Kw
R	R/Rh/Wr
S	S/C/Sh/Sch/Sc
T	T/D/Th
Th	Th/T/D
U	U/E/O
Ue	Ue/Oo/U/Ew
V	V/F
W	W/Wh
X	X/Z/Ek
Y	Y/I/J
Z	Z/S/C

Now look at the surname Sisler. The first sound is affiliated with the letter S. The above chart shows that the letters you should try are S/C/Sc/Sch/Sc. What you do is pronounce Sisler, Cisler, Shisler, Schisler, and Scisler. You will detect that all are similar. Hence, all these should be looked for in indexes and records.

The second and third sounds in a name are associated with internal (lower case) letters. The most likely substitutes are as follows:

For	Try
a	a/ai/ay/e/ea/eigh/ei/ey/i/o/u
ae	ae/e/ee/ea
ai	ai/a/ay/eight/ea/i/y/ey
ao	ao/o/a/au/aw
au	au/o/a/aw/ough/augh/oa
augh	augh/o/a/au/aw/ough
ay	ay/ai/eigh/e/ea/ei/ey
aw	aw/o/a/au/ough/augh/oa
b	b/bb/p/pp
c	c/k/ck/ch/cc/s/sc
ch	ch/t/tch/dg
d	d/dd/t
e	e/ee/ea/i/ie/ei/o/a/u

ea	ea/e/a/ee/ie/u/i/o
eau	eau/u/oa/ow/ew/ou/eu/ue
ee	ee/e/ea/i/ie/EI
ei	ei/e/i/a/ea/ai/ee/ay/ie/ey/eigh
eigh	eigh/a/ai/ay/i
eo	eo/o/a/i/e/ou/u
eou	eou/o/a/i/e/ou/u
eu	eu/u/ew/ue
ey	ey/i/y/a/ie/ai/ei
ew	ew/u/eu/ue
f	f/ph/ff/gh/v
g	g/gg/gh/j/x/k/ch
h	h/wh/omit h
i	i/y/igh/ie/a/e/u/ui/ai/ei/o
ie	ie/i/y/a/o/e/ou/u/igh/ea/ey/ee
ieu	ieu/u/ew/eu/ue/ui
iew	iew/u/ew/eu/ue/ui
igh	igh/i/y/ie
j	j/g/dg/d/dj
k	k/c/ck/ch/cc/x
l	l/ll
m	m/mm/mb/mp/lm/n
n	n/nn/ng/nd/nt/nk
o	o/e/u/i/a/oa/oo/oe/ou/ow/au/aw/ough/ew
oa	oa/o/ow/ou/oe/au
oe	oe/o/oa/ow/ou
oi	oi/oy
oo	oo/u/ou/o/ew/ue
ou	ou/o/a/i/e/u/oo/ow/oa
ough	ough/ou/ow/o/augh/ao
oy	oy/oi
ow	ow/o/a/i/e/u/oo/oa
p	p/pp/b/pb
qu	qu/kw
r	r/rr/wr/rh
s	s/ss/sc/st/c
sh	sh/ch/sch/s
t	t/tt/td/th/d/bt
th	th/t/d
u	u/a/i/e/o/ou/ea/ew/eu/ue/ou/oo/y
v	v/f
w	w/wh/r/a/e/i/o/u

x   x/ks

y   y/i/e/a/o/u

z   z/s/zz/ss/c

The second sound in the name Sisler is associated with the letter i. The possible substitutes from the above table are: i/y/igh/ ie/a/e/u/ui/ai/ei/o. This leads to <u>Sysler</u>, Sighsler, <u>Siesler</u>, Sasler, <u>Sesler</u>, <u>Susler</u>, <u>Suisler</u>, Saisler, <u>Seisler</u>, and Sosler. By sounding these out to determine which ones sound similar to Sisler, you get the underlined ones. They should be looked for. In the same fashion, you can obtain <u>Cysler</u>, Cighsler, <u>Ciesler</u>, Casler, <u>Cesler</u>, Cusler, Cuisler, Caisler, <u>Ceisler</u>, and Cosler. Also <u>Shysler</u>, Shighsler, <u>Shiesler</u>, Shasler, <u>Shesler</u>, <u>Shusler</u>, <u>Shuisler</u>, Shaisler, <u>Sheisler</u>, and Shoslar. And then <u>Schysler</u>, Schighsler, <u>Schiesler</u>, Schasler, <u>Scheslery</u>, <u>Schusler</u>, <u>Schuisler</u>, Schaisler, <u>Scheisler</u>, and Schosler. And, continuing with Scysler, Scighsler, <u>Sciesler</u>, Scasler, <u>Scesler</u>, Scusler, Scuisler, Scaisler, <u>Sceisler</u>, and Scosler. Again, the underlined versions should be looked for, since they can be pronounced somewhat like Sisler. Please notice that the various versions of Sisler that we have tried so far can be represented as S/C/Sh/Sch/Sc + i/y/igh/ie/a/e/u/ui/ai/ei/o + sler. Also recognize that some of the versions were ruled out by pronouncing them and discovering that they did not resemble the sound of the word Sisler.

The third sound in the name Sisler is associated with the lower case letter s. The chart indicates that these possibilities should be tried: s/ss/sc/st/c. Each of the <u>underlined</u> versions in the previous paragraph should be used and these possibilities added. For example, using <u>Sesler</u>, you will get <u>Sessler</u>, Sescler, <u>Sestler</u>, and Secler, with only the underlined ones sounding close to Sisler. All of these possible variations should be carefully examined and sounded out. The pattern of the possibilities can now be seen to be: S/C/Sh/Sch/Sc + i/y/igh/ie/a/e/u/ui/ai/ei/o + s/ss/sc/st/c + ler. This will give you 250 possibilities with only about 75 of them sounding close to Sisler. If you look these up, you will have only a small chance of missing spelling variations of Sisler.

This procedure is somewhat time consuming, but you will find that it pays off. After going through it with six or seven of your surnames, you will discover that you will be acquiring a very good sensitivity to surname spelling variations. And you will be finding your ancestor in places where you would have missed her/him before. Of course, this method is not fool-proof. Sometimes there will be spelling variations which you will miss, but not many. Be careful with double vowels such as ai/ee/oi/io/ oe.

Sometimes they represent one sound (h<u>ai</u>r, k<u>ee</u>n, b<u>oi</u>l), and sometimes they represent two (l<u>io</u>n, c<u>oe</u>d). If you care to go into the idea of spelling variations in more depth, consult:

_P. R. Hanna et al., PHONEME-GRAPHEME CORRESPONDENCES AS CUES TO SPELLING IMPROVEMENT, US Government Printing Office, Washington, DC, 1966.

---

117. State and special censuses

Before and in between the federal censuses (taken 1790, 1800, 1810, 1820, 1830, 1840, 1850, 1860, 1870, 1880, 1900, 1910, 1920, etc.) many censuses (lists of inhabitants) were taken in colonies, territories, states, and also in counties, cities, and towns. Quite a few of these are seriously incomplete because of losses, but even so, there have survived a considerable number which are 60-70% complete or better. Among the more important of these at the colony, territory, or state level are those of AL(1855, 1866), AK(various 1870-1907), AZ(1864, 1866),CA(missions 1796-8, 1852), CO(1860 in censuses of NE, NM, and KS Territories, 1861, 1885), CT(1670), DE(various 1665-97, 1782), DC(1867, 1878), FL(1885), HI(1878), ID(1870), IL(1855, 1865), IA(1851-6, 1885, 1895, 1905), KS(1860, 1865, 1875, 1885, 1895, 1905), LA(various 1699-1732, various 1758-96, various 1722-1803), MD(1776), MA(1855, 1865), MI(various 1710-1830, 1845, 1854, 1864, 1874, 1884, 1894), MN(1834 in census of MI Territory, 1836 in census of WI Territory, 1857, 1865, 1875, 1885, 1895, 1905), MS(various 1805-66), MT(1862-3), NE(1854, 1855, 1856, 1860, 1885), NV(1862-3, 1872, 1875), NH(1732, 1744, 1767, 1776), NJ(various 1773-80, 1855, 1865, 1875, 1885, 1895, 1905), NM(various 1750-1845, 1885), NY(1855, 1865, 1875, 1885, 1895, 1905), NC(1784-7), ND(1860, 1870, 1880, 1885), OK(1860 in census of AR, 1890), OR(various 1841-59), RI(1774, 1782, 1865, 1875, 1885, 1905), SD(1860, 1870, 1880, 1885, 1905), TX(various 1829-36, 1840), UT(1856), VT(1771), WA(various 1856-89), WI(1836, 1838, 1842, 1855, 1875, 1895, 1905), WY(1850 in census of UT Territory, 1860 in census of NE Territory, 1870, 1880). Some of these census records are synthetic, that is, they have been put together from non-census compilations, such as tax lists and voter registrations.

The best sources for the above censuses, as well as those of counties, cities, and towns, are the state archives, state libraries, state historical societies, and the Family History Library. Further listings and details on these special census records will be found in:

_A. S. Lainhart, STATE CENSUS RECORDS, Genealogical Publishing
Co., Baltimore, MD, 1992.
_US AND SPECIAL CENSUS CATALOG, Ancestry Publishing, Salt
Lake City, UT, 1985.
_A. Eichholz, ANCESTRY'S REDBOOK, Ancestry Publishing, Salt Lake
City, UT, 1989, see under the pertinent states.
In some cases involving the county, city, or town censuses, you will find
that they are available only in the county, city, or town.

118. State archives   Among the most important genealogical record
repositories in the US are the state archives.
These institutions collect, preserve, copy, and
index original colonial and state governmental
documents. Many of them also function to store originals or copies
(microform and published) of county, city, and town records, as well as
applicable federal records. And some of them also collect non-governmental records of numerous different types. When you write to state
archives, keep your letter brief, ask about only one or two items, and
enclose an SASE.

The state archives, along with their addresses, are:
_AL Department of Archives and History, 624 Washington Ave.,
Montgomery, AL 36130.
_AK State Archives and Record Service, 14 Willoughby Ave., Juneau,
AK 99801.
_AZ Department of Library, Archives, and Public Records, 1700 W.
Washington St., Phoenix, AZ 85007.
_AR History Commission, 1 Capitol Mall, Little Rock, AR 72201.
_CA State Archives, 1020 O St., Room 130, Sacramento, CA 95814.
_Division of [CO] State Archives and Public Records, 1313 Sherman St.,
Denver, CO 80203.
_CT State Library and Archives, 231 Capitol Ave., Hartford, CT 06106.
_DE State Archives, Hall of Records, Dover, DE 19901.
_FL State Archives, 500 S. Bronough St., Tallahassee, FL 32399.
_GA Department of Archives and History, 330 Capitol Ave., SE, Atlanta,
GA 30334.
_HI State Archives, 478 South King St., Honolulu, HI 96813.
_Contact for ID: ID Historical Society, 325 W. State St., Boise, ID 83702.
_IL State Archives, Archives Building, Springfield, IL 62756.
_IN State Archives, 140 North Senate Ave., Indianapolis, IN 46204.
_IA State Archives, Capitol Complex, Des Moines, IA 50319.
_KS State Historical Society, 120 W. 10th Ave., Topeka, KS 66612.

_KY Department for Libraries and Archives, 300 Coffee Tree Rd., Frankfort, KY 40602.

_LA State Archives and Records Service, PO Box 94125, Baton Rouge, LA 70804.

_ME State Archives, State House Station 84, August, ME 04333.

_MD State Archives, 350 Rowe Blvd., Annapolis, MD 21401.

_MA State Archives, 220 Morrissey Blvd., Boston, MA 02125.

_MI State Archives, 717 W. Allegan St., Lansing, MI 48918.

_MN Archives Division, 345 Kellogg Blvd. West, St. Paul, MN 55102.

_MS Department of Archives and History, PO Box 571, Jackson, MS 39205.

_MO State Archives, PO Box 778, Jefferson City, MO 65102.

_MT Historical Society, 225 N. Roberts St., Helena, MT 59620.

_NE State Historical Society, PO Box 82554, Lincoln, NE 68501.

_NV Division of Archives and Records, 100 Stewart St., Fall St., Carson City, NV 89710.

_NH Division of Records Management and Archives, 71 S. Fruit St., Concord, NH 03301.

_NJ State Archives, 185 West State St., CN-307, Trenton, NJ 08625.

_NM Records Center and Archives, 404 Montezuma St., Santa Fe, NM 87501.

_NY State Archives, Room 11 D-40 Cultural Education Center, Albany, NY 12230.

_NC Division of Archives and History, 109 East Jones St., Raleigh, NC 27601.

_State Archives of ND, ND Heritage Center, Bismarck, ND 58505.

_OH Historical Society, Archives-Library Division, 1982 Velma Ave., Columbus, OH 43211.

_OK State Archives and Records, 200 N.E. 18th St., Oklahoma City, OK 73105.

_OR State Archives, 800 Summer St., NE, Salem, OR 97130.

_PA State Archives Reference Section, 3rd and Forster Sts., Harrisburg, PA 17108.

_RI State Archives, Room 337 Westminster St., Providence, RI 02903.

_SC Department of Archives and History, 1430 Senate St., Columbia, SC 29211.

_SD Historical Society, Archives Division, 900 Governors Dr., Pierre, SD 57501.

_TN State Library and Archives, 403 Seventh Ave., North, Nashville, TN 37243.

_TX State Archives and Library, Capitol Station, Box 12927, Austin, TX 78711.

_UT State Archives, Room 28, State Capital, Salt Lake City, UT 84114.
_VT State Archives, State Office Building, Montpelier, VT 05609.
_VA State Archives, 11th and Capitol Sts., Richmond, VA 23219.
_WA State Archives, 1120 Washington St., Olympia, WA 98504.
_WV Archives and History Section, Cultural Center, Capitol Complex, Charleston, WV 25305.
_WI State Archives, 816 State St., Madison, WI 53706.
_WY State Archives Research Division, Barrett State Office Bldg., 2301 Central Ave., Cheyenne, WY 82002.

119. State indexes and finding aids

For most states there are extensive indexes to very important genealogical materials of numerous types. These indexes may be found in various formats: books, microfilms, microfiche, typescripts, manuscripts, card indexes, computer indexes. The types of records often include wills, military veterans, pensions, biographies, genealogies, land grants, cemetery records, tax lists, state censuses, genealogical periodicals, marriages, deeds, church records, immigrants, naturalizations, and local histories. To locate the published indexes, consult the listings under your ancestor's state in:
_P. W. Filby, AMERICAN AND BRITISH GENEALOGY AND HERALDRY, The New England Historic Genealogical Society, Boston, MA, 1983, with SUPPLEMENTS, 1987-. Be careful to consult all supplements.
To locate the other types of indexes, inquire at the appropriate state libraries and state archives, and examine the locality catalog at your nearest Family History Center to ascertain what is available from the Family History Library. Look under the state in the catalog. It is also advisable to examine the listings in state source guides. These guides will be treated in a later section of this Handbook.

120. State libraries

The state libraries (or similar non-governmental repositories) are of exceptional importance to genealogical researchers because they collect and make available published materials (books, microforms, typescripts, photocopies) dealing with ancestral investigation. Many of them also maintain extensive manuscript collections. When you write to state libraries, keep your letter brief, ask only one or two questions, and enclose an SASE.

The state libraries, along with their addresses, are:

_AL Department of Archives and History, 624 Washington Ave., Montgomery, AL 36130.

_AK State Library, State Office Bldg., Eighth Floor, Juneau, AK 99801.

_AZ State Genealogy Library, 1700 W. Washington St., Phoenix, AZ 85007.

_AR History Commission, 1 Capitol Mall, Little Rock, AR 72201.

_CA State Genealogical Library, Sutro Library, 480 Winston Dr., San Francisco, CA 94132.

_CO State Library, 201 East Colfax Ave., Denver, CO 80203.

_CT State Library and Archives, 231 Capitol Ave., Hartford, CT 06106.

_The Historical Society of DE, 505 Market St., Wilmington, DE 19801.

_State Library of FL, 500 S. Bronough St., Tallahassee, FL 32399.

_GA Department of Archives and History, 330 Capitol Ave., SE, Atlanta, GA 30334.

_HI State Library, 478 South King St., Honolulu, HI 96813.

_Contact for ID: ID Historical Society and ID Genealogical Society, 325 W. State St., Boise, ID 83702.

_IL State Library, 300 South Second St., Springfield, IL 62701.

_IN State Library, 140 North Senate Ave., Indianapolis, IN 46204.

_State Historical Society of IA Library, 600 East Locust, Capitol Complex, Des Moines, IA 50319.

_KS State Historical Society, 120 W. 10th Ave., Topeka, KS 66612.

_KY Historical Society, Old Capitol Annex, 300 Broadway, Frankfort, KY 40601.

_LA State Library, 760 North Third St., Baton Rouge, LA 70821.

_ME State Library, State House Station 64, Augusta, ME 04333.

_Contact for MD: MD Historical Society, 201 W. Monument St., Baltimore, MD 21201.

_State Library of MA, State House, Room 341, Beacon St., Boston, MA 02133.

_Library of MI, 717 West Allegan St., Lansing, MI 48189. Also contact Detroit Public Library, 5201 Woodward Ave., Detroit, MI 48202.

_MN Historical Society Library, 345 Kellogg Blvd., West, St. Paul, MN 55102.

_MS Department of Archives and History, PO Box 571, Jackson, MS 39205.

_State Historical Society of MO, 1020 Lowry St., Columbia, MO 65201.

_MT Historical Society, 225 N. Roberts, Helena, MT 59620.

_NE State Historical Society, 1500 R St., Lincoln, NE 68508.

_NV State Library, 100 Stewart St., Carson City, NV 89710,

_NH State Library, 20 Park St., Concord, NH 033301.

_NJ State Library, 185 West State St., CN 520, Trenton, NJ 08625.

_Contact for NM: Historical Society of NM, PO Box 1912, Santa Fe, NM 87504.
_NY State Library, Cultural Education Center, 7th Floor, Albany, NY 12230.
_NC Division of the State Library, 109 East Jones St., Raleigh, NC 27601.
_State Historical Society of ND, ND Heritage Center, Bismarck, ND 58505.
_OH Historical Society, Archives-Library Division, 1982 Velma Ave., Columbus, OH 43211.
_OK State Historical Society Library and Archives Division, 2100 North Lincoln Blvd., Oklahoma City, OK 73105.
_OR Historical Society, 1200 SW Park Ave., Portland, OR 97205.
_State Library of PA, Walnut St. and Commonwealth Ave., Harrisburg, PA 17105.
_State Historical Society of WI, 816 State St., Madison, WI 53706.
_WY State Library, Supreme Court and Library Bldg., Cheyenne, WY 82002.

121. State society libraries In many states, there are well-stocked state historical society and/or state genealogical society libraries which have excellent genealogical materials, especially for their own region. Some of these societies are state-run and others are private. There are also some regional society libraries which fit this category. You should not overlook these important potential sources of forebear data.

Among the better of the state and regional society libraries for genealogical materials are:
_AZ Historical Society, 949 E. Second St., Tucson, AZ 85719.
_Southern CA Genealogical Society, 122 S. Golden Mall, Burbank, CA 91503.
_CA Genealogical Society, 300 Brannan St., San Francisco, CA 94142.
_CO Historical Society, 1300 Broadway, Denver, CO 80203.
_CT Historical Society, 1 Elizabeth St., Hartford, CT 06105.
_Historical Society of DE, 505 Market St., Wilmington, DE 19801.
_GA Historical Society, 501 Whitaker St., Savannah, GA 31499.
_ID State Historical Society, 325 W. State St., Boise, ID 83702.
_IL State Historical Library, Old State Capitol, Springfield, IL 62701.
_IN Historical Society, 315 W. Ohio St., Indianapolis, IN 46202.
_State Historical Society of IA, 402 Iowa Ave., Iowa City, IA 52240.

_KS State Historical Society, 120 W. 10th, Topeka, KS 66612.
_(KS) Midwest Historical and Genealogical Society, PO Box 1121, Wichita, KS 67201.
_KY Historical Society, 300 Broadway, Frankfort, KY 40602.
_ME Historical Society, 485 Congress St., Portland, ME 04101.
_MD Historical Society, 201 W. Monument St., Baltimore, MD 21201.
_MA Historical Society, 1154 Boylston St., Boston, MA 02215.
_MN Genealogical Society, 678 Fort Rd., St. Paul, MN 55104.
_MN Historical Society, 690 Cedar St., St. Paul, MN 55101.
_State Historical Society of MO, 1020 Lowry St., Columbia, MO 65201.
_MO Historical Society, Forest Park, St. Louis, MO 63112.
_MT Historical Society, 225 N. Roberts St., Helena, MT 59620.
_NE State Historical Society, 1500 R. St., LIncoln, NE 65801.
_New England Historic Genealogical Society, 101 Newbury St., Boston, MA 02116.
_NH Historical Society, 30 Park St., Concord, NH 03301.
_NJ Historical Society, 230 Broadway, Newark, NJ 01924.
_NY Genealogical and Biographical Society, 122 E. 58th St., New York, NY 10022.
_NY Historical Society, 170 Central Park West, New York, NY 10024.
_State Historical Society of ND, Heritage Center, Bismarck, ND 58505.
_OH Historical Society, 1985 Velma Ave., Columbus, OH 43211.
_OH Genealogical Society, 419 W. Third St., Mansfield, OH 44906.
_OK Historical Society, 2100 N. Lincoln Blvd., Oklahoma City, OK 731-05.
_Genealogical Forum of OR, 1410 SW Morrison St., Portland, OR 97080.
_OR Historical Society, 1230 SW Park Ave., Portland, OR 97068.
_Genealogical Society of PA, 1300 Locust St., Philadelphia, PA 19107.
_SC Historical Society, 100 Meeting St., Charleston, SC 29401.
_SD State Historical Society, 500 E. Capitol, Pierre, SD 57501.
_TN Genealogical Society, 3340 Poplar Ave., Suite 327, Memphis, TN 12124.
_UT State Historical Society, 300 Rio Grande, Salt Lake City, UT 84101.
_VA Historical Society, 428 N. Boulevard, Richmond, VA 23220.
_WA State Historical Society, 315 N. Stadium Way, Tacoma, WA 98403.
_State Historical Society of WI, 816 State St., Madison, WI 53706.

122. State source guides

A number of guidebooks or extensive articles relating to state genealogical sources have been published. Such guidebooks or articles exist for almost all of the states. These writings usually describe the genealogical sources of the state, where they may be found, and how they are to be used.

Listed below is a selection of these guidebooks and articles. They vary in quality, some are brief, others are extensive, some are recent, others fairly old, but in general they can be of considerable help, saving you a great deal of time. Once you begin to dig into your ancestor's background in depth, you will find them quite valuable. The list below is not complete, but it contains many of the more useful publications. Scan down it until you find materials relating to the state or states you are interested in.

_For AL: M. D. Barefield, RESEARCHING IN AL, A GENEALOGI-CAL GUIDE, Southern Historical Press, Easley, SC, 1987.

_For AK: Family History Library, RESEARCH OUTLINE: AK, The Library, Salt Lake City, UT, latest edition; D. A. Radford, AK, in A. Eichholz, ANCESTRY'S REDBOOK, Ancestry Publishing, Salt Lake City, UT, 1992.

_For AZ: Family History Library, RESEARCH OUTLINE: AZ, The Library, Salt Lake City, UT, latest edition; N. S. Woodard, AZ, in A. Eichholz, ANCESTRY'S REDBOOK, Ancestry Publishing, Salt Lake City, UT, 1992.

_For AR: R. S. Norris, GENEALOGIST'S GUIDE TO AR RE-SEARCH, The Author, Russellville, AR, 1994,

_For CA: Family History Library, RESEARCH OUTLINE: CA, The Library, Salt Lake City, UT, latest edition; T. B. Walsmith and N. S. Woodard, CA, in A. Eichholz, ANCESTRY'S REDBOOK, Ancestry Publishing, Salt Lake City, UT, 1992.

_For CO: Family History Library, RESEARCH OUTLINE: CO, The Library, Salt Lake City, UT, latest edition; M. H. Rising, CO, in A. Eichholz, ANCESTRY'S REDBOOK, Ancestry Publishing, Salt Lake City, UT, 1992.

_For CT: T. J. Kemp, CT RESEARCHER'S HANDBOOK, Gale Research Co., Detroit, MI, 1981.

_For DE: DE Genealogical Society, DE GENEALOGICAL RE-SEARCH GUIDE, The Society, Wilmington, DE, 1980.

_For FL: FL Library Association, HISTORICAL AND GENEAL-OGICAL HOLDINGS IN THE STATE OF FL, The Association, Boca Raton, FL, 1992.

_For GA: R. S. Davis, Jr., RESEARCH IN GA, Southern Historical Press, Easley, SC, 1981; T. O. Brook, GA GENEALOGICAL WORKBOOK, Family Tree, LaGrange, GA, 1987; Geo. K. Schweit-zer, GA GENEALOGICAL RESEARCH, The Author, Knoxville,

TN, 1995.

_For HI: Family History Library, RESEARCH OUTLINE: HI, The Library, Salt Lake City, UT, latest edition; D. A. Radford, HI, in A. Eichholz, ANCESTRY'S REDBOOK, Ancestry Publishing, Salt Lake City, UT, 1992.

_For ID: Family History Library, RESEARCH OUTLINE: ID, The Library, Salt Lake City, UT, latest edition; D. A. Radford, ID, in A. Eichholz, ANCESTRY'S REDBOOK, Ancestry Publishing, Salt Lake City, UT, 1992.

_For IL: J. C. Wolf, A REFERENCE GUIDE FOR GENEALOGICAL AND HISTORICAL RESEARCH IN IL, Detroit Society for Genealogical Research, Detroit, MI, 1962; G. Beckstead and M. L. Kozub, SEARCHING IN IL, Everton Publishers, Logan, UT, 1985.

_For IN: M. Robinson, WHO'S YOUR HOOSIER ANCESTOR, IN University Press, Bloomington, IN, 1992.

_For IA: Family History Library, RESEARCH OUTLINE: IA, The Library, Salt Lake City, UT, latest edition; C. L. Maki, IA in A. Eichholz, ANCESTRY'S REDBOOK, Ancestry Publishing, Salt Lake City, UT, 1992.

_For KS: Family History Library, RESEARCH OUTLINE: KS, The Library, Salt Lake City, UT, latest edition; M. H. Rising, KS, in A. Eichholz, ANCESTRY'S REDBOOK, Ancestry Publishing, Salt Lake City, UT, 1992.

_For KY: Geo. K. Schweitzer, KY GENEALOGICAL RESEARCH, The Author, Knoxville, TN, 1995; R. R. Hogan, KY ANCESTRY, Ancestry, Salt Lake City, UT, 1992.

_For LA: Family History Library, RESEARCH OUTLINE: LA, The Library, Salt Lake City, UT, latest edition; S. S. Brown, LA, in A. Eichholz, ANCESTRY'S REDBOOK, Ancestry Publishing, Salt Lake City, UT, 1992; C. E. Ryan, LA PLUS GENEALOGY RE-SOURCES, The Author, Metairie, LA, 1987.

_For ME: J. E. Frost, ME GENEALOGY, in R. J. Crandell, GENEA-LOGICAL RESEARCH IN NEW ENGLAND, Genealogical Publishing Co., Baltimore, MD, 1984, pp. 15-41; M. W. Lindberg, ME, in GENEALOGIST'S HANDBOOK FOR NEW ENGLAND RESEARCH, New England Historic Genealogical Society, Boston, MA, 1985, pp. 23-56; Family History Library, RESEARCH OUT-LINE: ME, The Library, Salt Lake City, UT, latest edition; A. Eichholz, ME, in A. Eichholz, ANCESTRY'S REDBOOK, Ancestry PUblishing, Salt Lake City, UT, 1992.

_For MD: Geo. K. Schweitzer, MD GENEALOGICAL RESEARCH, Genealogical Sources, Unltd., Knoxville, TN, 1993; M. K. Meyer,

GENEALOGICAL RESEARCH IN MD, MD Historical Society, Baltimore, MD, 1983.

_For MA: Geo. K. Schweitzer, MA GENEALOGICAL RESEARCH, The Author, Knoxville, TN, 1990; E. W. Hanson and H. V. Rutherford, GENEALOGICAL RESEARCH IN MA, in R. J. Crandall, GENEALOGICAL RESEARCH IN NEW ENGLAND, Genealogical Publishing Co., Baltimore, MD, 1984, pp. 77-114.

_For MI: C. McGinnis, MI GENEALOGY SOURCES AND RESOURCES, Genealogical Publishing Co., Baltimore, MD, 1987.

_For MN: W. R. Pope, TRACING YOUR ANCESTORS IN MN, The Author, St. Paul, MN, 1989; M. Lind, CONTINUING YOUR GENEALOGICAL RESEARCH IN MN, Linden Tree, Cloquet, MN, 1986; MN Genealogical Society, MN GENEALOGY, The Society, St. Paul, MN, 1991.

_For MS: A. S. Lipscomb and K. S. Hutchinson, TRACING YOUR MS ANCESTORS, University Press of MS, Jackson, MS, 1994.

_For MO: R. E. Parkin, GUIDE TO TRACING YOUR FAMILY TREE IN MO, Genealogical Research and Productions, St. Louis, MO, 1979.

_For MT: D. L. Richards, MT'S GENEALOGICAL RECORDS, Gale Research Co., Detroit, MI, 1981.

_For NE: G. M. Sones, NE, A GUIDE TO GENEALOGICAL RESEARCH, The Author, Lincoln, NE, 1984; S. Nimmo, NE LOCAL HISTORY AND GENEALOGY REFERENCE GUIDE, The Author, Papillon, NE, 1987.

_For NV: Family History Library, RESEARCH OUTLINE: NV, The Library, Salt Lake City, UT, latest edition; N. S. Woodard, NV, in A. Eichholz, ANCESTRY'S REDBOOK, Ancestry Publishing, Salt Lake City, UT, 1992.

_For NH: L. C. Towle and A. N. Brown, NH GENEALOGICAL RESEARCH GUIDE, Heritage Books, Bowie, MD, 1983.

_For NJ: NJ Archives, GUIDE TO FAMILY HISTORY RESOURCES IN THE NJ STATE ARCHIVES, The Archives, Trenton, NJ, 1994; Family History Library, RESEARCH OUTLINE: NJ, The Library, Salt Lake City, UT, latest issue; R. D. Joslyn, NJ in A. Eichholz, ANCESTRY'S REDBOOK, Ancestry Publishing, Salt Lake City, UT, 1992.

_For NM: Family History Library, RESEARCH OUTLINE: NM, The Library, Salt Lake City, UT, latest edition; M. L. Windham and N. S, Woodard, NM, in A. Eichholz, ANCESTRY'S REDBOOK, Ancestry Publishing, Salt Lake City, UT, 1992.

_For NY: Geo. K. Schweitzer, NY GENEALOGICAL RESEARCH, The Author, Knoxville, TN, 1995.

_For NC: H. F. M. Leary and M. R. Stirewalt, NC RESEARCH, NC Genealogical Society, Raleigh, NC, 1980; Geo. K. Schweitzer, NC GENEALOGICAL RESEARCH, The Author, Knoxville, TN, 1991.

_For ND: C. A. Oihus, A GUIDE TO GENEALOGICAL/FAMILY HISTORY SOURCES, The Author, Grand Forks, ND, 1986.

_For OH: Geo. K. Schweitzer, OH GENEALOGICAL RESEARCH, Genealogical Sources, Unltd., Knoxville, TN, 1995; C. W. Bell, OH GUIDE TO GENEALOGICAL SOURCES, Genealogical Publishing Co., Baltimore, MD, 1988; C. W. Bell, OH GENEALOGICAL GUIDE, Bell Books, Youngstown, OH, 1995.

_For OK: M. M. O'Brien, OK GENEALOGICAL RESEARCH, O'Brien Bookshop, SAndy Springs, OK, 1986; W. L. Elliott, OK, in A. Eichholz, ANCESTRY'S REDBOOK, Ancestry Publishing, Salt Lake City, UT, 1992; Family History Library, RESEARCH OUTLINE: OK, The Library, Salt Lake City, UT, latest edition.

_For OR: C. Lenzen, OR GUIDE TO GENEALOGICAL SOURCES, Genealogical Forum of OR, Portland, OR, 1991; Family History Library, RESEARCH OUTLINE: OR, The Library, Salt Lake City, UT, latest edition; D. A. Radford, OR, in A. Eichholz, ANCESTRY'S REDBOOK, Ancestry Publishing, Salt Lake City, UT, 1992.

_For PA: Geo. K. Schweitzer, PA GENEALOGICAL RESEARCH, The Author, Knoxville, TN, 1993; Southwest PA Genealogical Services, PA LINE, A RESEARCH GUIDE TO PA GENEALOGY AND LOCAL HISTORY, The Services, Laughlintown, PA, 1994.

_For RI: J. F. Fiske, GENEALOGICAL RESEARCH IN RI, in R. J. Crandall, GENEALOGICAL RESEARCH IN NEW ENGLAND, Genealogical Publishing Co., Baltimore, MD, 1984, pp. 141-90; K. Sperry, RI SOURCES FOR FAMILY HISTORIANS AND GENEALOGISTS, Everton Publishers, Logan, UT, 1986.

_For SC: B. Holcomb, A GUIDE TO SC GENEALOGICAL RESEARCH, Ericson Books, Nacogdoches, TX, 1991; Geo. K. Schweitzer, SC GENEALOGICAL RESEARCH, The Author, Knoxville, TN, 1995; T. M. Hicks, SC, A GUIDE FOR GENEALOGISTS, Peppercorn Publications, Columbia, SC, 1985.

_For SD: Family History Library, RESEARCH OUTLINE: SD, The Library, Salt Lake City, UT, latest edition; M. H. Rising, SD, in A. Eichholz, ANCESTRY'S REDBOOK, Ancestry Publishing, Salt Lake City, UT, 1992.

_For TN: Geo. K. Schweitzer, TN GENEALOGICAL RESEARCH, The Author, Knoxville, TN, 1994; R. C. Fulcher, GUIDE TO COUNTY

RECORDS AND GENEALOGICAL RESOURCES IN TN, Genealogical Publishing Co., Baltimore, MD, 1987.
_For TX: I. K. and J. L. Kennedy, GENEALOGICAL RECORDS IN TX, Genealogical Publishing Co., Baltimore, MD, 1987; C. R. and J. E. Ericson, A GUIDE TO TX RESEARCH, Ericson Books, Nacogdoches, TX, 1994.
_For UT: UT State Archives and Records Service, GUIDE TO OFFICIAL RECORDS OF GENEALOGICAL VALUE IN THE STATE OF UT, The Service, Salt Lake City, UT, 1980; L. R. Jaussi and G. D. Chaston, GENEALOGICAL RECORDS OF UT, Deseret Book Co., Salt Lake City, UT, 1974.
_For VT: A Eichholz, COLLECTING VT ANCESTORS, New Trails, Montpelier, VT, 1985.
_For VA: Geo. K. Schweitzer, VA GENEALOGICAL RESEARCH, The Author, Knoxville, TN, 1994; C. McGinnis, VA GENEALOGY, Genealogical Publishing Co., Baltimore, MD, 1993.
_For WA: T. C. Eckert, GENEALOGICAL SOURCES IN WA STATE, Division of Archives and Records Management, Olympia, WA, 1983.
_For WV: C. McGinnis, WV GENEALOGY SOURCES AND RE-SOURCES, Genealogical Publishing Co., Baltimore, MD, 1988.
_For WI: J. P. Danky, GENEALOGICAL RESEARCH: AN INTRO-DUCTION TO THE RESOURCES OF THE STATE HISTORICAL SOCIETY OF WI, The Society, Madison, WI, 1986; C. W. Ryan, SEARCHING FOR YOUR WI ANCESTORS, The Author, Green Bay, WI, 1988.
_For WY: Family History Library, RESEARCH OUTLINE: WY, The Library, Salt Lake City, UT, latest edition; D. A. Radford, WY, in A. Eichholz, ANCESTRY'S REDBOOK, Ancestry Publishing, Salt Lake City, UT, 1992.

As you may have noticed, both books and also articles in compilations have been referred to above. There are five major compilations of articles on research in the various states. Three of them contain short treatments on states:
_Family History Library, STATE RESEARCH OUTLINES: [One for each state], The Library, Salt Lake City, UT, latest edition.
_A. Eichholz, editor, ANCESTRY'S REDBOOK, Ancestry Publishing, Salt Lake City, UT, 1992. [An article on each state.]
_National Genealogical Society, STATE RESEARCH ARTICLES: [Articles on research in many states reprinted from the NGS Quarterly.], The Society, Arlington, VA, various dates.
And two of these compilations treat only certain states:

_M. Rubincam and K. Stryker-Rodda, editors, GENEALOGICAL RE-
SEARCH, American Society of Genealogists, Washington, DC,
1980/3, 2 volumes. States treated: AL, AR, CT, DE, FL, GA, IA, IL,
IN, KY, LA, MA, MD, ME, MI, MO, MS, NC, NH, NJ, NY, OH,
PA, RI, SC, TN, VA, VT, WI.
_R. J. Crandall, editor, GENEALOGICAL RESEARCH IN NEW
ENGLAND, Genealogical Publishing Co., Baltimore, MD, 1984.
States treated: CT, MA, ME, NH, RI, VT.

---

123. State university libraries In some states, one or more of the libraries of the state universities may have a good genealogical collection (both published and manuscript materials). Often these state university libraries are excellent sources of histories, maps, newspapers, and private manuscripts. In short, these repositories should not be overlooked. In many cases, you will find important resources in them, but not always.

Among the more useful state libraries for genealogical and local history purposes are those at:
_Auburn University Library, Mell St., Auburn, AL 36849.
_University of CA at Los Angeles Library, 405 Hilgard Ave., Los Angeles, CA 90024.
_University of KY Library, Lexington, KY 40506.
_Murray State University Library, Murray, KY 42071.
_Western KY University Library, Bowling Green, KY 42101.
_University of MD, Baltimore County, Library, 5401 Wilkens Ave., Catonsville, MD 21228.
_University of MD Library, College Park, MD 20742.
_University of MN Library, Minneapolis, MN 55455.
_University of Southern MS Library, Hattiesburg, MS 39401.
_Keen State College Library, Keene, NH 03431.
_University of NC Library, Chapel Hill, NC 27514.
_ND State University Library, Fargo, ND 58105.
_OH University Library, Athens, OH 45701.
_University of SC, Caroliniana Library, Columbia, SC 29208.
_University of TX Library, Austin, TX 78713.
_University of VA Library, Charlottesville, VA 22903.
_University of WA Library, Seattle, WA 98195.

	Several organizations and a number of
124. Surname indexes	individuals have compiled surname indexes

Several organizations and a number of individuals have compiled surname indexes of varying sizes, some containing many names, others containing only a small number. These indexes refer you to data on ancestors which other people have compiled. You will be concerned only with those surname indexes which have a good probability of containing the name you seek. This means that the index should contain a large number of names, or cover a limited area, or deal with only one not-too-common surname. Among the more important of these indexes are the following:

_Family History Library Indexes, INTERNATIONAL GENEALOGI-
   CAL INDEX, FAMILY GROUP RECORDS COLLECTIONS, AN-
   CESTRAL FILE, Salt Lake City, UT. Accessed through Family
   History Centers. See previous sections in this Handbook.

_Everton Publishers Indexes, ROOTS CELLAR, FAMILY FILE, PO
   Box 368, Logan, UT 84321.

_K. A. Johnson and M. R. Sainty, GENEALOGICAL RESEARCH
   DIRECTORY, The Authors, Glendale, CA, annual edition. Search
   all editions.

_GENESIS: THE INTERNATIONAL FAMILY FILE, PO Box 2607,
   Salt Lake City, UT 84110.

In addition to the above surname indexes, you will find many others advertised in the Genealogical Helper, Heritage Quest, and similar genealogical magazines. Care should be exercised with regard to these, since they usually charge a fee, and they often are so small or so limited that the chance of them being of help to you is low. A further source of surname indexes, particularly those dealing with only one surname, is the various family organizations and family publications. For details refer to the two sections in this Handbook which deal with them. Surname indexes have also been compiled by state genealogical societies, and may be located by inquiring at the appropriate state library.

	Colonial governments, the federal government, state
125. Tax lists	governments, county governments, town govern-

Colonial governments, the federal government, state governments, county governments, town governments, and city governments at various times have assessed and collected taxes from their citizens. The taxes which led to records which are of the greatest value to genealogists include those on (1) real estate [land, quit rents, property], (2) individuals [poll, head, capitation, tithable], (3) personal property [such as horses, cattle, slaves, wagons, watches], and (4) income. Of course, there were other taxes [such as import, export, excise, tariff, crops, manufactured items, licenses, sales], but they are usually less helpful for ancestral research purposes.

Colonial government tax lists have in many cases been published, whereas others are available in the original forms or as microfilm copies in the state archives of the states which were formed from the thirteen colonies. The published tax lists appear as books and in journal articles, both of which can be located in the appropriate state libraries. Some of the published and some of the microfilmed colonial tax lists are also available at the Family History Library and may be borrowed through its branch Family History Centers.

The federal government set a direct tax on real property and slaves in 1798, and some of the records of assessment and collection have survived. Those for PA, MA, and ME are available on microfilm:
_National Archives, US DIRECT TAX OF 1798: TAX LISTS FOR PA, Microfilm M372, Washington, DC.
_New England Historic Genealogical Society, 1798 US DIRECT TAX CENSUS FOR ME AND MA, 18 reels of microfilm, Boston, MA, 1979.
Those for some of the other states, though usually quite incomplete may be found as follows: CT(CT Historical Society), DE(Historical Society of DE), GA(GA State Archives, very incomplete), MD(MD Hall of Records), NH(New England Historic Genealogical Society), RI(Rhode Island Historical Society), TN(TN State Library). There was another direct tax in 1814-6 to pay for the War of 1812, but few lists survive. Inquiries should be made at the pertinent state archives. Similar war-support taxes were levied during 1862-6, and the National Archives, which holds them, has microfilmed them.
_National Archives, INTERNAL REVENUE ASSESSMENT LISTS, 1862-6, for AL(Microfilm M754), AR(M755), CA(M756), CO(M757), CT(M758), DE(M759), DC(M760), FL(M761), GA(M762), ID(M763), IL(M764), IN(M765), IA(M766), KS(M767), KY(M768), LA(M769), ME(M770), MD(M771), MI(M773), MS(M775), MT-(M777), NV(M779), NH(M780), NM(M782), NY(M603), NJ(M603), NC(M784), PA(M787), RI(M788), SC(M789), TX(M791), VT(M792), VA(M793), WV(M795), Washington, DC. Original records for other states in National Archives Record Group 58.
Record Group 58 at the National Archives contains many more tax lists dating 1867-1910, and the Regional Branches of the National Archives also have many tax records up through 1917.

Counties, towns, and cities in the various states have also assessed and collected several types of taxes. These assessment and collection lists often provide a year-by-year record of your ancestor's taxation. The records usually record names of able-bodied males, the tax on individuals, the amount of land held, its location, and the tax on the land, plus other taxes in some cases. Many tax records have been lost or destroyed, but a surprising number have survived. Careful study of them can often indicate when a male become of age, when a property holder has died (the listing changes to the estate), when a person leaves, and who inherits land. These county, city, and town tax lists should be sought in the Family History Library (through its branch Family History Centers), in appropriate state archives and state libraries, and in the pertinent county court houses, city halls, and town halls. A few have been published in book form, and many more have appeared as articles in state and local genealogical periodicals. For a bit more detail on the tax records available in the various states, consult:

_A. Eichholz, ANCESTRY'S REDBOOK, Ancestry Publishing, Salt Lake City, UT, 1992.. See under the states.

For even more detail on tax records, consult the materials in the section entitled State source guides.

126. Territorial records

Many states of the US prior to their admission to the Union were for a number of years territories. Territories were governed very much as states except there was strong supervision by the federal government. Except for the thirteen colonies, CA, KY, ME, TX, VT, and WV, all the states went through a territorial stage before being admitted to the Union. The dates of the US territories (and the states into which they developed, if the territorial name differed) are: Northwest Territory (1787-1803, eastern part became OH), Territory Southwest of the River OH (1790-6, became TN), MS (1798-1817), IN (1800-16), Orleans (1804-12, became LA), MI (1805-37), LA-MO (1805-21), IL (1809-18), AL (1817-9), AR (1819-36), FL (1822-45), WI (1836-48), IA (1838-46), OR (1848-59), MN (1849-58), NM (1850-1912), WA (1853-89), NE (1854-61), KS (1854-61), CO (1861-76), NV (1861-4), Dakota (1861-89, became ND and SD), AZ (1863-1912), ID (1863-90), MT (1864-89), WY (1868-90), AK (district 1884-1912, territory 1912-59), OK (1890-1907), HI (1900-59). The records kept by these territories and their constituent counties or districts can be very helpful to genealogists.

Some years ago a series of volumes containing some records selected from some of the territories was published. This series includes records from the Northwest Territory, the Territory Southwest of the River OH, and the Territories of MS, IN, Orleans, MI, LA-MO, IL, AL, AR, FL, and WI. The records contain lists of early settlers, signers of petitions, correspondence, and other items which may mention your forebears.

_C. E. Carter and others, THE TERRITORIAL PAPERS OF THE US, AMS Press, New York, NY, 1973, 29 volumes. Also on National Archives Microfilm M721.

These volumes contain only a small fraction of the records of any of the territories. The National Archives is in the process of microfilming all the records they hold for each of the territories. So far, these have been done:

_National Archives, THE TERRITORIAL PAPERS OF THE US: The Territory of WI (Microfilm M236), The Territory of IA (M325), The Territory of MN (M1050), The Territory of OR (M1049), Washington, DC.

_National Archives, INTERIOR DEPARTMENT TERRITORIAL PAPERS: AK (M430), AZ(M429), CO(M431), Dakota(M310), HI-(M837), ID(M191), MT(M192), NM(M364), OK(M828), UT(M428), WA(M189), WY(M204), Washington, DC.

_National Archives, STATE DEPARTMENT TERRITORIAL PAPERS, AZ (M342), CO(M3), Dakota(M309), FL(M116), ID(M445), KS(M218), MO(M1134), MT(356), NE(M228), NV(M13), NM(T17), OR(M419), Orleans(T260), Territory Northwest of River OH(M470), Territory Southwest of River OH(M471), UT(M12), WA(M26), WY(M85), Washington, DC.

Some excellent guidebooks to the Territorial records in the National Archives are available:

_R. M. Kvasnicka, THE TRANS-MS WEST, 1804-1912, A GUIDE TO FEDERAL RECORDS FOR THE TERRITORIAL PERIOD, National Archives, Washington, DC, 1992-, several volumes.

The Interior and State Department records are far less useful genealogically than the others. The published volumes will be found in large genealogical libraries, state libraries, and state university libraries. The Territorial Papers microfilms are available at the National Archives and its regional branches, and sometimes in the appropriate state libraries or archives.

---

127. Town records

In most states, the most important governmental record-keeping subdivisions are the counties. However, in some states, towns, which are generally smaller in size than counties, also are important record-keeping jurisdictions. The states in which this is the case are CT, ME, MA, NH, RI, VT, and in a few places at early dates in NY. The types of records which might be found in the towns are appointments, birth, burial, church, death, freeman's oaths, land, marks, marriage, militia, mortgage, overseers of the poor, proprietors, school, selectmen, survey, tax, town meeting minutes, voter lists, warnings out (disclaimers of responsibility to provide care for persons not citizens of the town). In CT, the county kept court records (counties abolished 1959) and special districts keep probate records; almost all others are kept by the town. In ME, MA, and NH, the county keeps land, probate, and court records; almost all others are kept by the town. In RI, the county keeps court records, with all others being kept by the towns. In VT, the county keeps court records and some land records, districts within the counties keep probate records, and the towns keep some land records plus all others.

The originals of town records are usually in the town halls. The vital records (birth, marriage, death) for many of the towns have been published, with the records being supplemented by data from Bibles, cemeteries, and churches. The vital records for many of the towns have also been microfilmed by several agencies, and some of the other records have also been microfilmed. The published and microfilmed copies of the town records should be sought in large genealogical libraries, state libraries, state archives, and the Family History Library (through its branch Family History Centers). For further detail on town records, consult the materials referenced in the section of this Handbook entitled State source guides.

---

128. War of 1812 records

The War of 1812 was fought 1812-4 (some battles in 1815, before news of peace reached the areas) between the US and Great Britain. Approximately 187,000 fought in the US forces which means that 1 out of every 14 men participated. There are three main types of records that the war generated which are of use to genealogists: (1) service records, (2) bounty land records, and (3) pension records. Service records include rolls and rosters (enlistment, muster in, muster out, monthly, pay, discharge) and lists (description, wounded, death, deserter, casualty, missing, hospital, prisoner, burial, exchange, court martial, promotion). Among the items which may be found in service records are dates and places and events of service, and sometimes description, birthdate, birthplace, and place of residence. Bounty land records consist of an application with supporting documents, action taken on the application, a warrant for the land, and records of warrant redemption or sale. Pension records consist of an application with supporting documents, action taken on the application, and payment records, sometimes for a veteran, sometimes for his widow, sometimes both. Data may include birth, age, marriage, children, residences after the war, description, health, occupation, migrations, and death.

It is important to recognize that there were two major types of service in the War of 1812. The first was service in the federal US forces. The resulting service, bounty land, and pension records are chiefly in the National Archives, which has microfilmed indexes to them. These microfilms are available in large genealogical libraries, state libraries, state archives, or they may be borrowed from the Family History Library through its branch Family History Centers, or borrowed from the American Genealogical Lending Library, PO Box 329, Bountiful, UT 84011. The second type of military service was in the state militia or in other state-based forces. The originals of these records are in the pertinent state archives or offices of state adjutants general, a few got into the National Archives, and there are some published state lists. These records may be sought in state archives, state libraries, and the offices of the state adjutants general. In short, your search must involve both the federal and the state records or else you may miss your ancestor.

The first step you should take in your War of 1812 progenitor search is to examine three major indexes. These list most of the federal participants and some of the state forces:

_National Archives, INDEX TO THE COMPILED SERVICE RE-CORDS OF THE WAR OF 1812, Microfilm M602, 234 rolls, Washington, DC.

_National Archives, WAR OF 1812 BOUNTY LAND WARRANTS AND INDEXES, Microfilm M848, 14 rolls, Washington, DC.

_V. D. White, INDEX TO WAR OF 1812 PENSION FILES, National Historical Publishing Co., Waynesboro, TN, 1989; or National Archives, INDEX TO WAR OF 1812 PENSION RECORDS, Microfilm M313, 102 films, Washington, DC. Very few War of 1812 pensions were given before 1871, only some to the totally disabled.

Your second step is to obtain the materials to which the indexes above have led you: service records, pension applications and payment records, bounty land applications. Photocopies of these may be obtained from the National Archives by using their form NATF-80, by making a personal visit, or by dispatching a hired searcher. The service records are in Record Group 94, the bounty land applications in Record Group 15, the bounty land warrants in Record Group 49 and on Microfilm M848, and the pension applications in Record Group 15. Your third step is to visit, send a searcher to, or write the appropriate state library, state archives, and state adjutant general. Seek both federal and state information: service records, pay rolls, bounty land, pension records, claims, military unit histories. If you care to investigate further, it is often rewarding to search in the counties and/or towns where your veteran enlisted, lived after the war, and died. Seek Bible, cemetery, church, court, militia, tax, and newspaper records in local libraries, court houses, and town halls.

For further investigation, if that is your desire, you can consult the following volumes:
_Geo. K. Schweitzer, WAR OF 1812 GENEALOGY, Genealogical Sources, Unltd., Knoxville, TN, 1994.
_National Archives, GUIDE TO GENEALOGICAL RESEARCH IN THE NATIONAL ARCHIVES, The Archives, Washington, DC, 1985, Chapters 5-9.
_J. C. Neagles, US MILITARY RECORDS, Ancestry, Salt Lake City, UT, 1994.

129. Ward maps

As the cities of the US grew, it became necessary for administrative purposes to divide them into districts which were called wards. The boundaries of these wards changed fairly often and new wards were added during the years of largest growth. It is of considerable importance to the genealogist to know what ward an ancestor lived in if the contemporary census records are not indexed. The censuses which are most likely to be unindexed or partly unindexed are those of 1880 (families with no children under 11 are not indexed), and 1910 (many states not indexed). One of the best ways to avoid a page-by-page search of all the records for a large city during these census years is to use ward maps. The censuses were divided by wards, so the search can be narrowed down considerably if the ward is known. Ward maps in conjunction with street addresses permit this.

The approach to simplifying the census search is to first identify the street address by examining city directories. See the section in this Handbook entitled City directories. Then, once the street address is known, a ward map can be used to find the ward. Following this, the smaller part of the census corresponding to only one ward can be looked at. Ward maps, along with street indexes, for the larger US cities in the years 1860 and 1878 are printed in:

_E. K. Kirkham, A HANDY GUIDE TO RECORD SEARCHING IN THE LARGER CITIES OF THE US, Everton Publishers, Logan, UT, 1974.

Ward maps and/or descriptions of ward boundaries are also included in many city directories. Further, the large collection of ward maps in the Library of Congress is listed in the following publication:

_M. H. Shelley, WARD MAPS OF THE US CITIES, Library of Congress, Washington, DC, 1975.

The book contains instructions for ordering photocopies of the maps.

---

130. Will and probate records

Will and probate records relate to a court's distribution of a deceased person's estate (land, property, possessions, money) to the legal heirs and to the continuing care of the person's dependents (spouse, children, others designated in a will). These records will often reveal the death date of the deceased, the names of the spouse, the names of children, the residences of family members, the extent of the estate, and guardianship arrangements for minors. It is estimated that 9-11% of the adults living before 1900 made wills, and that the estates of 24-30% of heads of households were handled by the courts. The courts which carried out the probate action dealt with two types of situations: (1) cases in which there was a will, and (2) cases in which there was no will. These are called testate and intestate situations, respectively.

The present courts in the various states which handle probate matters are as follows: AL(County Probate Court), AK(Superior Court), AZ(Superior Court in the County), AR(County Probate Court), CA(County Superior Court), CO(District Court in the County), CT(Probate Court in the District), DE(County Registers Court), DC(Probate Division of the DC Superior Court), FL(Circuit Court in the County), GA(Probate Court in the County), HI(Circuit Court for the Island), ID(District Court in the County), IL(Circuit Court in the County), IN(County Probate Court or Superior Court in the County and/or Circuit Court in the County), KY(District Court in the County),

LA(District Court in the Parish), ME(County Probate Court), MD(Orphans Court in the County), MA(Probate Court in the County), MI(Probate Court in the County or District), MN(Probate Court in the County), MS(Chancery Court in the County), MO(Probate Division of Circuit Court in the County), MT(District Court in the County), NE(County Court), NV(District Court in the County), NH(County Probate Court), NJ(Chancery Division of Superior Court or Surrogate Court), NM(County Probate Court or District Court in the County), NY(County Surrogate Court), NC(County Superior Court), ND(County Court), OH(Probate Division of Court of Common Pleas in County), OK(District Court in the County), OR(County Court or Circuit Court in the County), PA(County Register of Wills), RI(City or Town Court of Probate), SC(County Probate Court), SD(Circuit Court in the County), TN(Probate Court or Chancery Court), TX(County Court or Probate Court), UT(District Court in the County), VT(District Probate Court, one or two districts in each county), VA(Circuit Court in the County or Independent City), WA(County Superior Court), WV(County Commission), WI(County Circuit Court), WY(District Court in the County).

The probate process in practically all colonies and states was very similar. An application to the court (a petition) is made by a concerned person to settle the estate. If there was a will, it was presented, proved by witnesses, and recorded in a book or register. The probate court then appointed an individual (executor, administrator) to settle the estate. This individual prepared an inventory or a list of the contents of the estate and had the various items appraised, that is, evaluated. The probate court then ordered the executor or administrator to distribute the estate in accordance with the will or in accordance with the state laws if there was no will. If necessary, the executor or administrator sold some or all of the estate in order to carry out the distribution and/or settle debts. The executor or administrator then reported all the transactions to the court. The actions of the court in appointing the executor or administrator, in supervising the settlement, and in closing the case were all recorded in the court records. And all the documents (appointment, letters, petitions, bonds, inventory, appraisal, accounts, receipts, list of heirs, distributions) were gathered into a probate packet or probate file which was stored by the court clerk. Some of these documents were sometimes copied or abstracted into record books.

Usually, the original will and probate records remain in the courts which were mentioned above. However, in several states, they are being gathered by the state archives. Further, many will and probate record books have been microfilmed, and these microfilms are available in state libraries, state archives, and at the Family History Library (from which they can be borrowed through the numerous Family History Centers). Many early will and probate records have been abstracted and indexed, and have appeared as books or as articles in genealogical periodicals. These may be found in the pertinent state libraries. The probate packets or probate files usually have not been microfilmed, and they often are available only in the counties or towns. However, it is well worth while to try to obtain them because they tend to be very valuable genealogically. All will and probate records for NH before 1771 were kept at the provincial level, all for NC before 1760 at the colony level, and all for SC before 1785 at the colony level.

---

131. WPA records

During the late 1930s and early 1940s the US WPA (Works Progress Administration) undertook the gigantic task of compiling lists of locations of vital records (birth, marriage, death), lists of the records in county archives, lists of records in churches, lists of cemetery and burial records, and lists of some state records. Many records in practically all states were inventoried. Some of these ended up as publications, some as typescript volumes, and many remained in manuscript form. They can be of value to you because they show what records were available at that time (late 1930s, early 1940s), what information they contained, and where they were located. They, therefore, provide you with a listing of materials which you should try to obtain. The published compilations are listed in:
_S. B. Child and D. P. Holmes, CHECK LIST OF HISTORICAL RECORDS SURVEY PUBLICATIONS, Genealogical Publishing Co., Baltimore, MD, 1969.
However, only some of the typescript volumes and none of the manuscript materials are listed here. The best places to find these compilations (published, typescript, manuscript) are in the appropriate state libraries, state archives, and state university libraries.

The WPA also transcribed and indexed many county records and some state records. These generally ended up as typescript volumes or manuscript materials. They, too, should be sought in state libraries, state archives, and state university libraries. A useful guide to the location of many of the unpublished materials, is:
__Society of American Archivists, THE WPA HISTORICAL RECORDS SURVEY, A GUIDE TO THE UNPUBLISHED INVENTORIES,

INDEXES, AND TRANSCRIPTS, The Society, Washington, DC, 1980.

---

132. Writing source citations

In doing genealogical research, it is very important to keep good records. Several different types of record-keeping systems are available from genealogical supply stores. Many of these advertise in the largest popular genealogical journal. Thus, to find their names and addresses check the latest issue of:

_V. N. Chambers, editor, THE GENEALOGICAL HELPER, Everton Publishers, Logan, UT.

Write them, asking for literature on record-keeping forms, notebooks, and systems. Be careful not to pay too much for these, especially for notebooks, since what you need is mainly some forms to show your lines of descent, some forms to record data on each family (husband-wife-children), some ordinary lined notebook paper, and an ordinary notebook or two.

One of the most aggravating and discouraging things that can happen to a genealogical researcher is to lose the information regarding where you found some important data. To prevent this, and to be able to authenticate your research, you need to carefully record and preserve the exact place where you obtained every bit of data. Without this, your genealogical data are utterly invalid. This act of backing your research up is called citing your sources. A valid source citation is one which will permit any competent genealogist to find the data in precisely the same way you did. In other words, your source citation must permit someone else to locate the same material you have located. There are numerous systems for source citations, and therefore the one suggested here is only one possibility. What is important, however, is that you adopt a systematic way of citing your sources, and that you keep in mind providing enough information to permit someone to verify your data easily.

The most conventional sources of genealogical information are oral statements of relatives and others,[1] personal observations,[2] family items,[3] original records,[4] microform copies of records,[5] books,[6] periodicals,[7] maps,[8] and manuscripts.[9] These things must be included in a reference in order to constitute it as a valid citation: what the record is, when it was constituted, where it can be located (for books and periodicals this is taken as implicit if the publisher is given, unless the item is rare or the publisher is private). Using the superscript numbers of the items at the beginning of this paragraph, some examples are shown below:

_[1]Personal communication from George Robert SCHWEITZER (1864-1962), Poplar Bluff, MO, 17 Dec 1960.

_[2]Personal observation of gravestone, Maple Grove Cemetery, Fremont, MI, 27 Jun 1990.

_[3]James Alonzo SISLER's (1834-94) family Bible, THE HOLY BIBLE, Nelson and Sons, Edinburgh, Scotland, 1860, in possession of Mrs. Ruth Finch, Doniphan, MO, 28 Feb 1989.

_[3]John Jacob HEINOLD's (1838-90) moustache cup, marked Altenburg, Saxony, in possession of Francis John SCHWEITZER, Jr., 14 Sandy Cove Rd., Clover, SC 19710, 16 Mar 1990.

_[4]Marriage Certificate (11 Feb 1860), White County, IN, County Clerk, Monticello, IN 47960.

_[4]Newaygo County, MI, Deed Book 21, page 242, 16 Sep 1876, located in Office of County Clerk, White Cloud, MI.

_[4]Birth Certificate, Registration District of St. Mary Magdalene, Bermondsey, Surrey (South London), 1847, No. 228, 25 Aug 1847, in St. Catherine's House, 10 Kingsway, London WC2B 6JP, England.

_[5]1850 MI Census Record, National Archives Microfilm M432, Reel 349, Eaton Township, page 119R.

_[5]Tax Books, Bradley County, TN, 1869-98, microfilm copy in Public Library, Cleveland, TN, 1969, Second District.

_[5]Civil War Pension Papers of Levi MASHBURN, File No. WC639775, National Archives, Washington, DC 20408.

_[6]National Genealogical Society, INDEX OF REVOLUTIONARY WAR PENSIONS APPLICATIONS IN THE NATIONAL AR-CHIVES, Bicentennial Edition, The Society, Washington, DC, 1976, page 557, column 3.

_[6]NATIONAL CYCLOPEDIA OF AMERICAN BIOGRAPHY, White Co., New York, NY, 1893-, volume 45, page 374.

_[6]L. W. Prewitt, THE DAWKINS AND STEWART FAMILIES OF VA AND KY, The Author, Fairfield, IA, 1968, available in the KY Historical Society Library, 200-2 Broadway, Frankfort, KY 40601.

_[6]J. I. Robertson, Jr., AN INDEX-GUIDE TO THE SOUTHERN HISTORICAL SOCIETY PAPERS, 1876-1959, Kraus International Publications, New York, NY, 1980, volume 2, page 958.

_[7]DIVISION OF LAND IN CASWELL COUNTY, NC, published in Bulletin of the VA-NC Piedmont Genealogical Society, Danville, VA, volume 1, number 4, 1979, page 115.

_[7]B. C. Richard, CIVIL WAR PRISONERS FROM IL BURIED AT ANDERSONVILLE, published in IL STATE GENEALOGICAL

SOCIETY QUARTERLY, Springfield, IL, volume 12, number 4, Dec 1980, page 187.

_[7]A VIOLENT DEATH: SUPERINTENDENT OF ST. LOUIS GAS WORKS KILLED BY EXPLOSION, St. Louis Daily Globe, Monday Morning, 14 Dec 1874, page 2, in collection of St. Louis Public Library, 1301 Olive St., St. Louis, MO 63103.

_[8]1878 LANDOWNER MAP OF BEDFORD COUNTY, TN, Special Collections, Main Library, University of TN, Knoxville, TN 37916.

_[9]BARNES PAPERS, letter of 12 Mar 1862 from Lt. Col. Milton Barnes (97th Ohio Volunteer Infantry) to his wife, Special Collections, Fenwick Library, George Mason University, Fairfax, VA 22030.

A useful manual which goes into more detail regarding source citations is:

__R. S. Lackey, CITE YOUR SOURCES, A MANUAL FOR DOCU-MENTING FAMILY HISTORIES AND GENEALOGICAL RECORDS, University Press of MS, Jackson, MS, latest edition.

Books by George K. Schweitzer

CIVIL WAR GENEALOGY. A 74-paged book of 316 sources for tracing your Civil War ancestor. Chapters include [I]: The Civil War, [II]: The Archives, [III]: National Publications, [IV]: State Publications, [V]: Local Sources, [VI]: Military Unit Histories, [VI]I: Civil War Events.

GEORGIA GENEALOGICAL RESEARCH. A 238-paged book containing 1303 sources for tracing your GA ancestor along with detailed instructions. Chapters include [I]: GA Background, [II]: Types of Records, [III]: Record Locations, [IV]: Research Procedure and County Listings (detailed listing of records available for each of the 159 GA counties).

GERMAN GENEALOGICAL RESEARCH. A 283-paged book containing 1984 sources for tracing your German ancestor along with detailed instructions. Chapters include [I]: German Background, [II]: Germans to America, [III]: Bridging the Atlantic, [IV]: Types of German Records, [V]: German Record Repositories, [VI]: The German Language.

HANDBOOK OF GENEALOGICAL SOURCES. A 252-paged book describing all major and many minor sources of genealogical information with precise and detailed instructions for obtaining data from them.

INDIANA GENEALOGICAL RESEARCH. A 156-paged book containing 1044 sources for tracing your IN ancestor along with detailed instructions. Chapters include [I]: IN Background, [II]: Types of Records, [III]: Record Locations, [IV]: Research Procedure and County Listings (detailed listing of records available for each of the 92 IN counties).

KENTUCKY GENEALOGICAL RESEARCH. A 167-paged book containing 1191 sources for tracing your KY ancestor along with detailed instructions. Chapters include [I]: KY Background, [II]: Types of Records, [III]: Record Locations, [IV]: Research Procedure and County Listings (detailed listing of records available for each of the 120 KY counties).

MARYLAND GENEALOGICAL RESEARCH. A 208-paged book containing 1176 sources for tracing your MD ancestor along with detailed instructions. Chapters inclùde [I]: MD Background, [II]: Types of Records, [III]: Record Locations, [IV]: Research Procedure and County Listings (detailed listing of records available for each of the 23 MD counties and for Baltimore City).

MASSACHUSETTS GENEALOGICAL RESEARCH. A 279-paged book containing 1709 sources for tracing your MA ancestor along with detailed instructions. Chapters include [I]: MA Background, [II]: Types of Records, [III]: Record Locations, [IV]: Research Procedure and County-Town-City Listings (detailed listing of records available for each of the 14 MA counties and the 351 cities-towns).

NEW YORK GENEALOGICAL RESEARCH. A 252-paged book containing 1426 sources for tracing your NY ancestor along with detailed instructions. Chapters include [I]: NY Background, [II]; Types of Records, [III]: Record Locations, [IV]: Research Procedure and NY City Record Listings (detailed listing of records available for the 5 counties of NY City), [V]: Record Listings for Other Counties (detailed listing of records available for each of the other 57 NY counties.)

NORTH CAROLINA GENEALOGICAL RESEARCH. A 169-paged book containing 1233 sources for tracing your NC ancestor along with detailed instructions. Chapters include [I]: NC Background, [II]: Types of Records, [III]: Record Locations, [IV]: Research Procedure and County Listings (detailed listing of records available for each of the 100 NC counties).

OHIO GENEALOGICAL RESEARCH, A 212-paged book containing 1241 sources for tracing your OH ancestor along with detailed instructions. Chapters include [I]: NC Background, [II]: Types of Records, [III]: Record Locations, [IV]: Research Procedure and County Listings (detailed listing of records available for each of the 100 OH counties).

PENNSYLVANIA GENEALOGICAL RESEARCH. A 201-paged book containing 1309 sources for tracing your PA ancestor along with detailed instructions. Chapters include [I]: PA Background, [II]: Types of Records, [III]: Record Locations, [IV]: Research Procedure and County Listings (detailed listing of records available for each of the 67 PA counties).

REVOLUTIONARY WAR GENEALOGY. A 110-paged book containing 407 sources for tracing your Revolutionary War ancestor. Chapters include [I]: Revolutionary War History, [II]: The Archives, [III]: National Publications, [IV]: State Publications, [V]: Local Sources, [VI]: Military Unit Histories, [VII]: Sites and Museums.

SOUTH CAROLINA GENEALOGICAL RESEARCH. A 170-paged book containing 1107 sources for tracing your SC ancestor along with detailed instructions. Chapters include [I]: SC Background, [II]: Types of Records, [III]: Record Locations, [IV]: Research Procedure and County Listings (detailed listing of records available for each of the 47 SC counties and districts).

TENNESSEE GENEALOGICAL RESEARCH. A 132-paged book containing 1073 sources for tracing your TN ancestor along with detailed instructions. Chapters include [I]: TN Background, [II]: Types of Records, [III]: Record Locations, [IV]: Research Procedure and County Listings (detailed listing of records available for each of the 96 TN counties).

VIRGINIA GENEALOGICAL RESEARCH. A 216-paged book containing 1273 sources for tracing your VA ancestor along with detailed instructions. Chapters include [I]: VA Background, [II]: Types of Records, [III]: Record Locations, [IV]: Research Procedure and County Listings (detailed listing of records available for each of the 100 VA counties and 41 major cities).

WAR OF 1812 GENEALOGY. A 75-paged book of 289 sources for tracing your War of 1812 ancestor. Chapters include [I]: History of the War, [II]: Service Records, [III]: Bounty Land and Pension Records, [IV]: National and State Publications, [V]: Local Sources, [VI]: Military Unit Histories, [VII]: Sites and Events.

All of the above books may be ordered from Dr. George K. Schweitzer at the address given on the title page. Or send a long SASE for a FREE descriptive leaflet on the books.